Chocolate

Chocolate

p

NOTE

Unless otherwise stated, milk is assumed to be whole fat, eggs are large, and pepper
is freshly ground black pepper.

Recipes using uncooked eggs should be
avoided by infants, the elderly, pregnant women, and anyone
suffering from an illness.

Contents

Introduction 8 Regional Cooking 10–13

Using Chocolate 14 How to Use This Book 17

Cakes, Gateaux & Loaves

Hot Desserts

Savories

Cold Desserts

Small Cakes & Cookies

Candies & Drinks

Introduction

Chocolate!—even the word is an enticing mixture of indulgence tinged with a touch of sinfulness, and the product itself more than lives up to its promise. The mere mention of anything associated with this mouthwatering confection can cause a dreamy look to come into the eyes of the chocoholic.

The cocoa tree, *Theobroma cacao*, originated in South America, and from the early 7th century it was cultivated by the Maya, who established a flourishing trade and even used the cocoa bean as currency. In 1502, Christopher Columbus took the cocoa bean to Spain, but it wasn't until later that Cortés introduced *xocotlatl*, a recipe brought from the Mexican court of Montezuma for a drink made from crushed roasted cocoa beans and cold water, thickened with cornstarch and frothed with a swizzle stick. Vanilla, spices, honey, and sugar were added to improve the flavor of this thick and bitter brew, and over time it came to be served hot. Cocoa was believed to cure a variety of physical illnesses, and to promote stamina.

In the 17th century, the popularity of cocoa spread to the rest of Europe. France was the first country to fall to its charms, then Holland, where Amsterdam became the most important cocoa port beyond Spain. From there cocoa went to Germany, then north to Scandinavia, and also south to Italy—by which time it had become a major source of revenue.

Cocoa arrived in England in the mid 17th century, and chocolate houses quickly began to rival the newly established coffee houses.

In the early 19th century, Dutch chemist Coenraad Van Houten invented a press to extract the fat from the beans, and developed a method of neutralizing the acids. In this way, he was able to produce almost pure cocoa butter, and a hard "cake," which could be milled to a powder for use as a flavoring. As a result, it became possible to eat chocolate as well as to drink it.

It was soon discovered that the rich cocoa butter made a delicious confection, and chocolate production began in earnest. In Britain, Fry's chocolate appeared in 1847, and in

Switzerland the famous chocolate companies were established. In 1875 chocolate was combined with condensed milk to produce the first milk chocolate. At around this time, Lindt found a way of making the smooth, melting chocolate still associated with his company today. About 20 years later, Hershey introduced his famous chocolate bar in the United States, where chocolate is perhaps better loved than anywhere else.

Today, cocoa trees are grown in Africa, the West Indies, the tropical areas of America, and the Far East. Harvested cocoa beans are left in the heat of the sun to develop their chocolate flavor, then afterward the beans are shelled, and the kernels are processed to produce cocoa solids. Finally, the cocoa butter is extracted and further processed to become chocolate, in all its many guises.

Regional Cooking

The Europeans, following their long association with cocoa as a drink, soon discovered the delights of chocolate, and set about using it to create some of the most delicious classic dessert recipes—rich, creamy, and incredibly good to eat.

In Austria, tortes are very popular, particularly Anna Sacher's delectable Sachertorte, which dates from 1883. The French offer a melting roulade, a light-as-air mixture that is cooked in a long rectangle, then rolled around a filling—there is plenty of scope for variations on this basic recipe. Also from France comes mousse, a melt-in-the-mouth dessert based on chocolate and eggs, to which can be added heavy cream, brandy, rum—or even champagne.

The Italians really know how to impress with their chocolate desserts. The frothy zabaglione, laced with marsala, is whisked over hot water until thick, and served immediately—so it needs patient guests and a confident cook! Tiramisu is based on a smooth and versatile cream cheese, mascarpone, which is layered with coffee-drenched sponge and chunks of chocolate. And the Italians are of course wonderful at making ice-cream—the combination of chocolate and mint is a classic favorite. For special occasions, two Tuscan specialities are Panforte di Siena—a rich, chocolate-flavored mixture of dried fruit, nuts, and honey—and Florentines, thin, crispy cookies topped with chocolate.

From Germany comes the Black Forest Gateau, a chocolate cake soaked in liqueur and filled with whipped cream and cherries. Adapted into a trifle, this makes a very special dessert.

Regional Cooking

It may seem a strange and newly fashionable idea to combine the creamy sweetness of chocolate with the hot and fiery chili, but in fact chili was one of the flavorings used in the original cocoa drink, *xocotlatl*, and the combination is still used in Mexican cooking today. That chocolate and chili have an affinity is evident in one of the most popular Mexican dishes, Mole Poblano (see

page 106), a blend of toasted fresh chilies, onions, garlic, tomatoes, spices, nuts, raisins—and chocolate, which is even used to garnish the dish. Chocolate also adds flavor and richness to Mexican beef stews.

More conventionally, chocolate is used in desserts such as Empanadas (see page 92), little parcels of banana and chocolate in phyllo pastry, and chocolate meringues, served with strawberries and chocolate-flavored cream. The Mexicans also make a modern version of the original cocoa drink, which is spiced with cinnamon and thickened with tortilla flour.

In North America, where home-baked cookies and traybakes are such a feature of everyday life and social occasions, chocolate is a very popular ingredient. From here come such tempting treats as the moist,

chewy, chocolate brownie, crisp chocolate chip cookies, and rocky road bites, which often find their way into ice-cream. Some recipes reflect the area in which a recipe originated—one that particularly catches the attention is Mississippi Mud Pie, definitely not a dish for the faint-hearted! And Devil's Food Cake, with its sumptuous chocolate frosting, is just as the name suggests—positively wicked!

Using Chocolate

Chocolate is delicious whether cooked or uncooked. It comes in many forms, of course, and here is a selection of some of the most popular ones, which can all be used in a wide variety of mouthwatering recipes.

Dark Chocolate

Dark chocolate that contains around 50% cocoa solids is ideal for most everyday cooking purposes. For special recipes, choose a luxury or continental chocolate with a cocoa solid content of 70–75% for a richer, more intense flavor.

White Chocolate

For color contrast, especially for cake decoration, white chocolate is unbeatable. However, white chocolate has a lower content of cocoa butter and cocoa solids, so choose a luxury cooking variety and take care not to overheat it when melting it.

Chocolate Chips

Available in dark, milk, or white chocolate, these chips are useful for baking and decoration. They are especially good in cookies, as well as candies and a whole range of delicious confections.

Milk Chocolate

This variety has a milder, creamier flavor. It is also useful for decorations. Care must be taken when melting it, however, because milk chocolate is more sensitive to heat than dark chocolate is.

Chocolate-Flavored Cake Covering

This product has an inferior flavor, but it is useful for making decorations because of its high fat content. As a compromise, add a few squares to a good-quality chocolate.

Unsweetened Cocoa

Unsweetened cocoa comes in powder form. It tastes bitter, and gives a good, strong chocolate flavor in cooking. It is mostly used in cakes.

Most chocolate, including unsweetened cocoa, can be stored for up to a year if it is kept in a cool, dry place away from direct heat or sunlight.

Preparing Chocolate

To melt chocolate on a stove:

1 Break the chocolate into small, equal-size pieces and put it into a heatproof bowl.

2 Place the bowl over a pan of hot, simmering water, making sure the base of the bowl does not come into contact with the water.

3 Once the chocolate starts to melt, stir gently until smooth, then remove from the heat.

Note: Do not melt chocolate over direct heat (unless melting with other ingredients—in this case, keep the heat very low).

To melt chocolate in a microwave oven:

1 Break chocolate into small pieces and place in a microwave-proof bowl.

2 Put the bowl in the microwave oven and melt. As a guide, melt 4½ oz/125g dark chocolate on High for 2 minutes, and white or milk chocolate on Medium for 2–3 minutes.

Note: As microwave oven temperatures and settings vary, you should consult the manufacturer's instructions first.

3 Stir the chocolate, let stand for a few minutes, then stir again. If necessary, return it to the microwave for 30 seconds more.

Chocolate Decorations

Decorations add a special touch to a cake or dessert. They can be interleaved with nonstick baking paper and stored in airtight containers. Dark chocolate will keep for 4 weeks, and milk or white chocolate for 2 weeks.

Caraque

1 Spread the melted chocolate over a clean acrylic chopping board and leave it to set.

2 When the chocolate has set, hold the board firmly, position a large, smooth-bladed knife on the chocolate, and pull the blade toward you at an angle of 45°, scraping along the chocolate to form the caraque. You should end up with irregularly shaped long curls (see below).

3 Using the knife blade, lift the caraque off the board.

Quick Curls

1 For quick curls, choose a thick bar of chocolate, and keep it at room temperature.

2 Using a sharp, swivel-bladed vegetable peeler, scrape lightly along the chocolate to form fine curls, or more firmly to form thicker curls.

Leaves

1 Use freshly-picked leaves with well-defined veins that are clean, dry, and pliable. Holding a leaf by its stem, paint a smooth layer of melted chocolate onto the underside with a small paint brush or pastry brush.

2 Repeat with the remaining leaves, then place them, chocolate side up, on a baking sheet lined with waxed paper.

3 Refrigerate for at least an hour until set. When set, peel each leaf away from its chocolate coating.

How to Use This Book

Each recipe contains a wealth of useful information, including a breakdown of nutritional quantities, preparation, and cooking times, and level of difficulty. All of this information is explained in detail below.

The number of chef's hats represents the difficulty of each recipe, ranging from easy (1 chef's hat) to difficult (5 chef's hats).

This amount of time represents the preparation of ingredients, including cooling, chilling, and soaking times.

This represents the cooking time.

The ingredients for each recipe are listed in the order that they are used.

The method is illustrated with step-by-step photographs, making the recipe easy to follow.

A full-color photograph of the finished dish.

Cook's tips and variations provide useful information regarding ingredients or cooking techniques.

The method is clearly explained with step-by-step instructions that are easy to follow.

Chocolate　55

Chocolate & Almond Torte

This torte is perfect for serving on a hot sunny day with double cream and a selection of fresh summer berries.

1 hr 25 mins　　40–45 mins

SERVES 10

INGREDIENTS

225 g/8 oz dark chocolate, broken into pieces

3 tbsp water

150 g/5½ oz soft brown sugar

175 g/6 oz butter, softened

25 g/1 oz ground almonds

3 tbsp self-raising flour

5 eggs, separated

100 g/3½ oz blanched almonds, finely chopped

icing sugar, for dusting

double cream, to serve (optional)

1 Grease a 23 cm/9 inch loose-bottomed cake tin and line the base with baking paper.

2 In a saucepan set over a very low heat, melt the chocolate with the water, stirring until smooth. Add the sugar and stir until dissolved, taking the pan off the heat to prevent it overheating.

3 Add the butter in small amounts until it has melted into the chocolate. Remove from the heat and lightly stir in the ground almonds and flour. Add the egg yolks one at a time, beating well after each addition.

4 In a large mixing bowl, whisk the egg whites until they stand in soft peaks, then fold them into the chocolate mixture with a metal spoon. Stir in the chopped almonds. Pour the mixture into the tin and level the surface.

5 Bake in a preheated oven, 180°C/350°F/Gas Mark 4, for 40–45 minutes until well risen and firm (the cake will crack on the surface during cooking).

6 Leave to cool in the tin for 30–40 minutes. Turn out on to a wire rack to cool completely. Dust with icing sugar and serve in slices with double cream, if using.

COOK'S TIP

For a nuttier flavour, toast the chopped almonds in a dry frying pan over a medium heat for about 2 minutes until lightly golden.

Cakes, Gateaux & Loaves

It is hard to resist the pleasure of a sumptuous piece of chocolate cake and no chocolate book would be complete without a selection of cakes, gateaux, and loaves—there are plenty to choose from in this chapter. The more experimental among you can vary the fillings or decorations according to what takes your fancy. Alternatively, follow our easy step-by-step instructions and look at our glossy pictures to guide you to perfect results.

The gateaux in this book are a feast for the eyes, and so are the delicious cakes, many of which can be made with surprising ease. The loaves are the perfect indulgence for snacktimes and can be made with very little effort. So next time you feel like a mouthwatering slice of something, these recipes are sure to be a success.

Chocolate Almond Cake

Chocolate and almonds complement each other perfectly in this delicious cake. Be warned though, one slice will never be enough!

3 hrs   40 mins

SERVES 8

INGREDIENTS

6 oz/175 g dark chocolate

3⁄4 cup butter

½ cup superfine sugar

4 eggs, separated

¼ tsp cream of tartar

⅓ cup self-rising flour

1¼ cups ground almonds

1 tsp almond extract

TOPPING

4½ oz/125 g light chocolate

2 tbsp butter

4 tbsp heavy cream

TO DECORATE

2 tbsp toasted flaked almonds

1 oz/25 g dark chocolate, melted

1 Lightly grease and line the bottom of a 9 inch/23 cm round springform pan. Break the chocolate into small pieces and place in a small pan with the butter. Heat gently, stirring until melted and well combined.

2 Place ½ cup of the superfine sugar in a bowl with the egg yolks and whisk until pale and creamy. Add the melted chocolate and butter mixture, beating until well combined.

3 Strain the cream of tartar and flour together and fold into the chocolate mixture with the ground almonds and almond extract.

4 Whisk the egg whites in a bowl until standing in soft peaks. Add the remaining superfine sugar and whisk for about 2 minutes by hand, or 45–60 seconds if using an electric whisk, until thick and glossy. Fold the egg whites into the chocolate mixture and spoon into the

pan. Bake in a preheated oven, 375°F/190°C, for 40 minutes, until just springy to the touch. Let cool.

5 Heat the topping ingredients in a bowl over a pan of hot water. Remove from the heat and beat for 2 minutes. Let chill for 30 minutes. Transfer the cake to a plate and spread with the topping. Scatter with the flaked almonds and drizzle with melted chocolate. Let the topping set for 2 hours before serving.

Chocolate Tray Bake

This is a good family cake that keeps well. Baked in a shallow rectangular cake pan, the squares are ideal for serving with morning coffee.

10 mins 30–40 mins

SERVES 15

INGREDIENTS

3 cups self-rising flour, strained

3 tbsp unsweetened cocoa, strained

1 cup superfine sugar

1 cup soft margarine

4 eggs, beaten

4 tbsp milk

1/3 cup light chocolate chips

1/3 cup dark chocolate chips

1/3 cup white chocolate chips

confectioners' sugar, to dust

1 Grease a 13 x 9 x 2 inch/33 x 24 x 5 cm cake pan with a little butter or margarine.

2 Place all of the ingredients except for the chocolate chips and confectioners' sugar in a large mixing bowl and beat together until smooth.

VARIATION

For an attractive finish, cut thin strips of paper and lay in a criss-cross pattern on top of the cake. Dust with confectioners' sugar, then remove the paper strips.

3 Beat in the light, dark, and white chocolate chips.

4 Spoon the mixture into the prepared cake pan and level the top. Bake in a preheated oven, 350°F/180°C, for 30–40 minutes until risen and springy to the touch. Let cool in the pan.

5 Once cool, dust with confectioners' sugar. Cut into squares to serve.

Chocolate & Pineapple Cake

Decorated with thick yogurt and canned pineapple, this is a low-fat cake, but it is by no means lacking in flavor.

🕙 40 mins   ⏱ 20–25 mins

SERVES 9

INGREDIENTS

⅔ cup low-fat spread

½ cup superfine sugar

¾ cup self-rising flour, strained

3 tbsp unsweetened cocoa, strained

1½ tsp baking powder

2 eggs

8 oz/225g canned pineapple pieces in natural juice

½ cup low-fat thick unsweetened yogurt

about 1 tbsp confectioners' sugar

grated chocolate, to decorate

1 Lightly grease an 8 inch/20 cm square cake pan.

2 Place the low-fat spread, superfine sugar, flour, unsweetened cocoa, baking powder, and eggs in a large mixing bowl. Beat with a wooden spoon or electric hand whisk until smooth.

3 Pour the cake mixture into the prepared pan and level the surface. Bake in a preheated oven, 325°F/190°C, for 20–25 minutes or until springy to the touch. Let the cake cool slightly in the tin pan before transferring to a wire rack to cool completely.

4 Drain the pineapple, chop the pineapple pieces, and drain again. Reserve a little pineapple for decoration,

then stir the rest of the pineapple into the yogurt and sweeten to taste with confectioners' sugar.

5 Spread the pineapple and yogurt mixture over the cake and decorate with the reserved pineapple pieces. Sprinkle with the grated chocolate.

COOK'S TIP

Store the cake, undecorated, in an airtight container for up to 3 days. Once decorated, refrigerate and use within 2 days.

Chocolate & Orange Cake

An all-time favorite combination of flavors makes this cake ideal for a treat. Omit the icing, if preferred, and sprinkle with confectioners' sugar.

🍰 1 hr   ⏱ 25 mins

SERVES 8

INGREDIENTS

¾ cup superfine sugar

¾ cup butter or block margarine

3 eggs, beaten

1½ cups self-rising flour, strained

2 tbsp unsweetened cocoa, strained

2 tbsp milk

3 tbsp orange juice

grated zest of ½ orange

ICING

1½ cups confectioners' sugar

2 tbsp orange juice

1 Lightly grease an 8 inch/20 cm deep round cake pan.

2 Beat together the sugar and butter or margarine in a bowl until light and fluffy. Gradually add the eggs, beating well after each addition. Carefully fold in the flour.

3 Divide the mixture in half. Add the cocoa and milk to one half, stirring until well combined. Flavor the other half with the orange juice and zest.

4 Place spoonfuls of each mixture into the prepared pan and swirl together with a skewer, to create a marbled effect. Bake in a preheated oven, 375°F/190°C, for 25 minutes or until the cake is springy to the touch.

5 Let the cake cool in the pan for a few minutes before transferring to a wire rack to cool completely.

6 To make the icing, sift the confectioners' sugar into a mixing bowl and mix in enough of the orange juice to form a smooth icing. Spread the icing over the top of the cake and let set before serving.

VARIATION

Add 2 tablespoons of rum or brandy to the chocolate mixture instead of the milk. The cake also works well when flavored with grated lemon zest and juice instead of the orange.

Family Chocolate Cake

A simple to make family cake ideal for an everyday treat. Keep the decoration simple—you could use a store-bought icing or filling, if liked.

1 hr   20 mins

SERVES 8

INGREDIENTS

½ cup soft margarine

½ cup superfine sugar

2 eggs

1 tbsp light corn syrup

1 cup self-rising flour, strained

2 tbsp unsweetened cocoa, strained

FILLING AND TOPPING

4 tbsp confectioners' sugar, strained

2 tbsp butter

3½ oz/100 g white or light cooking chocolate

a little light or white chocolate, melted (optional)

1 Lightly grease two 7 inch/18 cm shallow cake pans.

2 Place all of the ingredients for the cake in a large mixing bowl and beat with a wooden spoon or electric hand whisk to form a smooth mixture.

3 Divide the mixture between the prepared pans and level the tops. Bake in a preheated oven, 325°F/190°C, for 20 minutes or until springy to the touch. Cool for a few minutes in the pans before transferring to a wire rack to cool completely.

4 To make the filling, beat the confectioners' sugar and butter together in a bowl until light and fluffy.

Melt the cooking chocolate and beat half into the icing mixture. Use the filling to sandwich the 2 cakes together.

5 Spread the remaining melted cooking chocolate over the top of the cake. Pipe circles of contrasting melted light or white chocolate and feather into the cooking chocolate with a toothpick, if desired. Let the cake set before serving.

COOK'S TIP
Ensure that you eat this cake on the day of baking, because it does not keep well.

Chocolate & Vanilla Loaf

An old-fashioned favorite, this cake will keep well if stored in an airtight container or wrapped in foil in a cool place.

50 mins | 30 mins

SERVES 10

INGREDIENTS

¾ cup superfine sugar

¾ cup soft margarine

½ tsp vanilla extract

3 eggs

2 cups self-rising flour, strained

1¾ oz/50 g dark chocolate

confectioners' sugar, to dust

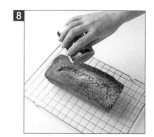

1 Lightly grease a 1 lb/450 g loaf pan.

2 Beat together the sugar and soft margarine in a bowl until the mixture is light and fluffy.

3 Beat in the vanilla extract. Gradually add the eggs, beating well after each addition. Carefully fold the self-rising flour into the mixture.

4 Divide the mixture in half. Melt the dark chocolate and stir into one half of the mixture until well combined.

5 Place the vanilla mixture in the pan and level the top. Spread the chocolate layer over the vanilla layer.

6 Bake in a preheated oven, 375°F/ 190°C, for 30 minutes or until springy to the touch.

7 Let the loaf cool in the pan for a few minutes before transferring to a wire rack to cool completely.

8 Serve the loaf dusted with confectioners' sugar.

COOK'S TIP

Freeze the loaf undecorated for up to 2 months. Thaw at room temperature.

Chocolate Fruit Bread

What better in the afternoon than to sit down with a cup of coffee and a slice of fruit bread, and when it's made of chocolate it's even better.

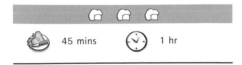

45 mins   1 hr

SERVES 4

INGREDIENTS

¾ cup butter, softened

⅔ cup light brown sugar

4 eggs, lightly beaten

8 oz/225 g dark chocolate chips

½ cup raisins

½ cup chopped walnuts

finely grated zest of 1 orange

2 cups self-rising flour

1 Lightly grease a 2 lb/900 g loaf pan and line the bottom with baking parchment.

2 Cream together the butter and sugar in a bowl until light and fluffy.

3 Gradually add the eggs, beating well after each addition. If the mixture begins to curdle, beat in 1–2 tablespoons of the flour.

4 Stir in the chocolate chips, raisins, walnuts, and orange zest. Strain the flour and carefully fold it into the mixture.

5 Spoon the mixture into the prepared loaf pan and then make a slight dip in the center of the top with the back of a spoon.

6 Bake in a preheated oven, 325°F/ 170°C, for 1 hour or until a fine skewer inserted into the center of the loaf comes out clean.

7 Let the loaf cool in the pan for 5 minutes before carefully turning out on to a wire rack to cool completely.

8 To serve the fruit bread, cut it into thin slices.

VARIATION

Use white or light chocolate chips instead of dark chocolate chips, or a mixture of all three, if desired. Dried cranberries instead of the raisins also work well in this recipe.

Apricot & Chocolate Ring

A tasty fruit bread in the shape of a ring. You could use sultanas instead of the apricots, if preferred.

🍐 1 hr 🕐 30 mins

SERVES 12

INGREDIENTS

⅓ cup diced butter

4 cups self-rising flour, strained

4 tbsp superfine sugar

2 eggs, beaten

⅔ cup milk

FILLING AND DECORATION

2 tbsp butter, melted

5½ oz/150 g no-soak dried apricots, chopped

3½ oz/100 g dark chocolate chips

1–2 tbsp milk, to glaze

1 oz/25 g dark chocolate, melted

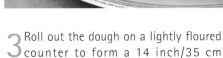

1 Grease a 10 inch/25 cm round cake pan and line the bottom with baking parchment.

2 Rub the butter into the flour until the mixture resembles fine bread crumbs. Stir in the superfine sugar, eggs, and milk to form a soft dough.

3 Roll out the dough on a lightly floured counter to form a 14 inch/35 cm square.

4 Brush the melted butter over the surface of the dough. Mix together the apricots and chocolate chips and spread them over the dough to within 1 inch/2.5 cm of the top and bottom.

5 Roll up the dough tightly, like a jelly roll, and cut it into 1 inch/2.5 cm slices. Stand the slices in a ring around the edge of the prepared pan at a slight tilt. Brush with a little milk.

6 Bake in a preheated oven, 350°F/ 180°C, for 30 minutes or until cooked and golden. Let the bread cool in the pan for about 15 minutes, then transfer to a wire rack to cool.

7 Drizzle the melted chocolate over the ring, to decorate.

COOK'S TIP

This cake is best served very fresh, ideally on the day it is made. It is fabulous served slightly warm.

Chocolate Fruit Loaf

A very moreish loaf that smells divine while cooking. It is best eaten warm.

1 hr 40 mins   30 mins

SERVES 10

INGREDIENTS

3 cups white bread flour

¼ cup unsweetened cocoa

2 tbsp superfine sugar

6 g sachet active dry yeast

¼ tsp salt

1 cup lukewarm water

2 tbsp butter, melted

5 tbsp roughly chopped candied cherries

½ cup dark chocolate chips

⅓ cup golden raisins

2¾ oz/75 g no-soak dried apricots, roughly chopped

GLAZE

1 tbsp superfine sugar

1 tbsp water

1 Lightly grease a 2 lb/900 g loaf pan. Strain the flour and cocoa into a large mixing bowl. Stir in the sugar, dry yeast, and salt.

2 Mix together the lukewarm water and butter. Make a well in the center of the dry ingredients and add the liquid. Mix well with a wooden spoon, then use your hands to bring the dough together. Turn out on to a lightly floured counter and knead for 5 minutes, until a smooth elastic dough forms. Return to a clean bowl, cover with a damp dish towel and let rise in a warm place for about 1 hour or until doubled in size.

3 Turn the dough out on to a floured counter and knead for 5 minutes. Roll out to a rectangle about ½ inch/1 cm thick and the same width as the length of the pan. Scatter the cherries, chocolate chips, golden raisins, and chopped apricots over the dough. Carefully roll up the dough, like a jelly roll, enclosing the filling. Transfer to the loaf pan, cover with a damp dish towel and let rise for 20 minutes or until the top of the dough is level with the top of the pan.

4 To make the glaze, mix together the sugar and water, then brush it over the top of the loaf. Bake in a preheated oven, 400°F/200°C, for 30 minutes or until well risen. Serve.

Mocha Layer Cake

Chocolate cake and a creamy coffee-flavored filling are combined in this delicious mocha cake.

🍰 50 mins   ⏱ 35–45 mins

SERVES 8

INGREDIENTS

1¾ cups self-rising flour

¼ tsp baking powder

4 tbsp unsweetened cocoa

½ cup superfine sugar

2 eggs

2 tbsp light corn syrup

⅔ cup sunflower oil

⅔ cup milk

FILLING

1 tsp instant coffee powder

1 tbsp boiling water

1¼ cups heavy cream

2 tbsp confectioners' sugar

TO DECORATE

1¾ oz/50 g flock chocolate

chocolate caraque (see page 15)

confectioners' sugar, to dust

1 Lightly grease three 7 inch/18 cm cake pans.

2 Strain the flour, baking powder, and cocoa into a large mixing bowl. Stir in the sugar. Make a well in the center and stir in the eggs, syrup, oil, and milk. Beat with a wooden spoon, gradually mixing in the dry ingredients to make a smooth batter. Divide the mixture between the prepared pans.

3 Bake in a preheated oven, 350°F/ 180°C, for 35–45 minutes or until springy to the touch. Let cool in the pans for 5 minutes, then turn out on to a wire rack to cool completely.

4 Dissolve the instant coffee in the boiling water and place in a bowl with the cream and confectioners' sugar. Whip until the cream is just holding its shape. Use half of the cream to sandwich the 3 cakes together. Spread the remaining cream over the top and sides of the cake. Lightly press the flock chocolate into the cream around the edge of the cake.

5 Transfer to a serving plate. Lay the caraque over the top of the cake. Cut a few thin strips of baking parchment and place on top of the caraque. Dust lightly with confectioners' sugar, then carefully remove the paper. Serve.

Chocolate Lamington Cake

This cake is based on an Australian cake named after Lord Lamington, a former Governor of Queensland.

50 mins   40 mins

SERVES 8

INGREDIENTS

¾ cup butter or block margarine

¾ cup superfine sugar

3 eggs, lightly beaten

1¼ cups self-rising flour

2 tbsp unsweetened cocoa

¾ cup confectioners' sugar

1¾ oz/50 g dark chocolate, broken into pieces

5 tbsp milk

1 tsp butter

about 8 tbsp shredded coconut

⅔ cup heavy cream, whipped

1 Lightly grease a 1 lb/450 g loaf pan – preferably a long, thin pan measuring about 3 x 10 inches/7.5 x 25 cm.

2 Cream together the butter and sugar in a bowl until light and fluffy. Gradually add the eggs, beating well after each addition. Strain together the flour and cocoa. Fold into the mixture.

3 Pour the mixture into the prepared pan and level the top. Bake in a preheated oven, 350°F/180°C, for 40 minutes or until springy to the touch. Let cool for 5 minutes in the pan, then turn out on to a wire rack to cool completely.

4 Place the chocolate, milk, and butter in a heatproof bowl set over a pan of hot water. Stir until the chocolate has melted. Add the confectioners' sugar and beat until smooth. Let the icing cool until it is thick enough to spread, then spread it all over the cake. Sprinkle with the shredded coconut and allow the icing to set.

5 Cut a V-shape wedge from the top of the cake. Put the cream in a pastry bag fitted with a plain or star tip. Pipe the cream down the center of the wedge and replace the wedge of cake on top of the cream. Pipe another line of cream down either side of the wedge of cake. Serve.

Rich Chocolate Layer Cake

Thin layers of delicious light chocolate cake sandwiched together with a rich chocolate icing.

🍳 1 hr 5 mins 🕐 30–35 mins

SERVES 10

INGREDIENTS

7 eggs

scant 1 cup superfine sugar

1¼ cups all-purpose flour

½ cup unsweetened cocoa

4 tbsp butter, melted

FILLING

7 oz/200 g dark chocolate

½ cup butter

¼ cup icing confectioners' sugar

TO DECORATE

¾ cup lightly crushed, toasted flaked almonds

quick chocolate curls (see page 15) or grated chocolate

1 Grease a deep 9 inch/23 cm square cake pan and line the bottom with baking parchment.

2 Whisk the eggs and superfine sugar in a mixing bowl with an electric whisk for about 10 minutes, or until the mixture is very light and foamy and the whisk leaves a trail that lasts a few seconds when lifted.

3 Strain the flour and cocoa together and fold half into the mixture. Drizzle over the melted butter and fold in the rest of the flour and cocoa. Pour into the prepared pan and bake in a preheated oven, 350°F/180°C, for 30–35 minutes or until springy to the touch. Let the cake cool slightly, then remove from the pan and cool completely on a wire

rack. Wash and dry the pan and return the cake to it.

4 While the cake is cooling, make the filling. Melt the chocolate and butter together, then remove from the heat. Stir in the confectioners' sugar, let cool, then beat until thick enough to spread.

5 Halve the cooled cake lengthwise and cut each half into 3 layers. Sandwich the layers together with three-quarters of the chocolate filling. Spread the remainder over the cake and mark a wavy pattern on the top. Press the almonds on to the sides. Decorate with chocolate curls or grated chocolate.

Chocolate & Mango Layer

Canned peaches can be used instead of mangoes for this deliciously moist cake, if you prefer.

1¼ hrs   1 hr

SERVES 12

INGREDIENTS

½ cup unsweetened cocoa

⅔ cup boiling water

6 large eggs

1½ cups superfine sugar

2½ cups self-rising flour

1 lb 12 oz/800 g canned mangoes

1 tsp cornstarch

generous 1¾ cups heavy cream

2¾ oz/75 g dark flock chocolate or grated chocolate

1 Grease a deep 9 inch/23 cm round cake pan and line the bottom with baking parchment.

2 Place the cocoa in a small bowl and gradually add the boiling water; blend to form a smooth paste.

3 Place the eggs and superfine sugar in a mixing bowl and whisk until the mixture is very light and foamy and the whisk leaves a trail that lasts a few seconds when lifted. Fold in the cocoa mixture. Strain the self-rising flour and fold into the mixture.

4 Pour the mixture into the pan and level the top. Bake in a preheated oven, 325°F/170°C, for about 1 hour or until springy to the touch.

5 Let the cake cool in the pan for a few minutes then turn out and cool completely on a wire rack. Peel off the lining paper and cut the cake into 3 layers.

6 Drain the mangoes and place a quarter of them in a food processor and blend until smooth. Mix the cornstarch with about 3 tablespoons of the mango juice to form a smooth paste. Add to the blended mangoes. Transfer to a small pan and heat gently, stirring until the paste thickens. Let cool.

7 Chop the remaining mango. Whip the cream and reserve about one quarter. Fold the mango into the remaining cream and use to sandwich the layers of cake together. Place on a serving plate. Spread some of the remaining cream around the side of the cake. Press the flock or grated chocolate lightly into the cream. Pipe cream rosettes around the top. Spread the mango paste over the center.

Devil's Food Cake

This is a classic recipe, consisting of a rich melt-in-the-mouth chocolate cake with a citrus-flavored frosting.

🍰 1 hr   🕐 30 mins

SERVES 6

INGREDIENTS

3½ oz/100 g dark chocolate

2¼ cups self-rising flour

1 tsp baking soda

1 cup butter

2⅔ cups dark brown sugar

1 tsp vanilla extract

3 eggs

½ cup buttermilk

scant 1 cup boiling water

FROSTING

1¼ cups superfine sugar

2 egg whites

1 tbsp lemon juice

3 tbsp orange juice

candied orange zest, to decorate

1 Lightly grease 2 shallow 8 inch/20 cm round cake pans and line the bottoms. Melt the chocolate in a pan. Strain the flour and baking soda together.

2 Beat the butter and sugar in a bowl until pale and fluffy. Beat in the vanilla extract and the eggs one at a time, beating well after each addition. Add a little flour if the mixture begins to curdle.

3 Fold the melted chocolate into the mixture until well blended. Gradually fold in the remaining flour, then stir in the buttermilk and boiling water.

4 Divide the mixture between the pans and level the tops. Bake in a preheated oven, 375°F/190°C, for 30 minutes, until springy to the touch. Let the cake cool in the pan for 5 minutes, then transfer to a wire rack to cool completely.

5 Place the frosting ingredients in a large bowl set over a pan of gently simmering water. Whisk, preferably with an electric beater, until thickened and forming soft peaks. Remove from the heat and whisk until the mixture is cool.

6 Sandwich the 2 cakes together with a little of the frosting, then spread the remainder over the sides and top of the cake, swirling it as you do so. Decorate with the candied orange zest.

Chocolate Passion Cake

What could be nicer than passion cake with added chocolate?
Rich and moist, this cake is fabulous with afternoon tea.

45 mins   45 mins

SERVES 6

INGREDIENTS

5 eggs

⅔ cup superfine sugar

1¼ cups all-purpose flour

⅓ cup unsweetened cocoa

2 carrots, peeled, finely grated and
   squeezed until dry

⅓ cup chopped walnuts

2 tbsp sunflower oil

12 oz/350 g medium fat soft cheese

1½ cups confectioners' sugar

6 oz/175 g light or dark chocolate, melted

1 Lightly grease and line the bottom of an 8 inch/20 cm deep round cake pan.

2 Place the eggs and sugar in a large mixing bowl set over a pan of gently simmering water and whisk until very thick. Lift the whisk up and let the mixture drizzle back—it will leave a trail for a few seconds when thick enough.

3 Remove the bowl from the heat. Strain the flour and cocoa into the bowl and carefully fold in. Fold in the grated carrots, walnuts, and oil until they are just combined.

4 Pour into the prepared pan and bake in a preheated oven, 375°F/190°C, for 45 minutes. Let the cake cool slightly then turn out on to a wire rack to cool completely.

5 Beat together the soft cheese and confectioners' sugar until combined. Beat in the melted chocolate. Split the cake in half and sandwich together again with half of the chocolate mixture. Cover the top of the cake with the remainder of the chocolate mixture, swirling it with a knife. Let chill, or serve at once.

COOK'S TIP

The undecorated cake can be frozen for up to 2 months. Thaw at room temperature for 3 hours or overnight in the refrigerator.

Chocolate Yogurt Cake

Adding yogurt to the cake mixture gives the baked cake a deliciously moist texture.

55 mins   45–50 mins

SERVES 8

INGREDIENTS

⅔ cup vegetable oil

⅔ cup whole milk unsweetened yogurt

1¼ cups light brown sugar

3 eggs, beaten

¾ cup whole-wheat self-rising flour

1 cup self-rising flour, strained

2 tbsp unsweetened cocoa

1 tsp baking soda

1¾ oz/50 g dark chocolate, melted

FILLING AND TOPPING

⅔ cup whole milk unsweetened yogurt

⅔ cup heavy cream

8 oz/225 g fresh soft fruit, such as strawberries or raspberries

1 Grease a deep 9 inch/23 cm round cake pan and line the bottom with baking parchment.

2 Place the oil, yogurt, sugar, and beaten eggs in a large mixing bowl and beat together until well combined. Strain the flours, cocoa, and baking soda together and beat into the bowl until well combined. Beat in the melted chocolate.

3 Pour into the prepared pan and bake in a preheated oven, 350°F/180°C, for 45–50 minutes or until a fine skewer inserted into the center comes out clean. Let the cake cool in the pan for 5 minutes, then turn out on to a wire rack to cool completely. When cold, split the cake into 3 layers.

4 To make the filling, place the yogurt and cream in a large mixing bowl and whisk well until the mixture stands in soft peaks.

5 Place one layer of cake on to a serving plate and spread with some of the cream. Top with a little of the fruit (slicing larger fruit such as strawberries). Repeat with the next layer. Top with the final layer of cake and spread with the rest of the cream. Arrange more fruit on top and cut the cake into wedges to serve.

Chocolate Layer Log

This unusual cake is very popular with children who love the appearance of the layers when it is sliced.

🍳 55 mins 🕐 40 mins

SERVES 8

INGREDIENTS

½ cup soft margarine

½ cup superfine sugar

2 eggs

¾ cup self-rising flour

¼ cup unsweetened cocoa

2 tbsp milk

WHITE CHOCOLATE BUTTER CREAM

2¾ oz/75 g white chocolate

2 tbsp milk

⅔ cup butter

¾ cup confectioners' sugar

2 tbsp orange-flavored liqueur

quick chocolate curls (see page 15), to decorate

1 Grease and line the sides of two 14 oz/400 g food cans.

2 Beat together the margarine and sugar in a bowl until light and fluffy. Gradually add the eggs, beating well after each addition. Strain together the flour and cocoa powder and fold into the cake mixture. Fold in the milk.

3 Divide the mixture between the two prepared cans. Stand the cans on a cookie sheet and bake in a preheated oven, 350°F/180°C, for 40 minutes or until springy to the touch. Leave to cool for about 5 minutes in the cans, then turn out and cool completely on a wire rack.

4 Meanwhile, make the butter cream. Put the chocolate and milk in a pan and heat gently until the chocolate has melted, stirring until well combined. Let cool slightly. Beat together the butter and confectioners' sugar until light and fluffy. Beat in the orange liqueur. Gradually beat in the chocolate mixture.

5 To assemble, cut both cakes into ½ inch/1 cm thick slices, then reassemble them by sandwiching the slices together with some of the butter cream.

6 Place the cake on a serving plate and spread the remaining butter cream over the top and sides. Decorate with the chocolate curls, then serve the cake cut diagonally into slices.

Mousse Cake

With a dark chocolate sponge sandwiched together with a light, creamy orange mousse, this spectacular cake is irresistible.

🥧 1¼ hrs ⏰ 40 mins

SERVES 12

INGREDIENTS

¾ cup butter

¾ cup superfine sugar

4 eggs, lightly beaten

1¾ cups self-rising flour

1 tbsp unsweetened cocoa

1¾ oz/50 g dark, orange-flavored chocolate, melted

ORANGE MOUSSE

2 eggs, separated

4 tbsp superfine sugar

generous ¾ cup freshly squeezed orange juice

2 tsp gelatin

3 tbsp water

1¼ cups heavy cream

peeled orange slices, to decorate

1 Grease an 8 inch/20 cm springform cake pan and and line the bottom. Beat the butter and sugar in a bowl until light and fluffy. Gradually add the eggs, beating well after each addition. Strain together the cocoa and flour and fold into the cake mixture. Fold in the chocolate.

2 Pour into the prepared pan and level the top. Bake in a preheated oven, 350°F/180°C, for 40 minutes or until springy to the touch. Let the cake cool for 5 minutes in the pan, then turn out and cool completely on a wire rack.

3 Meanwhile, make the orange mousse. Beat the egg yolks and sugar until light, then whisk in the orange juice. Sprinkle the gelatin over the water in a

small bowl and allow to go spongy, then place over a pan of hot water and stir until the gelatin has dissolved. Stir into the mousse.

4 Whip the cream until holding its shape, reserve a little for decoration and fold the rest into the mousse. Whisk the egg whites until standing in soft

peaks, then fold in. Let stand a cool place until starting to set, stirring occasionally.

5 Cut the cold cake into 2 layers. Place half of the cake in the pan. Pour in the mousse and press the second cake layer on top. Chill until set. Transfer to a dish, pipe cream rosettes on the top and arrange orange slices in the center.

Chocolate Roulade

Don't worry if the cake cracks when rolled, this is quite normal. If it doesn't crack, consider yourself a real chocolate wizard in the kitchen!

SERVES 6

INGREDIENTS

5½ oz/150 g dark chocolate

2 tbsp water

6 eggs

¾ cup superfine sugar

¼ cup plain flour

1 tbsp unsweetened cocoa

FILLING

1¼ cups heavy cream

2¾ oz/75 g sliced strawberries

TO DECORATE

confectioners' sugar

chocolate leaves (see page 15)

1 Line a 15 x 10 inch/37.5 x 25 cm jelly roll pan. Melt the chocolate in the water, stirring. Let cool slightly.

2 Place the eggs and sugar in a bowl and whisk for 10 minutes, or until the mixture is pale and foamy and the whisk leaves a trail when lifted. Whisk in the chocolate in a thin stream. Strain the flour and cocoa together and fold into the mixture. Pour into the tin; level the top.

3 Bake in a preheated oven, 400°F/ 200°C, for 12 minutes. Dust a sheet of baking parchment with a little confectioners' sugar. Turn out the roulade and remove the lining paper. Roll up the roulade with the fresh parchment inside. Place on a wire rack, cover with a damp dish towel and let cool.

4 Whisk the cream. Unroll the roulade and scatter over the fruit. Spread three-quarters of the cream over the roulade and re-roll. Dust with confectioners' sugar.

5 Place the roulade on a plate. Pipe the rest of the cream down the center. Make the chocolate leaves (see page 15) and use them to decorate the roulade.

Chocolate & Coconut Roulade

A coconut-flavored roulade is encased in a rich chocolate coating. A fresh raspberry coulis contrasts with the sweetness of the roulade.

55 mins   10–12 mins

SERVES 8

INGREDIENTS

3 eggs

⅓ cup superfine sugar

⅓ cup self-rising flour

1 tbsp block creamed coconut, softened with 1 tbsp boiling water

¼ cup shredded coconut

6 tbsp good raspberry conserve

CHOCOLATE COATING

7 oz/200 g dark chocolate

5 tbsp butter

2 tbsp light corn syrup

RASPBERRY COULIS

8 oz/225 g fresh or frozen raspberries, thawed if frozen

2 tbsp water

4 tbsp confectioners' sugar

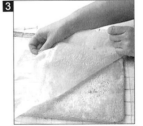

1 Grease and line a 9 x 12 inch/ 23 x 30 cm jelly roll pan. Whisk the eggs and superfine sugar in a large mixing bowl with an electric whisk for about 10 minutes or until the mixture is very light and foamy and the whisk leaves a trail that lasts a few seconds when lifted.

2 Strain the flour and fold in with a metal spoon or a spatula. Fold in the creamed coconut and shredded coconut. Pour into the prepared tin pan and bake in a preheated oven, 400°F/200°C, for 10–12 minutes, or until springy to the touch.

3 Sprinkle a sheet of baking parchment with a little superfine sugar and place on top of a damp dish towel. Turn the cake out on to the paper and carefully peel away the lining parchment. Spread the raspberry conserve over the sponge and roll up from one of the short ends, using the dish towel to help you. Place the roulade seam-side down on a wire rack and let cool completely.

4 Meanwhile, make the coating. Melt the chocolate and butter, stirring. Stir in the syrup and let the mixture cool for 5 minutes. Spread it over the roulade and let stand until set. To make the coulis, blend the fruit to a paste in a food processor with the water and sugar, and strain to remove the seeds. Cut the roulade into slices and serve with the coulis.

Almond & Hazelnut Gateau

This is a light, nutty cake made with a rich chocolate cream. Simple to create, it is a gateau you are sure to make again and again.

2 hrs   15–20 mins

SERVES 8

INGREDIENTS

4 eggs

½ cup superfine sugar

½ cup ground almonds

½ cup ground hazelnuts

⅓ cup all-purpose flour

½ cup flaked almonds

FILLING

3½ oz/100 g dark chocolate

1 tbsp butter

1¼ cups heavy cream

confectioners' sugar, to dust

1 Grease 2 round 7 inch/18 cm layer cake pans and line the bottoms with baking parchment.

2 Whisk the eggs and superfine sugar in a large mixing bowl with an electric whisk for about 10 minutes, or until the mixture is very light and foamy and the whisk leaves a trail that lasts a few seconds when lifted.

3 Fold in the ground nuts, strain the flour and fold in with a metal spoon or spatula. Pour into the prepared pans.

4 Scatter the flaked almonds over the top of one of the cakes. Bake both of the cakes in a preheated oven, 375°F/190°C, for 15–20 minutes or until springy to the touch.

5 Let the cakes cool slightly in the pans. Carefully remove the cakes from the pans and transfer them to a wire rack to cool completely.

6 Meanwhile, make the filling. Melt the chocolate, remove from the heat and stir in the butter. Let the mixture cool slightly. Whip the cream until just holding its shape, then fold in the melted chocolate until mixed.

7 Place the cake without the extra almonds on a serving plate and spread the filling over it. Let the filling set slightly, then place the almond-topped cake on top and chill for about 1 hour. Dust with confectioners' sugar and serve.

Chocolate & Walnut Cake

This walnut-studded chocolate cake has a tasty chocolate butter icing. It is perfect for coffee mornings because it can easily be made the day before.

🍰 1 hr   🕐 30–35 mins

SERVES 8

INGREDIENTS

4 eggs

½ cup superfine sugar

1 cup all-purpose flour

1 tbsp unsweetened cocoa

2 tbsp butter, melted

2¾ oz/75 g dark chocolate, melted

1¼ cups finely chopped walnuts

ICING

2¾ oz/75 g dark chocolate

½ cup butter

1¼ cups confectioners' sugar

2 tbsp milk

walnut halves, to decorate

1 Grease a 7 inch/18 cm deep round cake pan and line the bottom. Place the eggs and superfine sugar in a mixing bowl and beat with an electric whisk for 10 minutes, or until the mixture is light and foamy and the whisk leaves a trail that lasts a few seconds when lifted.

2 Strain together the flour and cocoa powder and fold in with a metal spoon or spatula. Fold in the melted butter and chocolate, and the chopped walnuts. Pour into the prepared pan and bake in a preheated oven, 325°F/160°C, and bake for 30–35 minutes or until the cake is springy to the touch.

3 Let cool in the pan for 5 minutes, then transfer to a wire rack to cool completely.

4 Meanwhile, make the icing. Melt the dark chocolate and let it cool slightly. Beat together the butter, confectioners' sugar, and milk in a bowl until the mixture is pale and fluffy. Whisk in the melted chocolate.

5 Cut the cold cake into 2 layers. Sandwich the 2 layers with some of the icing and place on a serving plate. Spread the remaining icing over the top of the cake with a spatula, swirling it slightly as you do so. Decorate the cake with the walnut halves and serve.

Dobos Torte

This wonderful cake originates from Hungary and consists of thin layers of light sponge topped with a crunchy caramel layer.

40 mins　　10–16 mins

SERVES 8

INGREDIENTS

3 eggs

½ cup superfine sugar

1 tsp vanilla extract

¾ cup all-purpose flour

FILLING

6 oz/175 g dark chocolate

¾ cup butter

2 tbsp milk

3 cups confectioners' sugar

CARAMEL

½ cup granulated sugar

4 tbsp water

1 Draw four 7 inch/18 cm circles on sheets of baking parchment. Place 2 of them upside down on 2 cookie sheets.

2 Beat the eggs and superfine sugar in a large mixing bowl with an electric whisk for 10 minutes, or until the mixture is light and foamy and the whisk leaves a trail. Fold in the vanilla extract. Strain the flour and fold in with a metal spoon.

3 Spoon a quarter of the mixture on to one of the cookie sheets and spread out to the size of the circle. Repeat with the other circle. Bake in a preheated oven, 400°F/200°C, for 5–8 minutes or until golden brown. Cool on wire racks. Repeat with the remaining mixture.

4 To make the filling, melt the chocolate and cool slightly. Beat the butter, milk, and confectioners' sugar until pale and fluffy. Whisk in the chocolate.

5 Place the sugar and water for the caramel in a heavy-based pan. Heat gently, stirring, to dissolve the sugar. Boil gently until pale golden in color. Remove from the heat. Pour over one cake layer as a topping. Let harden slightly, then mark into 8 portions with an oiled knife.

6 Remove the cakes from the parchment. Trim the edges. Sandwich the layers together with some of the filling, finishing with the caramel-topped cake. Place on a serving plate, spread the sides with the filling mixture, and pipe rosettes around the top of the cake.

Bistvitny Torte

This is a Russian marbled chocolate cake that is soaked in a delicious flavored syrup and decorated with chocolate and cream.

1 hr 10 mins   30 mins

SERVES 10

INGREDIENTS

CHOCOLATE TRIANGLES

1 oz/25 g dark chocolate, melted

1 oz/25 g white chocolate, melted

CAKE

¾ cup soft margarine

¾ cup superfine sugar

½ tsp vanilla extract

3 eggs, lightly beaten

2 cups self-rising flour

1¾ oz/50 g dark chocolate

SYRUP

½ cup granulated sugar

6 tbsp water

3 tbsp brandy or sherry

⅔ cup heavy cream

1 Grease a 9 inch/23 cm ring pan. To make the triangles, place a sheet of baking parchment on to a cookie sheet and place alternate spoonfuls of the dark and white chocolate on to the paper. Spread together to form a thick marbled layer, and let the chocolate set. Cut into squares, then into triangles.

2 To make the cake, beat the margarine and sugar until light and fluffy. Beat in the vanilla extract. Gradually add the eggs, beating well after each addition. Fold in the flour. Divide the mixture in half. Melt the dark chocolate and stir into one half.

3 Place spoonfuls of each mixture into the prepared pan and swirl together with a skewer to create a marbled effect.

4 Bake in a preheated oven, 375°F/190°C, for 30 minutes, or until the cake is springy to the touch. Let cool in the pan for a few minutes, then transfer to a wire rack to cool completely.

5 To make the syrup, place the sugar in a small pan with the water and heat until the sugar has dissolved. Boil for 1–2 minutes. Remove from the heat and stir in the brandy or sherry. Let the syrup cool slightly then spoon it slowly over the cake, allowing it to soak into the sponge. Whip the cream and pipe swirls of it on top of the cake. Decorate with the marbled chocolate triangles.

Sachertorte

This rich melt-in-the mouth cake originates in Austria. Make sure you have a steady hand when writing the name on the top.

🍰 3½ hrs   🕐 1–1¼ hrs

SERVES 10

INGREDIENTS

6 oz/175 g dark chocolate

⅔ cup sweet butter

⅔ cup superfine sugar

6 eggs, separated

1¼ cups all-purpose flour

ICING AND FILLING

6 oz/175 g dark chocolate

5 tbsp strong black coffee

1 cup icing confectioners' sugar

6 tbsp good apricot preserve

1¾ oz/50 g dark chocolate, melted

1 Grease a 9 inch/23 cm springform cake pan and line the bottom. Melt the chocolate. Beat the butter and ⅓ cup of the sugar until pale and fluffy. Add the egg yolks and beat well. Add the chocolate in a thin stream, beating well. Strain the flour; fold it into the mixture. Whisk the egg whites until they stand in soft peaks. Add the remaining sugar and whisk for 2 minutes by hand, or 45–60 seconds if using an electric whisk, until glossy. Fold half into the chocolate mixture, then fold in the remainder.

2 Spoon into the prepared pan and level the top. Bake in a preheated oven, 300°F/150°C, for 1–1¼ hours until a skewer inserted into the center comes out clean. Cool in the pan for 5 minutes, then transfer to a wire rack to cool completely.

3 To make the icing, melt the chocolate and beat in the coffee until smooth. Strain the confectioners' sugar into a bowl. Whisk in the melted chocolate mixture to give a thick icing. Halve the cake. Warm the apricot preserve, spread over one half of the cake and sandwich together. Invert the cake on a wire rack. Spoon the icing over the cake and spread to coat the top and sides. Let the icing set

for 5 minutes, allowing any excess to drop through the rack. Transfer to a serving plate and allow to set for at least 2 hours.

4 To decorate, spoon the melted chocolate into a small pastry bag and pipe the word 'Sacher' or 'Sachertorte' on the top of the cake. Let it harden before serving the cake.

Dark & White Chocolate Torte

If you can't decide if you prefer bitter dark chocolate or rich creamy white chocolate, then this gateau is for you.

🍰 1 hr 5 mins 🕐 35–40 mins

SERVES 6

INGREDIENTS

4 eggs

½ cup superfine sugar

¾ cup all-purpose flour

DARK CHOCOLATE CREAM

⅔ cup heavy cream

5½ oz/150 g dark chocolate, broken into small pieces

WHITE CHOCOLATE ICING

2¾ oz/75 g white chocolate

1 tbsp butter

1 tbsp milk

4 tbsp confectioners' sugar

chocolate caraque (see page 15)

1 Grease an 8 inch/20 cm round springform pan and line the bottom. Beat the eggs and superfine sugar in a large mixing bowl with an electric whisk for about 10 minutes, or until the mixture is very light and foamy and the whisk leaves a trail that lasts a few seconds when lifted.

2 Strain the flour and fold in with a metal spoon or spatula. Pour into the prepared pan and bake in a preheated oven, 350°F/180°C, for 35–40 minutes or until springy to the touch. Let the cake cool slightly, then transfer to a wire rack to cool completely.

3 While the cake is cooling, make the chocolate cream. Place the cream in a pan and bring to a boil, stirring. Add the chocolate and stir until melted and well combined. Remove from the heat, transfer to a bowl, and let cool. Beat with a wooden spoon until thick.

4 Cut the cold cake into 2 layers horizontally. Sandwich the layers back together with the chocolate cream and place on a wire rack.

5 To make the icing, melt the chocolate and butter together and stir until blended. Whisk in the milk and confectioners' sugar, and continue whisking until cool. Pour over the cake and spread with a spatula to coat the top and sides. Decorate with chocolate caraque and let the icing set.

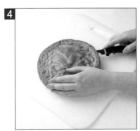

Chocolate Ganache Cake

Ganache—a divine mixture of chocolate and cream—is used to fill and decorate this rich chocolate cake, making it a chocolate-lover's dream.

🍲 2 hrs 5 mins   🕐 40 mins

SERVES 10

I N G R E D I E N T S

¾ cup butter

¾ cup superfine sugar

4 eggs, lightly beaten

1¾ cups self-rising flour

1 tbsp unsweetened cocoa

1¾ oz/50 g dark chocolate, melted

G A N A C H E

2 cups heavy cream

13 oz/375 g dark chocolate, broken into pieces

T O   F I N I S H

7 oz/200 g chocolate-flavored cake covering

1 Lightly grease an 8 inch/20 cm springform cake pan and line the bottom. Beat the butter and sugar until light and fluffy. Gradually add the eggs, beating well after each addition. Strain together the flour and cocoa. Fold into the cake mixture. Fold in the melted chocolate.

2 Pour into the prepared pan and level the top. Bake in a preheated oven, 350°F/180°C, for 40 minutes or until springy to the touch. Let the cake cool for 5 minutes in the pan, then turn out on to a wire rack and let cool completely. Cut the cold cake into 2 layers.

3 To make the ganache, place the cream in a pan and bring to a boil, stirring. Add the chocolate and stir until melted and combined. Pour into a bowl and whisk

for about 5 minutes or until the ganache is fluffy and cool.

4 Reserve one-third of the ganache. Use the remaining ganache to sandwich the cake together and spread over the top and sides of the cake.

5 Melt the cake covering and spread it over a large sheet of baking

parchment. Let cool until just set. Cut into strips a little wider than the height of the cake. Place the strips around the edge of the cake, overlapping them slightly.

6 Pipe the reserved ganache in tear drops or shells to cover the top of the cake. Chill for 1 hour.

Bûche de Noël

This is the traditional French Christmas cake. It consists of a chocolate cake roll filled with and encased in a delicious rich chocolate icing.

🍰 1 hr   🕐 12 mins

SERVES 10

INGREDIENTS

CAKE

4 eggs

½ cup superfine sugar

⅔ cup self-rising flour

2 tbsp unsweetened cocoa

ICING

5½ oz/150 g dark chocolate

2 egg yolks

⅔ cup milk

½ cup butter

4 tbsp confectioners' sugar

2 tbsp rum, optional

TO DECORATE

a little white candied or royal icing

confectioners' sugar, to dust

holly leaves

1 Grease and line a 12 x 9 inch/ 30 x 23 cm jelly roll pan.

2 Beat the eggs and superfine sugar in a bowl with an electric whisk for 10 minutes, or until the mixture is very light and foamy and the whisk leaves a trail. Strain the flour and cocoa and fold in. Pour into the prepared pan and bake in a preheated oven, 400°F/200°C, for 12 minutes or until springy to the touch. Turn out on to baking parchment sprinkled with a little superfine sugar. Peel off the lining parchment and trim the edges. Cut a small slit halfway into the cake, ½ inch/1 cm from one of the short ends. Starting at that end, roll up tightly, enclosing the parchment. Place on a wire rack to cool.

3 To make the icing, break the chocolate into pieces and melt in a heatproof bowl over a pan of hot water. Beat in the egg yolks, whisk in the milk and cook until the mixture thickens enough to coat the back of a wooden spoon, stirring. Cover with dampened waxed paper and cool. Beat the butter and sugar until pale. Beat in the custard and rum, if using.

4 Unroll the sponge, spread with one-third of the icing and roll up. Place on a serving plate. Spread the remaining icing over the cake and mark with a fork to give the effect of bark. Let the icing set. Pipe white icing to form the rings of the log. Sprinkle with sugar and decorate.

Chocolate Truffle Cake

Soft chocolate sponge topped with a rich chocolate truffle mixture makes a cake that chocoholics will die for.

4¾ hrs   20–25 mins

SERVES 12

INGREDIENTS

⅓ cup butter

⅓ cup superfine sugar

2 eggs, lightly beaten

⅔ cup self-rising flour

½ tsp baking powder

¼ cup unsweetened cocoa

½ cup ground almonds

TRUFFLE TOPPING

12 oz/350 g dark chocolate

½ cup butter

1¼ cups heavy cream

1¼ cups plain cake crumbs

3 tbsp dark rum

TO DECORATE

ground cherries

1¾ oz/50 g dark chocolate, melted

1 Lightly grease an 8 inch/20 cm round springform pan and line the bottom. Beat together the butter and sugar until light and fluffy. Gradually add the eggs, beating well after each addition.

2 Strain the flour, baking powder, and cocoa together and fold into the mixture along with the ground almonds. Pour into the prepared pan and bake in a preheated oven, 350°F/180°C, for 20–25 minutes or until springy to the touch. Let the cake cool slightly in the pan, then transfer to a wire rack to cool completely. Wash and dry the pan and return the cooled cake to the pan.

3 To make the topping, heat the chocolate, butter, and cream in a heavy-based pan over a low heat and stir until smooth. Cool, then chill for 30 minutes. Beat well with a wooden spoon and chill for a further 30 minutes. Beat the mixture again, then add the cake crumbs and rum, beating until well combined. Spoon over the sponge cake and chill for 3 hours.

4 Meanwhile, dip the ground cherries in the melted chocolate until partially covered. Set aside on baking parchment to set. Transfer the cake to a serving plate; decorate with ground cherries.

White Truffle Cake

A light white sponge, topped with a rich creamy-white chocolate truffle mixture, makes an out-of-this-world gateau.

🍰 3¼ hrs 🕐 25 mins

SERVES 12

INGREDIENTS

2 eggs

4 tbsp superfine sugar

⅓ cup all-purpose flour

1¾ oz/50 g white chocolate, melted

TRUFFLE TOPPING

1¼ cups heavy cream

12 oz/350 g white chocolate, broken into pieces

9 oz/250 g Quark or mascarpone cheese

TO DECORATE

dark, light, or white chocolate caraque (see page 15)

unsweetened cocoa, to dust

1 Grease an 8 inch/20 cm round springform pan and line the bottom.

2 Whisk the eggs and superfine sugar in a mixing bowl for 10 minutes, or until the mixture is very light and foamy and the whisk leaves a trail that lasts a few seconds when lifted. Strain the flour and fold in with a metal spoon. Fold in the melted white chocolate. Pour into the pan and bake in a preheated oven, 350°F/180°C, for 25 minutes or until springy to the touch. Let cool slightly, then transfer to a wire rack until completely cold. Return the cold cake to the pan.

3 To make the topping, place the cream in a pan and bring to a boil, stirring to prevent it sticking to the bottom of the pan. Cool slightly, then add the white chocolate pieces and stir until melted and combined. Remove from the heat and stir until almost cool, then stir in the Quark or mascarpone. Pour the mixture on top of the cake and chill for 2 hours.

4 Remove the cake from the pan and transfer to a serving plate. Make the caraque (see page 15) and then use it to decorate the top of the cake.

Raspberry Vacherin

A vacherin is made of layers of crisp meringue sandwiched together with fruit and cream. It makes a fabulous gateau for special occasions.

1¾ hrs   1½ hrs

SERVES 10

INGREDIENTS

3 egg whites

¾ cup superfine sugar

1 tsp cornstarch

1 oz/25 g dark chocolate, grated

FILLING

6 oz/175 g dark chocolate

2 cups heavy cream, whipped

12 oz/350 g fresh raspberries

a little melted chocolate, to decorate

1 Draw 3 rectangles, 4 x 10 inches/ 10 x 25 cm, on sheets of baking parchment, and place on 2 cookie sheets.

2 Whisk the egg whites in a mixing bowl until standing in soft peaks, then gradually whisk in half of the sugar and continue whisking until the mixture is very stiff and glossy.

3 Carefully fold in the rest of the sugar, the cornstarch, and the grated chocolate with a metal spoon or a spatula.

4 Spoon the meringue mixture into a pastry bag fitted with a ½ inch/1 cm plain tip and pipe lines across the rectangles.

5 Bake in a preheated oven, 275°F/ 140°C, for 1½ hours, changing the positions of the cookie sheets halfway through. Without opening the oven door, turn off the oven and let the meringues cool inside the oven, then peel away the baking parchment.

6 To make the filling, melt the chocolate and spread it over 2 of the meringue layers. Let the filling harden.

7 Place 1 chocolate-coated meringue on a plate and top with about one-third of the cream and raspberries. Gently place the second chocolate-coated meringue on top and spread with half of the remaining cream and raspberries.

8 Place the last meringue on the top and decorate with the remaining cream and raspberries. Drizzle a little melted chocolate over the top and serve.

Tropical Fruit Vacherin

Meringue layers are sandwiched with a rich chocolate cream and topped with tropical fruit. Prepare in advance and make up just before required.

 1½ hrs   1½ hrs

SERVES 10

INGREDIENTS

6 egg whites

1¼ cups superfine sugar

¾ cup shredded coconut

FILLING AND TOPPING

3 oz/85 g dark chocolate, broken into pieces

3 egg yolks

3 tbsp water

1 tbsp rum, optional

4 tbsp superfine sugar

2 cups heavy cream

selection of tropical fruits, sliced or cut into bite-sized pieces

1 Draw 3 circles, each 8 inches/20 cm across, on baking parchment, and place on cookie sheets.

2 Whisk the egg whites until standing in soft peaks, then gradually whisk in half of the sugar and continue whisking until the mixture is very stiff and glossy. Carefully fold in the remaining sugar and the coconut.

  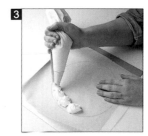

3 Spoon the mixture into a pastry bag fitted with a star tip and cover the circles with piped swirls. Bake in a preheated oven, 275°F/140°C, for 1½ hours, changing the position of the cookie sheets halfway through. Without opening the oven door, turn off the oven and let the meringues cool inside the oven, then peel away the baking parchment.

4 While the meringues are cooling, make the filling. Place the chocolate pieces, egg yolks, water, rum, if using, and sugar in a small bowl and place it over a pan of gently simmering water. Cook over a low heat, stirring, until the chocolate has melted and the mixture has thickened. Cover with a disc of baking parchment and set aside until cold.

5 Whip the cream and fold two-thirds of it into the chocolate mixture. Sandwich the meringue layers together with the chocolate mixture. Place the remaining cream in a pastry bag fitted with a star tip and pipe around the edge of the meringue. Arrange the tropical fruits in the center.

Chocolate Brownie Roulade

The addition of nuts and raisins has given this dessert extra texture, making it similar to that of chocolate brownies.

1 hr   25 mins

SERVES 8

INGREDIENTS

5 ½ oz/150 g dark chocolate, broken into pieces

3 tbsp water

¾ cup superfine sugar

5 eggs, separated

2 tbsp raisins, chopped

2 tbsp chopped pecan nuts

pinch of salt

1¼ cups heavy cream, lightly whipped

confectioners' sugar, for dusting

1 Grease a 12 x 8 inch/30 x 20 cm jelly roll pan, line with baking parchment and grease the parchment.

2 Melt the chocolate with the water in a small pan over a low heat until the chocolate has just melted. Let cool.

3 In a bowl, whisk the sugar and egg yolks for 2–3 minutes with a hand-held electric whisk until thick and pale.

4 Fold in the cooled chocolate, raisins, and pecan nuts.

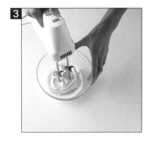

5 In a separate bowl, whisk the egg whites with the salt. Fold one quarter of the egg whites into the chocolate mixture, then fold in the rest of the whites, working lightly and quickly.

6 Transfer the mixture to the prepared pan and bake in a preheated oven, 350°F/180°C, for 25 minutes, until risen and just firm to the touch. Let the cake cool before covering with a sheet of non-stick baking parchment and a damp clean dish towel. Set aside until completely cold.

7 Turn the roulade out on to another piece of baking parchment dusted with confectioners' sugar and remove the lining paper.

8 Spread the cream over the roulade. Starting from a short end, roll the sponge away from you using the parchment to guide you. Trim the ends of the roulade to make a neat finish and transfer to a serving plate. Chill in the refrigerator until ready to serve. Dust with a little confectioners' sugar before serving.

Chocolate & Apricot Squares

The white chocolate makes this a very rich cake, so serve it cut into small squares or bars, or sliced thinly.

50 mins 25–30 mins

SERVES 12

I N G R E D I E N T S

½ cup butter

6 oz/175 g white chocolate, chopped

4 eggs

½ cup superfine sugar

1¾ cups all-purpose flour, strained

1 tsp baking powder

pinch of salt

3½ oz/100 g no-soak dried apricots, chopped

1 Lightly grease a 9 inch/20 cm square cake pan and line the bottom with baking parchment.

2 Melt the butter and chocolate in a heatproof bowl set over a pan of simmering water. Stir frequently with a wooden spoon until the mixture is smooth and glossy. Let the mixture cool slightly.

3 Beat the eggs and superfine sugar into the butter and chocolate mixture until well combined.

4 Fold in the flour, baking powder, salt, and chopped dried apricots, and mix together well.

5 Pour the mixture into the pan and bake in a preheated oven, 350°F/180°C, for 25–30 minutes.

6 The center of the cake may not be completely firm, but it will set as it cools. Let it cool in the pan.

7 When the cake is completely cold turn it out and slice into squares or bars.

VARIATION
Replace the white chocolate with light or dark chocolate, if you prefer.

Chocolate Slab Cake

This chocolate slab cake gets its moist texture from the sour cream which is stirred into the beaten mixture.

55 mins

40–45 mins

SERVES 10

INGREDIENTS

1 cup butter

3½ oz/100 g dark chocolate, chopped

⅔ cup water

2½ cups all-purpose flour

2 tsp baking powder

1⅔ cups soft brown sugar

⅔ cup sour cream

2 eggs, beaten

FROSTING

7 oz/200 g dark chocolate

6 tbsp water

3 tbsp light cream

1 tbsp butter, chilled

1 Grease a 13 x 8 inch/33 x 20 cm square cake pan and line the bottom with baking parchment. In a pan, melt the butter and chocolate with the water over a low heat, stirring frequently.

2 Strain the flour and baking powder into a mixing bowl and stir in the sugar.

3 Pour the hot chocolate liquid into the bowl and then beat well until all of the ingredients are evenly mixed. Stir in the sour cream, followed by the eggs.

4 Pour the mixture into the prepared pan and bake in a preheated oven, 375°F/190°C, for 40–45 minutes.

5 Let the cake cool in the pan before turning it out on to a wire rack to cool completely.

6 To make the frosting, melt the chocolate with the water in a pan over a very low heat, stir in the cream and remove from the heat. Stir in the chilled butter, then pour the frosting over the cooled cake, using a spatula to spread it evenly over the top of the cake.

COOK'S TIP
Frost the cake on the wire rack, and place a large cookie sheet underneath to catch any drips.

Chocolate & Almond Torte

This torte is perfect for serving on a hot sunny day with heavy cream and a selection of fresh summer berries.

1 hr 25 mins   40–45 mins

SERVES 10

INGREDIENTS

8 oz/225 g dark chocolate, broken into pieces

3 tbsp water

1 cup soft brown sugar

¾ cup butter, softened

¼ cup ground almonds

3 tbsp self-rising flour

5 eggs, separated

⅔ cup finely chopped blanched almonds

confectioners' sugar, for dusting

heavy cream, to serve (optional)

1 Grease a 9 inch/23 cm loose-bottomed cake pan and line the bottom with baking parchment.

2 In a pan set over a very low heat, melt the chocolate with the water, stirring until smooth. Add the sugar and stir until dissolved, taking the pan off the heat to prevent it overheating.

3 Add the butter in small amounts until it has melted into the chocolate. Remove from the heat and lightly stir in the ground almonds and flour. Add the egg yolks one at a time, beating well after each addition.

4 In a large mixing bowl, whisk the egg whites until they stand in soft peaks, then fold them into the chocolate mixture with a metal spoon. Stir in the chopped almonds. Pour the mixture into the pan and level the surface.

5 Bake in a preheated oven, 350°F/180°C, for 40–45 minutes until well risen and firm (the cake will crack on the surface during cooking).

6 Let cool in the pan for 30–40 minutes, then turn out on to a wire rack to cool completely. Dust with confectioners' sugar and serve in slices with heavy cream.

COOK'S TIP
For a nuttier flavor, toast the chopped almonds in a dry skillet over a medium heat for about 2 minutes until lightly golden.

Marbled Chocolate Cake

Separate chocolate and orange cake mixtures are combined in a ring mold to achieve the marbled effect in this light sponge.

🥧 1¼ hrs   🕐 30–35 mins

SERVES 8

INGREDIENTS

¾ cup butter, softened

¾ cup superfine sugar

3 eggs, beaten

1¼ cups self-rising flour, strained

¼ cup unsweetened cocoa, strained

5–6 tbsp orange juice

grated zest of 1 orange

1 Lightly grease a 10 inch/25 cm ovenproof ring mold.

2 In a mixing bowl, cream together the butter and sugar with an electric whisk for about 5 minutes.

3 Add the beaten egg a little at a time, whisking well after each addition.

4 Using a metal spoon, fold the flour into the creamed mixture carefully, then spoon half of the mixture into a separate mixing bowl.

5 Fold the cocoa and half of the orange juice into one bowl and mix gently.

6 Fold the orange rind and remaining orange juice into the other bowl and mix gently.

7 Place spoonfuls of each of the mixtures alternately into the mold, then drag a skewer through the mixture to create a marbled effect.

8 Bake in a preheated oven, 350°F/ 180°C, for 30–35 minutes until well risen and a skewer inserted into the center comes out clean.

9 Let the cake cool in the mold before turning out on to a wire rack.

VARIATION

For a richer chocolate flavor, add ¼ cup chocolate drops to the cocoa mixture.

Chocolate Bread

For the chocoholics among us, this bread is great fun to make and even better to eat.

2 hrs   25–30 mins

MAKES 1 LOAF

INGREDIENTS

4 cups white bread flour

¼ cup unsweetened cocoa

1 tsp salt

1 sachet active dry yeast

2 tbsp soft brown sugar

1 tbsp oil

1¼ cups lukewarm water

1   Lightly grease a 2 lb/900 g loaf pan.

2   Strain the flour and cocoa into a large mixing bowl.

3   Stir in the salt, dry yeast, and brown sugar.

4   Pour in the oil along with the lukewarm water and mix the ingredients together to make a dough.

5   Place the dough on a lightly floured counter and knead for 5 minutes.

6   Place the dough in a greased bowl, cover and let rise in a warm place for

about 1 hour or until the dough has doubled in size.

7   Punch down the dough and shape it into a loaf. Place the dough in the prepared pan, cover and let rise in a warm place for a further 30 minutes.

8   Bake in a preheated oven, 400°F/200°C, for 25–30 minutes, or until a hollow sound is heard when the bottom of the bread is tapped.

9   Transfer the bread to a wire rack and let cool. Cut into slices to serve.

COOK'S TIP

This bread can be sliced and spread with butter or it can be lightly toasted.

Raspberry Croissants

Simple to prepare, these tasty croissants are popped on a barbecue grill to warm through until the chocolate melts.

10 mins   10–15 mins

SERVES 4

INGREDIENTS

4 butter croissants

4 tsp raspberry preserve

2¾ oz/75 g dark chocolate

4½ oz/125 g raspberries

oil, for greasing

1 Slice the croissants in half. Spread the bottom half of each croissant with 1 teaspoon of the raspberry preserve.

2 Grate or finely chop the chocolate and sprinkle over the raspberry preserve.

3 Lightly grease 4 sheets of kitchen foil, brushing with a little oil.

4 Divide the raspberries equally among the croissants and replace the top half of each croissant. Place each croissant on to a sheet of foil, wrapping the foil to enclose the croissant completely.

VARIATION

For a delicious chocolate and strawberry filling for the croissants, use sliced strawberries and strawberry preserve instead of the raspberries.

5 Place the rack 6 inches/15 cm above hot coals. Transfer the croissants to the rack and let them heat through for 10–15 minutes or until the chocolate just begins to melt.

6 Remove the foil and transfer the croissants to individual serving plates. Serve hot.

Italian Chocolate Chip Bread

Serve this tasty snack plain with butter or jelly, or Italian-style with mascarpone cheese.

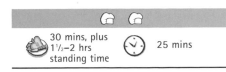
30 mins, plus 1½–2 hrs standing time   25 mins

MAKES 1 LOAF

INGREDIENTS

1 tsp vegetable oil, for brushing

2 cups all-purpose flour, plus extra for dusting

1 tbsp unsweetened cocoa

pinch of salt

1 tbsp sweet butter, plus ½ tsp extra, melted, for brushing

1 tbsp superfine sugar

1 tsp active dry yeast

⅔ cup lukewarm water

⅓ cup dark chocolate chips

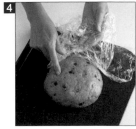

1 Brush a cookie sheet with ½ teaspoon of the oil. Strain the flour, cocoa, and salt into a bowl. Add the butter and cut it into the flour mixture, then stir in the sugar and yeast.

2 Gradually add the water, stirring well to mix. When the dough becomes too firm to stir with a spoon, gather it together with your hands. Turn it out on to a lightly floured counter and knead thoroughly until smooth and elastic.

3 Knead the chocolate chips into the dough, distributing them throughout. Form into a round loaf, then place on the cookie sheet, cover with oiled plastic wrap and set aside in a warm place for 1½–2 hours, until doubled in bulk.

4 Remove and discard the plastic wrap and bake the loaf in a preheated oven, 425°F/220°C, for 10 minutes. Lower the temperature to 375°F/190°C and bake for a further 15 minutes.

5 Transfer the loaf to a wire rack and brush with melted butter. Cover with a clean dish towel until cooled.

Chocolate Marshmallow Cake

The sweetness of whipped marshmallow frosting complements the mouthwatering flavor of this moist dark chocolate sponge.

30 mins, plus 1 hr cooling

55 mins

MAKES 1 x 6 INCH/15 CM CAKE

INGREDIENTS

6 tbsp sweet butter, plus extra for greasing

generous 1 cup superfine sugar

½ tsp vanilla extract

2 eggs, lightly beaten

3 oz/85 g dark chocolate, broken into pieces

⅔ cup buttermilk

1¼ cups self-rising flour

½ tsp baking soda

pinch of salt

2 oz/55 g milk chocolate, grated, to decorate

FROSTING

6 oz/175 g white marshmallows

1 tbsp milk

2 egg whites

2 tbsp superfine sugar

1 Grease an 3¾ cup ovenproof bowl with butter. Cream the butter, sugar and vanilla together until pale and fluffy, then gradually beat in the eggs.

2 Melt the dark chocolate in a heatproof bowl over a pan of simmering water. When the chocolate has melted, stir in the buttermilk gradually, until well combined. Remove the pan from the heat and cool slightly.

3 Strain the flour, baking soda, and salt into a separate bowl.

4 Alternately add the chocolate mixture and the flour mixture to the creamed mixture, a little at a time. Spoon the mixture into the ovenproof bowl and smooth the surface.

5 Bake in a preheated oven, 325°F/ 160°C, for about 50 minutes, until a skewer inserted into the center of the cake comes out clean. Turn out on to a wire rack to cool.

6 Meanwhile, make the frosting. Put the marshmallows and milk in a small pan and heat very gently until the marshmallows have melted. Remove the pan from the heat and set aside to cool.

7 Whisk the egg whites until soft peaks form, then add the sugar and continue whisking, until stiff peaks form. Fold the egg white into the cooled marshmallow mixture and set aside for 10 minutes.

8 When the cake is cool, cover the top and sides with the marshmallow frosting. Top with grated milk chocolate.

Layered Meringue Gateau

Surprisingly easy, but somewhat time-consuming to make, this magnificent gateau makes a wonderfully impressive dinner party dessert.

 40 mins, plus 1 hr cooling   6 hrs, or overnight

MAKES 1 x 7 INCH/18 CM CAKE

I N G R E D I E N T S

6 egg whites

¾ cup superfine sugar

1½ cups confectioners' sugar

2 tbsp cornstarch

F I L L I N G

1 cup heavy cream

5 oz/140 g dark chocolate, broken into small pieces

4 tsp dark rum

D E C O R A T I O N

⅔ cup heavy cream

4 tsp superfine sugar

1–2 tsp unsweetened cocoa, for dusting

1 Prepare 5 sheets of baking parchment by drawing an 7 inch/18 cm circle on each, then use them to line cookie sheets.

2 Whisk the egg whites until they form soft peaks. Mix together the sugar and cornstarch and strain it into the egg whites, a little at a time, whisking constantly until firm peaks form.

3 Spoon the meringue mixture into a pastry bag fitted with a round tip. Starting from the center, pipe five spirals, measuring 7 inches/18 cm, on each of the prepared pieces of baking parchment.

4 Bake in a preheated oven, at the lowest possible temperature with the door slightly ajar, for 6 hours or overnight.

5 After baking, carefully peel the meringue spirals from the baking parchment and place on wire racks to cool.

6 To make the filling, pour the cream into a small pan and place over a low heat. Add the chocolate and stir until melted. Remove the pan from the heat and beat the mixture with a hand-held whisk. Beat in the rum, then cover with plastic wrap and refrigerate overnight or for as long as the meringues are baking.

7 To assemble the gateau, beat the filling with an electric mixer until thick and smooth. Place three of the meringue layers on a counter and spread the filling over them. Stack the three layers, one on top of the other, and place an uncovered meringue layer on top. Crush the fifth meringue into crumbs.

8 To make the decoration, whisk the cream with the sugar until thick. Carefully spread the mixture over the top of the gateau. Sprinkle the meringue crumbs on top of the cream and dust the center of the gateau with cocoa. Serve within 1–2 hours.

No-Bake Refrigerator Cake

Ideal for children to make, this cake does not require an oven and it is prepared very rapidly—but it does need to chill overnight.

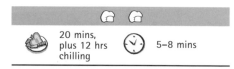   

20 mins, plus 12 hrs chilling

5–8 mins

MAKES AN 8½ X 4¼ INCH/ 22 X 11 CM CAKE

INGREDIENTS

1 cup sweet butter, diced

8 oz/225 g dark chocolate, broken into pieces

⅓ cup chopped candied cherries

½ cup chopped walnuts

12 rectangular semi-sweet chocolate cookies

1 Line a 1 lb/450 g loaf pan with greaseproof paper or baking parchment.

2 Put the butter and chocolate into the top of a double boiler or in a heatproof bowl set over a pan of barely simmering water. Stir constantly over a low heat until they have melted and the mixture is smooth. Remove from the heat and cool slightly.

3 In a separate bowl, mix together the cherries and walnuts. Spoon one-third of the chocolate mixture into the prepared pan, cover with a layer of cookies and top with half the cherries and walnuts. Make further layers, ending with the chocolate mixture. Cover with plastic wrap and chill in the refrigerator for at least 12 hours. When chilled, turn the cake out onto a serving dish.

Swedish Chocolate Cake

This is the ideal snack to eat with a mid-morning cup of coffee. Serve with whipped cream for a special treat.

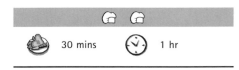

🍰 30 mins   🕐 1 hr

MAKES 1 x 9 INCH/23 CM CAKE

INGREDIENTS

5 tbsp sweet butter, plus 2 tsp extra for greasing

⅓ cup dry white breadcrumbs

3 oz/85 g dark chocolate, broken into pieces

scant 1 cup superfine sugar

2 eggs, separated

1 tsp vanilla extract

1½ cups all-purpose flour

1 tsp baking powder

½ cup light cream

1 Grease a deep 9 inch/23 cm round cake pan with butter. Sprinkle the breadcrumbs into the pan and press them on to the bottom and sides.

2 Place the chocolate in the top of a double boiler or in a heatproof bowl set over a pan of barely simmering water. Stir over a low heat until melted, then remove from the heat.

3 Cream the butter with the sugar until pale and fluffy. Beat in the egg yolks, one at a time, and add the vanilla.

4 Strain one-third of the flour with the baking powder, then beat into the egg mixture. Mix together the cream and melted chocolate, then beat one-third of this mixture into the egg mixture. Continue adding the flour and the chocolate mixture alternately, beating well after each addition.

5 Whisk the egg whites in a separate bowl until they form stiff peaks. Fold the egg whites into the chocolate mixture.

6 Pour into the prepared tin and bake in a preheated oven, 300°F/150°C, for about 50 minutes, until a skewer inserted into the center of the cake comes out clean. Turn the cake out on to a wire rack to cool before serving.

Date & Chocolate Cake

Moist and moreish, this fruity chocolate cake will prove to be a popular after-school snack.

25 mins, plus 20 mins cooling

40 mins

MAKES 1 X 7 INCH /18 CM CAKE

INGREDIENTS

½ cup sweet butter, plus 2 tsp extra for greasing

⅔ cup self-rising flour, plus 1 tbsp extra for dusting

4 oz/115 g dark chocolate, broken into pieces

1 tbsp grenadine

1 tbsp light corn syrup

4 tbsp superfine sugar

2 large eggs

2 tbsp ground rice

1 tbsp confectioners' sugar, to decorate

FILLING

⅔ cup chopped dried dates

1 tbsp lemon juice

1 tbsp orange juice

1 tbsp raw brown sugar

¼ cup chopped blanched almonds

2 tbsp apricot jelly

1 Grease and flour two 7 inch/18 cm layer cake pans. Put the chocolate, grenadine, and syrup in the top of a double boiler or in a heatproof bowl set over a pan of barely simmering water. Stir over a low heat until the chocolate has melted and the mixture is smooth. Remove from the heat and let cool.

2 Cream together the butter and superfine sugar together until pale and fluffy, then gradually beat in the eggs and then the cooled chocolate mixture.

3 Strain the flour into another bowl and stir in the ground rice. Fold the flour mixture into the creamed mixture.

4 Divide the mixture between the prepared pans and smooth the surface. Bake in a preheated oven, 350°F/180°C, for 20–25 minutes, until golden and firm to the touch. Turn out on to a wire rack to cool.

5 To make the filling, Put all the ingredients into a pan and stir over a low heat for 4–5 minutes, until fully incorporated. Remove from the heat, let cool and then use it to sandwich the cakes together. Dust the top of the cake with confectioners' sugar to decorate.

Chocolate Bread Dessert

This chocolate sponge is served with hot fudge sauce, making it the most delicious way to use up bread that is slightly stale.

2¼ hours   45 mins

SERVES 4

INGREDIENTS

6 thick slices white bread, crusts removed

scant 2 cups milk

6 oz/175 g canned evaporated milk

2 tbsp unsweetened cocoa

2 eggs

2 tbsp dark muscovado sugar

1 tsp vanilla extract

confectioners' sugar, for dusting

HOT FUDGE SAUCE

2 oz/60 g dark chocolate, broken into pieces

1 tbsp unsweetened cocoa

2 tbsp light corn syrup

¼ cup butter or margarine

2 tbsp dark muscovado sugar

⅔ cup milk

1 tbsp cornstarch

1 Grease a shallow ovenproof dish. Cut the bread into squares and layer them in the dish.

2 Put the milk, evaporated milk, and unsweetened cocoa in a pan and heat gently, stirring occasionally, until the mixture is lukewarm.

3 Whisk together the eggs, sugar, and vanilla extract. Add the warm milk mixture and beat well.

4 Pour into the prepared dish, making sure that all the bread is completely covered. Cover the dish with plastic wrap and chill in the refrigerator for 1–2 hours.

5 Transfer to an oven preheated to 350°F/180°C, and bake for 35–40 minutes, until set. Let stand for 5 minutes.

6 To make the sauce, put the chocolate, unsweetened cocoa, syrup, butter or margarine, sugar, milk, and cornstarch into a pan. Heat gently, stirring until smooth.

7 Dust the dessert with confectioners' sugar and serve immediately with the hot fudge sauce.

Hot Desserts

Chocolate is comforting at any time but no more so than when served in a steaming hot sponge. It is hard to think of anything more warming, comforting, and homey than tucking into a steamed hot Chocolate Fudge Dessert or a Hot Chocolate Soufflé, and children will love the chocolate addition to nursery favorites such as Chocolate Bread & Butter Sponge. In fact, there are several old favorites that have been given the chocolate treatment, bringing them

bang up to date and putting them on the chocolate lover's map.

When you are feeling in need of something a little more sophisticated, try the new-style Chocolate Apple Pancake Stack, or Chocolate Pear & Almond Tart, or Chocolate Zabaglione for a sophisticated creamy, warm dessert set to get your tastebuds in a whirl!

This chapter is packed full of chocolate delights, with different tastes and textures to add warmth to any day.

Chocolate Queen of Desserts

An old time favorite with an up-to-date twist, this dessert makes the perfect end to a special family meal.

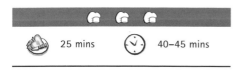

25 mins   40–45 mins

SERVES 4

INGREDIENTS

1¾ oz/ 50 g dark chocolate

2 cups chocolate-flavored milk

1¾ cups fresh white or whole-wheat breadcrumbs

½ cup superfine sugar

2 eggs, separated

4 tbsp black cherry jelly

1 Break the chocolate into small pieces and place in a pan with the chocolate-flavored milk. Heat gently, stirring until the chocolate melts. Bring almost to a boil, then remove the pan from the heat.

2 Place the breadcrumbs in a large mixing bowl with 5 teaspoons of the sugar. Pour over the chocolate milk and mix well. Beat in the egg yolks.

3 Spoon into a 5 cup pie dish and bake in a preheated oven, 350°F/180°C, for 25–30 minutes or until set and firm to the touch.

4 Whisk the egg whites in a large grease-free bowl until standing in soft peaks. Gradually whisk in the remaining

superfine sugar and whisk until you have a glossy, thick meringue.

5 Spread the black cherry jelly over the surface of the chocolate mixture and pile or pipe the meringue on top. Return the dessert to the oven for about 15 minutes or until the meringue is crisp and golden.

VARIATION
If you prefer, add ½ cup shredded coconut to the breadcrumbs and omit the jelly.

Chocolate Eve's Dessert

Eve's Dessert is traditionally made with apples, but here it is made with raspberries and white chocolate sponge, with a bitter chocolate sauce.

15 mins

40–45 mins

SERVES 4

INGREDIENTS

8 oz/225 g fresh or frozen raspberries

2 eating apples, peeled, cored, and thickly sliced

4 tbsp seedless raspberry jelly

2 tbsp port, optional

SPONGE TOPPING

4 tbsp soft margarine

4 tbsp superfine sugar

⅔ cup self-rising flour, strained

1¾ oz/50 g white chocolate, grated

1 egg

2 tbsp milk

BITTER CHOCOLATE SAUCE

3 oz/85 g dark chocolate

⅔ cup light cream

1 Place the apple slices and raspberries in a shallow 5 cup ovenproof dish.

2 Place the raspberry jelly and port (if using) in a small pan and heat gently until the jelly melts and combines with the port. Pour the mixture over the fruit.

3 Place all of the ingredients for the sponge topping in a large mixing bowl and beat until the mixture is smooth.

4 Spoon the sponge mixture over the fruit and level the top. Bake in a preheated oven, 350°F/180°C, for 40–45 minutes or until the sponge is springy to the touch.

5 To make the sauce, break the chocolate into small pieces and place in a heavy-based pan with the cream. Heat gently, beating until a smooth sauce is formed. Serve warm with the dessert.

VARIATION

Use dark chocolate in the sponge and top with apricot halves, covered with peach schnapps and apricot jelly.

Mini Chocolate Gingers

Individually made desserts look professional and are quick to cook. If you do not have small ovenproof bowls, use small teacups instead.

20 mins · 45 mins

SERVES 4

INGREDIENTS

generous ⅓ cup soft margarine

¾ cup self-rising flour, strained

½ cup superfine sugar

2 eggs

¼ cup unsweetened cocoa, strained

1 oz/25 g dark chocolate

1¾ oz/50 g preserved ginger

CHOCOLATE CUSTARD

2 egg yolks

1 tbsp superfine sugar

1 tbsp cornstarch

1¼ cups milk

3½ oz/100 g dark chocolate, broken into pieces

confectioners' sugar, to dust

1 Lightly grease 4 small individual ovenproof bowls. Place the margarine, flour, sugar, eggs, and cocoa in a mixing bowl and beat until well combined and smooth. Chop the chocolate and ginger and stir into the mixture.

2 Spoon the cake mixture into the prepared bowls and level the top. The mixture should three-quarters fill the bowls. Cover the bowls with discs of baking parchment and cover with a pleated sheet of foil. Steam for 45 minutes until the sponges are cooked and springy to the touch.

3 Meanwhile, make the custard. Beat together the egg yolks, sugar, and cornstarch to form a smooth paste. Heat the milk until boiling and pour over the egg mixture. Return to the pan and cook over a very low heat, stirring until thick. Remove from the heat and beat in the chocolate. Stir until the chocolate melts.

4 Lift the mini chocolate gingers from the steamer, run a knife around the edge of the bowls and turn out on to serving plates. Dust with sugar and drizzle chocolate custard over the top. Serve the remaining custard separately.

Bread & Butter Dessert

Brioche gives this dessert a lovely rich flavor, but this recipe also works well with soft-baked batch bread.

2¼ hours   35–40 mins

SERVES 4

INGREDIENTS

8 oz/225 g brioche

1 tbsp butter

1¾ oz/50 g dark chocolate chips

1 egg

2 egg yolks

4 tbsp superfine sugar

15 fl oz/425 ml canned light evaporated milk

1 Cut the brioche into thin slices. Lightly butter one side of each slice.

2 Place a layer of brioche, buttered-side down, in the bottom of a shallow ovenproof dish. Sprinkle a few chocolate chips over the top.

3 Continue layering the brioche and chocolate chips, finishing with a layer of bread on top.

4 Whisk together the egg, egg yolks, and sugar until well combined. Heat the milk in a small pan until it just begins to simmer. Gradually add to the egg mixture, whisking well.

VARIATION

For a double-chocolate dessert, heat the milk with 1 tbsp of unsweetened cocoa, stirring until well dissolved then continue from step 4.

5 Pour the custard over the bread and let stand for 5 minutes. Press the brioche down into the milk.

6 Place the dish the in a roasting pan and fill with boiling water to come halfway up the side of the dish (this is known as a bain-marie). Bake in a preheated oven, 350°F/180°C, for 30 minutes, or until the custard has set. Let the dessert cool for about 5 minutes before serving.

Chocolate French Toasties

There is something very moreish about these delicious chocolate toasties, served with whipped cream and a raspberry and rum sauce.

10–15 mins   10–20 mins

SERVES 4

INGREDIENTS

1¾ oz/50 g dark chocolate

⅔ cup milk

1 egg

4 tbsp seedless raspberry jelly

2 tbsp rum, optional

8 thick slices white bread

butter or oil, for shallow-frying

½ tsp ground cinnamon

3 tbsp superfine sugar

a little whipped cream, to serve

1 Break the chocolate into small pieces and place in a small pan with the milk. Heat gently, stirring, until the chocolate melts. Let the mixture cool slightly.

2 Beat the egg in a large mixing bowl and whisk in the warm chocolate milk.

3 Heat the raspberry jelly gently and stir in the rum, if using. Set aside and keep warm.

4 Remove the crusts from the bread, cut into triangles and dip each one into the chocolate mixture. Heat the butter or oil in a skillet and cook the bread triangles for 2–3 minutes, turning once, until they are just crispy.

5 Mix together the cinnamon and superfine sugar and sprinkle it over the toasties. Serve with the hot raspberry and rum sauce and a little whipped cream.

COOK'S TIP

Young children adore this dessert. Cut the bread into fingers to make it easier for them to handle.

Chocolate Fudge Dessert

This fabulous steamed sponge, served with a rich chocolate fudge sauce, is perfect for cold winter days.

10 mins   35–40 mins

SERVES 6

INGREDIENTS

generous ⅓ cup soft margarine

1¼ cups self-rising flour

½ cup light corn syrup

3 eggs

¼ cup unsweetened cocoa

CHOCOLATE FUDGE SAUCE

3½ oz/100 g dark chocolate

½ cup condensed milk

4 tbsp heavy cream

1 Lightly grease a 5 cup/1.2 liter heatproof bowl.

2 Place the ingredients for the sponge in a separate mixing bowl and beat until well combined and smooth.

3 Spoon into the prepared bowl and level the top. Cover with a disk of waxed paper and tie a pleated sheet of aluminum foil over the bowl. Steam for 1½-2 hours until the sponge is cooked and springy to the touch.

4 To make the sauce, break the chocolate into small pieces and place in a small pan with the condensed milk. Heat gently, stirring until the chocolate melts.

5 Remove the pan from the heat and stir in the heavy cream.

6 To serve the dessert, turn it out on to a serving plate and pour over a little of the chocolate fudge sauce. Serve the remaining sauce separately.

Chocolate Fruit Crumble

The addition of chocolate to a crumble topping makes it even more of a treat, and is a good way of enticing children to eat a fruit dessert.

5–10 mins 40–45 mins

SERVES 4

INGREDIENTS

14 oz/400 g canned apricots, in natural juice

1 lb/450 g cooking apples, peeled and thickly sliced

¾ cup all-purpose flour

6 tbsp butter

⅔ cup porridge oats

4 tbsp superfine sugar

⅔ cup chocolate chips

1 Lightly grease an ovenproof dish with a little butter or margarine.

2 Drain the apricots, reserving 4 tablespoons of the juice. Place the apples and apricots in the prepared ovenproof dish with the reserved apricot juice and toss to mix.

3 Strain the flour into a mixing bowl. Cut the butter into small cubes and rub in with your fingertips until the mixture resembles fine breadcrumbs. Stir in the porridge oats, sugar, and chocolate chips.

VARIATION

Other fruits can be used to make this crumble—fresh pears mixed with fresh or frozen raspberries work well. If you do not use canned fruit, add 4 tablespoons of orange juice to the fresh fruit.

4 Sprinkle the crumble mixture over the apples and apricots and level the top roughly. Do not press the crumble into the fruit.

5 Bake in a preheated oven, 180°C/ 350°F, for 40–45 minutes or until the topping is golden. Serve hot or cold.

Poached Pears in Chocolate

This elegant dessert can be served hot or cold. The pears can be poached 2 days in advance and stored in their poaching juices in the refrigerator.

🕙 10 mins   🕐 25 mins

SERVES 6

INGREDIENTS

6 firm ripe pears

½ cup superfine sugar

2 cinnamon sticks

zest of 1 orange

2 cloves

1 bottle rosé wine

CHOCOLATE SAUCE

6 oz/175 g dark chocolate

9 oz/250 g mascarpone cheese

2 tbsp orange-flavored liqueur

1 Carefully peel the pears, leaving the stalks intact.

2 Place the sugar, cinnamon, sticks, orange zest, cloves, and wine in a pan that will hold the 6 pears snugly.

3 Heat gently until the sugar has dissolved, then add the pears to the liquid and bring to a simmer. Cover and poach gently for 20 minutes. If

COOK'S TIP

There is no need to waste the poaching liquid. Boil it rapidly in a clean pan for about 10 minutes to reduce to a syrup. Use the syrup to sweeten a fresh fruit salad or spoon it over ice cream.

serving them cold, let the pears cool in the liquid, then chill until required. If serving hot, leave the pears in the hot liquid whilst preparing the chocolate sauce.

4 To make the sauce, melt the chocolate. Beat together the cheese and the orange-flavored liqueur. Beat the cheese mixture into the chocolate.

5 Remove the pears from the poaching liquid and place on a serving plate. Add a generous spoonful of sauce on the side and serve the remainder separately.

Saucy Chocolate Dessert

In this recipe, the mixture separates out during cooking to produce a cream sponge topping and a delicious chocolate sauce on the bottom.

15 mins   40 mins

SERVES 4

INGREDIENTS

1¼ cups milk

2¾ oz/75 g dark chocolate

½ tsp vanilla extract

½ cup superfine sugar

generous ⅓ cup butter

1¼ cups self-raising flour

2 tbsp unsweetened cocoa

confectioners' sugar, to dust

FOR THE SAUCE

3 tbsp unsweetened cocoa

⅓ cup light brown sugar

1¼ cups boiling water

1 Lightly grease a 3¾ cup oven-proof dish.

2 Place the milk in a small pan. Break the chocolate into pieces and add to the milk. Heat gently, stirring until the chocolate melts. Let the mixture cool slightly. Stir in the vanilla extract.

3 Beat together the superfine sugar and butter in a bowl until light and fluffy. Strain the flour and cocoa together. Add to the bowl with the chocolate milk and beat until smooth, using an electric whisk if you have one. Pour the mixture into the prepared dish.

4 To make the sauce, mix together the cocoa and sugar. Add a little boiling water and mix to a smooth paste, then stir in the remaining water. Pour the sauce over the dessert mixture but do not mix in.

5 Place the dish on to a cookie sheet and bake in a preheated oven, 350°F/180°C, for 40 minutes or until the dessert is dry on top and springy to the touch. Let stand for 5 minutes, then dust with a little confectioners' sugar just before serving.

VARIATION

For a mocha sauce, add 1 tablespoon of instant coffee to the cocoa and sugar in Step 4, before mixing to a paste with the boiling water.

Pecan Fudge Ring

Although this can be served cold as a cake, it is absolutely delicious served as a hot dessert.

🖐 35 mins   🕐 35 mins

SERVES 6

INGREDIENTS

FUDGE SAUCE

3 tbsp butter

3 tbsp light brown sugar

4 tbsp light corn syrup

2 tbsp milk

1 tbsp unsweetened cocoa

1½ oz/40 g dark chocolate

⅓ cup finely chopped pecan nuts

CAKE

generous ⅓ cup soft margarine

⅔ cup light brown sugar

1 cup self-raising flour

2 eggs

2 tbsp milk

1 tbsp light corn syrup

1 Lightly grease an 8 inch/20 cm ovenproof ring pan.

2 To make the fudge sauce, place the butter, sugar, syrup, milk, and cocoa in a small pan and heat gently, stirring until combined.

3 Break the chocolate into pieces, add to the mixture and stir until melted. Stir in the chopped nuts. Pour into the bottom of the pan and let cool.

4 To make the cake, place all of the ingredients in a mixing bowl and beat until smooth. Carefully spoon the cake mixture over the chocolate fudge sauce.

5 Bake in a preheated oven, 350°F/ 180°C, for 35 minutes or until the cake is springy to the touch.

6 Let the fudge ring cool in the pan for 5 minutes, then turn out on to a serving dish and serve.

Chocolate Meringue Pie

Crumbly cracker base, rich creamy chocolate filling topped with fluffy meringue—what could be more indulgent than this fabulous dessert?

25 mins   35 mins

SERVES 6

INGREDIENTS

8 oz/225 g dark chocolate graham crackers

4 tbsp butter

FILLING

3 egg yolks

4 tbsp superfine sugar

4 tbsp cornstarch

2½ cups milk

3½ oz/100 g dark chocolate, melted

MERINGUE

2 egg whites

½ cup superfine sugar

¼ tsp vanilla extract

1 Place the graham crackers in a plastic bag and crush with a rolling pin. Pour into a mixing bowl. Melt the butter and stir it into the cracker crumbs until well mixed. Press the biscuit mixture firmly into the bottom and up the sides of a 23 cm/9 inch tart pan or dish.

2 To make the filling, beat the egg yolks, superfine sugar, and cornstarch in a large bowl until they form a smooth paste, adding a little of the milk if necessary. Heat the milk until almost boiling, then slowly pour it on to the egg mixture, whisking well.

3 Return the mixture to the pan and cook gently, whisking constantly until it thickens. Remove from the heat. Whisk in the melted chocolate, then pour it on to the graham cracker pie shell.

4 To make the meringue, whisk the egg whites in a large mixing bowl until standing in soft peaks. Gradually whisk in about two-thirds of the sugar until the mixture is stiff and glossy. Fold in the remaining sugar and vanilla extract.

5 Spread the meringue over the filling, swirling the surface with the back of a spoon to give it an attractive finish. Bake in the center of a preheated oven, 375°F/170°C, for 30 minutes or until the meringue is golden. Serve the pie hot or just warm.

Chocolate Apple Pie

Easy-to-make crumbly chocolate pie dough encases a delicious apple filling studded with chocolate chips—a guaranteed family favorite.

45 mins   40 mins

SERVES 6

INGREDIENTS

CHOCOLATE PIE DOUGH

4 tbsp unsweetened cocoa

1¾ cups all-purpose flour

generous ⅓ cup softened butter

4 tbsp superfine sugar

2 egg yolks

a few drops of vanilla extract

cold water, to mix

FILLING

1 lb10 oz/750 g cooking apples

2 tbsp butter

½ tsp ground cinnamon

¾ cup dark chocolate chips

a little egg white, beaten

½ tsp superfine sugar

whipped cream or vanilla ice cream,
  to serve

3 Peel, core, and thickly slice the apples. Place half of the apple slices in a pan with the butter and cinnamon and cook over a gentle heat, stirring occasionally until the apples soften.

4 Stir in the uncooked apple slices, let cool slightly, then stir in the chocolate chips. Prick the base of the pie shell and pile the apple mixture into it. Arrange the pie dough leaves on top. Brush the leaves with a little egg white and sprinkle with superfine sugar.

5 Bake in a preheated oven, 350°F/180°C, for 35 minutes until the pastry is crisp. Serve warm or cold, with whipped cream or vanilla ice cream.

1 To make the pie dough, strain the cocoa and flour into a mixing bowl and rub in the butter until the mixture resembles fine breadcrumbs. Stir in the sugar. Add the egg yolks, vanilla extract, and enough water to mix to a dough.

2 Roll out the dough on a lightly floured counter and use to line a deep 8 inch/20 cm flan or cake pan. Chill for 30 minutes. Roll out any trimmings and cut out some pie dough leaves to decorate the top of the pie.

Chocolate Pear & Almond Tart

This attractive dessert consists of a tart filled with pears cooked in a chocolate, almond-flavored sponge. It is delicious served hot or cold.

30 mins   35 mins

SERVES 6

INGREDIENTS

¾ cup all-purpose flour

¼ cup ground almonds

5 tbsp block margarine

about 3 tbsp water

FILLING

400 g/14 oz canned pear halves, in natural juice

4 tbsp butter

4 tbsp superfine sugar

2 eggs, beaten

1 cup ground almonds

2 tbsp unsweetened cocoa

a few drops of almond extract

confectioners' sugar, to dust

CHOCOLATE SAUCE

4 tbsp superfine sugar

3 tbsp light corn syrup

generous ⅓ cup water

6 oz/175 g dark chocolate, broken into pieces

2 tbsp butter

1 Lightly grease an 8 inch/20 cm tart pan. Strain the flour into a mixing bowl and stir in the almonds. Rub in the margarine with your fingertips until the mixture resembles breadcrumbs. Add enough water to mix to a soft dough. Cover, chill in the freezer for 10 minutes, then roll out and use to line the pan. Prick the bottom and chill.

2 Meanwhile, make the filling. Drain the pears well. Beat the butter and sugar until light and fluffy. Beat in the eggs. Fold in the almonds, cocoa, and almond extract. Spread the chocolate mixture in the pie shell and arrange the pears on top, pressing down lightly. Bake in the center of a preheated oven, 400°F/200°C, for 30 minutes or until the filling has risen. Cool slightly and transfer to a serving dish, if wished. Dust with sugar.

3 To make the sauce, place the sugar, syrup, and water in a pan and heat gently, stirring until the sugar dissolves. Boil gently for 1 minute. Remove from the heat, add the chocolate and butter and stir until melted. Serve with the tart.

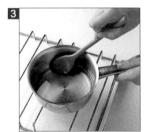

Chocolate & Banana Crêpes

Crêpes are given the chocolate treatment here to make a fabulous dinner party dessert. Prepare them ahead of time for trouble-free entertaining.

🍳 10 mins   🕐 15 mins

SERVES 4

INGREDIENTS

3 large bananas

6 tbsp orange juice

grated zest of 1 orange

2 tbsp orange- or banana-flavored liqueur

HOT CHOCOLATE SAUCE

1 tbsp unsweetened cocoa

2 tsp cornstarch

3 tbsp milk

1½ oz/40 g dark chocolate

1 tbsp butter

½ cup light corn syrup

¼ tsp vanilla extract

PANCAKES

¾ cup all-purpose flour

1 tbsp unsweetened cocoa

1 egg

1 tsp sunflower oil

1¼ cups milk

oil, for frying

1 Peel and slice the bananas and arrange them in a dish with the orange juice and rind and the liqueur. Set aside.

2 Mix the cocoa and cornstarch in a bowl, then stir in the milk. Break the dark chocolate into pieces and place in a pan with the butter and light corn syrup. Heat gently, stirring until well blended. Add the cocoa mixture and bring to a boil over a gentle heat, stirring. Simmer for 1 minute, then remove from the heat and stir in the vanilla extract.

3 To make the crêpes, strain the flour and cocoa into a mixing bowl and make a well in the center. Add the egg and oil. Gradually whisk in the milk to form a smooth batter. Heat a little oil in a heavy-based skillet and pour off any excess. Pour in a little batter and tilt the pan to coat the bottom. Cook over a medium heat until the underside is browned. Flip over and cook the other side. Slide the crêpe out of the pan and keep warm. Repeat until all the batter has been used.

4 To serve, reheat the chocolate sauce for 1–2 minutes. Fill the crêpes with the bananas and fold in half or into triangles. Pour over a little chocolate sauce and serve.

Apple Crêpe Stacks

If you cannot wait to get your first chocolate "fix" of the day, serve these crêpes for breakfast. They also make a perfect family dessert.

20 mins   **45 mins**

SERVES 4

INGREDIENTS

2 cups all-purpose flour

1½ tsp baking powder

4 tbsp superfine sugar

1 egg

1 tbsp butter, melted

1¼ cups milk

1 eating apple

1¾ oz/50 g dark chocolate chips

Chocolate Sauce (see page 80) or
  maple syrup, to serve

1 Strain the flour and baking powder into a mixing bowl. Stir in the superfine sugar. Make a well in the center and add the egg and melted butter. Gradually whisk in the milk to form a smooth batter.

2 Peel, core, and grate the apple and stir it into the batter with the chocolate chips.

3 Heat a griddle pan or heavy-based skillet over a medium heat and grease it lightly. For each crêpe, place about 2 tablespoons of the batter on to the griddle or skillet and spread to make a 3 inch/7.5 cm circle.

4 Cook for a few minutes until you see bubbles appear on the surface of the crêpe. Turn over and cook for a further 1 minute. Remove from the pan and keep warm. Repeat with the remaining batter to make about 12 crêpes.

5 To serve, stack 2 or 3 crêpes on an individual serving plate and serve them with the hot chocolate sauce or maple syrup.

COOK'S TIP

To keep the cooked crêpes warm, pile them on top of each other with waxed paper in between to prevent them from sticking to one another.

Chocolate Fondue

This is a fun dessert to serve at the end of the meal. Prepare in advance, then just warm through before serving.

5 mins   5 mins

SERVES 4

INGREDIENTS

CHOCOLATE FONDUE

8 oz/225 g dark chocolate

generous ¾ cup heavy cream

2 tbsp brandy

TO SERVE

selection of fruit

white and pink marshmallows

sweet cookies

1 Break the chocolate into small pieces and place in a small pan with the heavy cream.

2 Heat the mixture gently, stirring constantly until the chocolate has melted and blended with the cream.

3 Remove the pan from the heat and stir in the brandy.

4 Pour into a fondue pot or a small flameproof dish and keep warm, preferably over a small burner.

5 Serve with a selection of fruit, marshmallows, and cookies for dipping. The fruit and marshmallows can be spiked on fondue forks, wooden skewers, or ordinary forks, for dipping into the chocolate fondue.

COOK'S TIP

To prepare the fruit for dipping, cut larger fruit into bite-sized pieces. Fruit that discolors, such as bananas, apples, and pears, should be dipped in a little lemon juice as soon as it is cut.

Hot Chocolate Soufflé

Served with hot chocolate custard this is a chocoholic's dream. Do not be put off by the mystique of soufflés—this one is not difficult to make.

15 mins   50–55 mins

SERVES 4

INGREDIENTS

3½ oz/100 g dark chocolate

1¼ cups milk

2 tbsp butter

4 large eggs, separated

1 tbsp cornstarch

4 tbsp superfine sugar

½ tsp vanilla extract

⅔ cup dark chocolate chips

superfine and confectioners' sugar, to dust

CHOCOLATE CUSTARD

2 tbsp cornstarch

1 tbsp superfine sugar

scant 2 cups milk

1¾ oz/50 g dark chocolate

1 Grease a 5 cup soufflé dish and sprinkle with superfine sugar. Break the chocolate into pieces.

2 Heat the milk with the butter in a pan until almost boiling. Mix the egg yolks, cornstarch, and superfine sugar in a bowl and pour on some of the hot milk, whisking. Return it to the pan and cook gently, stirring constantly until thickened. Add the chocolate and stir until melted. Remove from the heat and stir in the extract.

3 Whisk the egg whites until standing in soft peaks. Fold half of the egg whites into the chocolate mixture. Fold in the rest with the chocolate chips. Pour into the dish and bake in a preheated oven, 350°F/180°C, for 40–45 minutes until well risen.

4 Meanwhile, make the custard. Put the cornstarch and sugar in a small bowl and mix to a smooth paste with a little of the milk. Heat the remaining milk until almost boiling. Pour a little of the hot milk on to the cornstarch, mix well, then pour back into the pan. Cook gently, stirring until thickened. Break the chocolate into pieces and add to the custard, stirring until melted.

5 Dust the soufflé with sugar and serve immediately with the chocolate custard.

Chocolate Zabaglione

As this recipe only uses a little chocolate, choose one with a minimum of 70 percent cocoa solids for a good flavor.

🕙 10 mins   🕐 5 mins

SERVES 4

INGREDIENTS

4 egg yolks

4 tbsp superfine sugar

1¾ oz/50 g dark chocolate

½ cup Marsala wine

unsweetened cocoa, to dust

1 In a large glass mixing bowl, whisk together the egg yolks and superfine sugar until you have a very pale mixture, using an electric whisk.

2 Grate the chocolate finely and fold into the egg mixture.

3 Fold the Marsala wine into the chocolate mixture.

4 Place the mixing bowl over a pan of gently simmering water and set the electric whisk on the lowest speed or change to a hand-held balloon whisk. Cook gently, whisking continuously until the mixture thickens; take care not to overcook or the mixture will curdle.

5 Spoon the hot mixture into warmed individual glass dishes or coffee cups (as here) and dust with cocoa. Serve the zabaglione as soon as possible so that it is warm, light, and fluffy.

COOK'S TIP

Make the dessert just before serving as it will separate if you let it stand. If it begins to curdle, remove it from the heat immediately and place it in a bowl of cold water to stop the cooking. Whisk furiously until the mixture comes together.

Steamed Coffee Sponge

This sponge dessert is very light and is delicious with a chocolate or coffee sauce.

🍮 10 mins   🕐 1–1¼ hrs

SERVES 4

INGREDIENTS

2 tbsp margarine

2 tbsp soft brown sugar

2 eggs

⅓ cup all-purpose flour

¾ tsp baking powder

6 tbsp milk

1 tsp coffee extract

SAUCE

1¼ cups milk

1 tbsp soft brown sugar

1 tsp unsweetened cocoa

2 tbsp cornstarch

1 Lightly grease a 2½ cup heatproof bowl. Cream the margarine and sugar until light and fluffy and beat in the eggs.

2 Gradually stir in the flour and baking powder and then the milk and coffee extract, to make a smooth batter.

COOK'S TIP

The sponge is covered with pleated paper and foil to allow it to rise. The foil will react with the steam and must therefore not be placed directly against the sponge.

3 Spoon the mixture into the prepared heatproof bowl and cover with a pleated piece of baking parchment and then a pleated piece of foil, securing around the bowl with string. Place in a steamer or large pan and half fill with boiling water. Cover and steam for 1–1¼ hours or until cooked through.

4 To make the sauce, put the milk, soft brown sugar, and cocoa in a pan and heat until the sugar dissolves. Blend the cornstarch with 4 tablespoons of cold water to make a paste and stir into the pan. Bring to a boil, stirring, until thickened. Cook over a gentle heat for 1 minute.

5 Turn the dessert out on to a serving plate and spoon the sauce over the top. Serve.

Fudge Dessert

This dessert has a hidden surprise when cooked because it separates to give a rich chocolate sauce at the bottom of the dish.

10 mins   35–40 mins

SERVES 4

INGREDIENTS

4 tbsp margarine, plus extra for greasing

½ cup soft light brown sugar

2 eggs, beaten

1¼ cups milk

⅓ cup chopped walnuts

¼ cup all-purpose flour

2 tbsp unsweetened cocoa

confectioners' sugar and unsweetened cocoa, to dust

1 Lightly grease a 4 cup ovenproof dish.

2 Cream together the margarine and sugar in a large mixing bowl until fluffy. Beat in the eggs.

3 Gradually stir in the milk and add the walnuts.

4 Sieve the flour and cocoa into the mixture and fold in gently, with a metal spoon, until well mixed.

VARIATION

Add 1–2 tablespoons of brandy or rum to the mixture for a slightly alcoholic dessert, or 1–2 tablespoons of orange juice for a child-friendly version.

5 Spoon the mixture into the dish and cook in a preheated oven, 350°F/180°C, for 35–40 minutes or until the sponge is cooked.

6 Dust with confectioners' sugar and cocoa and serve.

Toasted Tropical Fruit

Spear some chunks of exotic tropical fruits onto kabob sticks, sear them over a barbecue grill, and serve with this amazing chocolate dip.

45 mins   5 mins

SERVES 4

INGREDIENTS

DIP

4½ oz/125 g dark chocolate, broken into pieces

2 tbsp light corn syrup

1 tbsp unsweetened cocoa

1 tbsp cornstarch

generous ¾ cup milk

KABOBS

1 mango

1 papaya

2 kiwi fruit

½ small pineapple

1 large banana

2 tbsp lemon juice

⅔ cup white rum

1 Put all the ingredients for the chocolate dip into a heavy-based pan. Heat over the barbecue grill or a low heat, stirring constantly, until thickened and smooth. Keep warm at the edge of the barbecue grill.

2 Slice the mango on each side of its large, flat pit. Cut the flesh into chunks, removing the peel. Halve, seed, and peel the papaya and cut it into chunks. Peel the kiwi fruit and slice into chunks. Peel and cut the pineapple into chunks. Peel and slice the banana and dip the pieces in the lemon juice to prevent it from discoloring.

3 Thread the pieces of fruit alternately on to 4 wooden skewers. Place them in a shallow dish and pour over the rum. Set aside to soak up the flavor of the rum for at least 30 minutes, until ready to cook.

4 Cook the kabobs over the hot coals, turning frequently, for about 2 minutes, until seared. Serve, accompanied by the hot chocolate dip.

Sticky Chocolate Sponges

These rich individual desserts with a cream sauce always look and taste impressive at the end of a meal.

20 mins   1 hr

SERVES 6

INGREDIENTS

½ cup butter, softened

1 cup soft brown sugar

3 eggs, beaten

pinch of salt

¼ cup unsweetened cocoa

1 cup self-rising flour

1 oz/25 g dark chocolate, finely chopped

2¾ oz/75 g white chocolate, finely chopped

SAUCE

⅔ cup heavy cream

½ cup soft brown sugar

2 tbsp butter

1 Lightly grease 6 individual ¾ cup individual dessert molds.

2 In a bowl, cream together the butter and sugar until pale and fluffy. Beat in the eggs a little at a time, beating well after each addition.

3 Strain the salt, cocoa, and flour into the creamed mixture, and fold through the mixture. Stir the chopped chocolate into the mixture until evenly combined throughout.

4 Divide the mixture between the prepared molds. Lightly grease 6 squares of foil and use them to cover the tops of the molds. Press around the edges to seal.

5 Place the molds in a roasting pan and pour in boiling water to come halfway up the sides of the molds.

6 Bake in a preheated oven, 350°F/ 180°C, for 50 minutes, or until a skewer inserted into the center of the sponges comes out clean.

7 Remove the molds from the roasting pan and set aside while you prepare the sauce.

8 To make the sauce, put the cream, sugar and butter into a pan and bring to a boil over a gentle heat. Simmer gently until the sugar has dissolved.

9 To serve, run a knife around the edge of each sponge, then turn out on to serving plates. Pour the sauce over the top of the chocolate sponges and serve immediately.

Chocolate Fruit Dip

These warm, lightly grilled fruit kabobs are served with a delicious chocolate dipping sauce.

🕙 10 mins ⏱ 5–10 mins

SERVES 4

INGREDIENTS

selection of fruit (choose from oranges, bananas, strawberries, pineapple chunks (fresh or canned), apricots (fresh or canned), apples, pears, kiwi fruit)

1 tbsp lemon juice

CHOCOLATE SAUCE

4 tbsp butter

1¾ oz/50 g dark chocolate, broken into small cubes

½ tbsp unsweetened cocoa

2 tbsp light corn syrup

BASTE

4 tbsp clear honey

grated zest and juice of ½ orange

1 To make the chocolate sauce, place the butter, chocolate, cocoa, and syrup in a small pan. Heat gently on a stove or at the side of a barbecue grill, stirring continuously, until all of the ingredients have melted and combined.

2 To prepare the fruit, peel and core if necessary, then cut into large, bite-sized pieces or wedges as appropriate. Dip apples, pears, and bananas in lemon juice to prevent discoloration. Thread the pieces of fruit on to skewers.

3 To make the baste, mix together the honey, orange zest, and orange juice, heat gently if required and brush over the fruit.

4 Grill the fruit skewers over warm coals for 5–10 minutes until hot. Serve with the chocolate dipping sauce.

COOK'S TIP

If the coals are too hot, raise the rack so that it is about 6 inches/15 cm above the coals, or spread out the coals a little to reduce the heat. Do not assemble the fruit kabobs more than 1–2 hours before they are required.

Italian Drowned Ice Cream

A classic vanilla ice cream is topped with steaming coffee to make a wonderful instant dessert. Remember to serve in heatproof bowls.

7½ hrs   10 mins

SERVES 4

INGREDIENTS

2 cups freshly made espresso coffee

chocolate-covered coffee beans,
   to decorate

VANILLA ICE CREAM

1 vanilla bean

6 large egg yolks

⅔ cup superfine sugar, or vanilla-flavored
   sugar (sugar that has been stored with a
   vanilla bean)

2¼ cups milk

1 cup plus 2 tbsp heavy cream

1 To make the ice cream, slit the vanilla bean lengthwise and scrape out the tiny brown seeds. Set aside.

2 Put the yolks and sugar in a heatproof bowl that will sit over a pan with plenty of room underneath. Beat the eggs and sugar together until thick and creamy.

3 Put the milk, cream, and vanilla seeds in the pan over a low heat and bring to a simmer. Pour the milk over the egg mixture, whisking. Pour 1 inch/2.5 cm of water in the bottom of a pan. Place the bowl on top, ensuring that the base does not touch the water. Turn the heat to medium–high.

4 Cook the mixture, stirring constantly, until it is thick enough to coat the back of the spoon. Remove from the heat, transfer to a bowl and let cool.

5 Churn the mixture in an ice-cream maker, following the manufacturer's instructions. Alternatively, place it in a freezerproof container and freeze for 1 hour. Turn out into a bowl and whisk to break up the ice crystals, then return to the freezer. Repeat 4 times at 30-minute intervals.

6 Transfer the ice cream to a freezerproof bowl, smooth the top and cover with plastic wrap or foil. Freeze for up to 3 months.

7 Soften in the refrigerator for 20 minutes before serving. Place scoops of ice cream in each bowl. Pour over coffee and sprinkle with coffee beans.

Banana Empanadas

Phyllo pastry makes these empanadas light and crisp on the outside, while the filling melts into a scrumptious hot banana-chocolate goo.

10 mins   15 mins

SERVES 4

INGREDIENTS

about 8 sheets of phyllo pastry, cut into half lengthwise

melted butter or vegetable oil, for brushing

2 ripe sweet bananas

1–2 tsp sugar

juice of ½ lemon

6–7 oz/175–200 g dark chocolate, broken into small pieces

confectioners' sugar and ground cinnamon, for dusting

COOK'S TIP
You could use ready-made puff pie dough instead of phyllo for a more puffed-up effect.

1 Working one at a time, lay a long rectangular sheet of phyllo pastry out in front of you and then brush it with butter or oil.

2 Peel and dice and bananas and place in a bowl. Add the sugar and lemon juice and stir well to combine. Stir in the chocolate.

3 Place a couple of teaspoons of the banana and chocolate mixture in one corner of the phyllo pastry, then fold over into a triangle shape to enclose the filling. Continue to fold in a triangular shape,

until the pastry is completely wrapped around the filling.

4 Dust the parcels with confectioners' sugar and cinnamon. Place them on a cookie sheet and continue the process with the remaining phyllo pastry and filling.

5 Bake in a preheated oven, 375°F/190°C, for about 15 minutes or until the empanadas are golden. Remove from the oven and serve immediately—warn people that the filling is very hot.

Chocolate Fudge Pears

Melt-in-the-mouth, spicy poached pears are enveloped in a wonderfully self-indulgent chocolate fudge sauce.

10 mins   30–35 mins

SERVES 4

INGREDIENTS

4 eating pears

1–2 tbsp lemon juice

1¼ cups water

5 tbsp superfine sugar

2 inch/5 cm piece of cinnamon stick

2 cloves

scant 1 cup heavy cream

½ cup milk

scant 1 cup light brown sugar

2 tbsp sweet butter, diced

2 tbsp maple syrup

7 oz/200 g dark chocolate, broken into pieces

1 Peel the pears using a swivel vegetable peeler. Carefully cut out the cores from underneath, but leave the stalks intact because they look more attractive. Brush the pears with the lemon juice to prevent discoloration.

2 Pour the water into a large, heavy-based pan and add the superfine sugar. Stir over a low heat until the sugar has dissolved. Add the pears, cinnamon, and cloves and bring to a boil. (Add a little more water if the pears are not almost covered.) Lower the heat and simmer for 20 minutes.

3 Meanwhile, pour the cream and milk into another heavy-based pan and add the brown sugar, butter, and maple syrup. Stir over a low heat until the sugar

has dissolved and the butter has melted. Still stirring, bring to a boil and continue to boil, stirring constantly, for 5 minutes, until thick and smooth. Remove the pan from the heat and stir in the chocolate, a little at a time, waiting until each batch has melted before adding the next. Set aside.

4 Transfer the pears to individual serving plates using a draining spoon and keep warm. Bring the poaching syrup back to a boil and cook until reduced. Remove and discard the cinnamon and cloves, then fold the syrup into the chocolate sauce. Pour the sauce over the pears and serve immediately.

Individual Soufflés

Light-as-air, these delicious little soufflés are the perfect choice for a dinner party dessert.

15 mins

20 mins

SERVES 6

INGREDIENTS

⅔ cup sweet butter, plus 1 tbsp extra for greasing

3 tbsp superfine sugar, plus 1 tbsp extra for sprinkling

6 oz/175 g dark chocolate, broken into small pieces

4 large eggs, separated

2 tbsp orange liqueur

¼ tsp cream of tartar

1 tbsp confectioners' sugar, for dusting

1¼ cups French Chocolate Sauce (see page 102), to serve

1 Butter 6 custard pots or individual heatproof bowls and sprinkle with superfine sugar to coat the bottoms and sides. Tip out any excess. Stand the ramekins on a cookie sheet.

2 Chop the butter and place it in a heavy-based pan with the chocolate. Stir over a very low heat until melted and smooth. Remove the pan from the heat and cool slightly. Beat in the egg yolks, one at a time, and stir in the orange liqueur. Set aside, stirring occasionally.

3 Gently whisk the egg whites until they are frothy, then sprinkle in the cream of tartar and whisk rapidly until they form soft peaks. Add 1 tablespoon of superfine sugar and whisk rapidly again. Add the remaining superfine sugar, one

tablespoon at a time, whisking until the whites form stiff, glossy peaks. Gently stir about one-quarter of the whites into the cooled chocolate mixture, then fold the chocolate mixture into the remaining whites using a metal spoon.

4 Divide the mixture among the ramekins and bake in a preheated oven, 425°F/220°C, for about 10 minutes, until risen and just set. Dust the soufflés with confectioners' sugar and serve immediately, handing the sauce separately.

Chocolate Crêpes

Serve these sweet soufflé-filled, golden chocolate crêpes with flambéed summer berries for a superb contrast.

40 mins, plus 30 mins cooling · 1 hr

SERVES 6

INGREDIENTS

⅔ cup all-purpose flour

1 tbsp unsweetened cocoa

1 tsp superfine sugar

2 eggs, lightly beaten

¾ cup milk

2 tsp dark rum

6 tbsp sweet butter

confectioners' sugar, to dust

FILLING

5 tbsp heavy cream

8 oz/225 g dark chocolate

3 eggs, separated

2 tbsp superfine sugar

BERRIES

2 tbsp butter

4 tbsp superfine sugar

⅔ cup orange juice

2 cups mixed berries, such as raspberries, blackberries and strawberries

3 tbsp white rum

1 To make the crêpes, strain the flour, cocoa, and superfine sugar into a bowl. Make a well in the center and add the eggs, beating them in a little at a time. Add the milk and beat until smooth. Stir in the rum.

2 Melt all the butter and stir 2 tablespoonfuls into the batter. Cover with plastic wrap and let stand for 30 minutes.

3 To cook the crêpes, brush the bottom of a 7 inch/18 cm crêpe pan or non-stick skillet with melted butter and set over a medium heat Stir the batter and pour 3 tablespoonfuls into the pan, swirling it to cover the bottom. Cook for 2 minutes or until the underside is golden, flip over, cook for 30 seconds, then slide on to a plate. Cook another 11 crêpes in the same way. Stack them interleaved with baking parchment.

4 For the filling, pour the cream into a heavy-based pan, add the chocolate and melt over a low heat, stirring. Remove from the heat. In a heatproof bowl, beat the egg yolks with half of the superfine sugar until creamy, beat in the chocolate cream and let the mixture cool.

5 In a separate bowl, whisk the egg whites into soft peaks, add the rest of the superfine sugar, and beat into stiff peaks. Stir a spoonful of the whites into the chocolate mixture, then fold the mixture into the remaining egg whites with a spoon.

6 Preheat the oven to 400°F/200°C. Brush a cookie sheet with melted butter. Spread 1 crêpe with 1 tablespoon of the filling, then fold it in half and in half again to make a triangle. Place on the cookie sheet. Repeat with the remaining crêpes. Brush the tops with the remaining melted butter and bake for 20 minutes.

7 For the berry sauce, melt the butter in a heavy-based skillet over a low heat, stir in the sugar and cook until golden. Stir in the orange juice and cook until syrupy. Add the berries and warm through, stirring gently. Add the rum, heat gently for 1 minute, then ignite. Shake the pan until the flames have died down. Transfer the crêpes to serving plates with the sauce and serve.

Chocolate Ravioli

Tempting squares of home-made chocolate pasta are filled with a mouthwatering mixture of mascarpone cheese and white chocolate.

25 mins, plus 1 hr chilling/resting

10 mins

SERVES 4

INGREDIENTS

1½ cups all-purpose flour, plus 2 tbsp extra for dusting

4 tbsp unsweetened cocoa

2 tbsp confectioners' sugar

2 eggs, lightly beaten, plus extra for brushing

1 tbsp vegetable oil

FILLING

6 oz/175 g white chocolate, broken into pieces

1 cup mascarpone cheese

1 egg

1 tbsp finely chopped preserved ginger

fresh mint sprigs, to decorate

heavy cream, to serve

1 Strain together the flour, cocoa, and sugar on to a clean counter. Make a well in the center and pour the 2 beaten eggs and the oil into it. Gradually draw in the flour with your fingertips until it is fully incorporated. Alternatively, strain the flour, cocoa, and sugar into a food processor, add the eggs and oil and process until mixed. Knead the dough until it is smooth and elastic, then cover with plastic wrap and place in the refrigerator for 30 minutes to chill.

2 Meanwhile, to make the filling, put the white chocolate in the top of a double boiler or in a heatproof bowl set over a pan of barely simmering water. When the chocolate has melted, remove it from the heat and cool slightly, then beat in the mascarpone and the egg. Stir in the chopped ginger.

3 Remove the pasta dough from the refrigerator, cut it in half and keep one half tightly wrapped in plastic wrap. Roll out the first half of the dough into a rectangle on a lightly floured counter, then cover with a clean, damp dish towel. Roll out the other half into a rectangle. Spoon the chocolate and ginger filling into a pastry bag and pipe small mounds in even rows at intervals of about 1½ inches/4 cm over 1 dough rectangle. Brush the spaces between the mounds with beaten egg, then, using a rolling pin to lift it, position the second dough rectangle on top of the first. Press firmly between the mounds with your finger to

seal and push out any pockets of air. Cut the dough into squares around the mounds using a serrated ravioli or dough cutter or a sharp knife. Transfer the ravioli to a lightly floured dish towel and let rest for 30 minutes.

4 Bring a large pan of water to a boil, then lower the heat to medium and cook the ravioli, in batches, stirring to prevent them from sticking together, for 4–5 minutes, until tender but still firm to the bite. Remove with a slotted spoon. Serve immediately on individual plates, garnished with mint sprigs, and hand the cream separately.

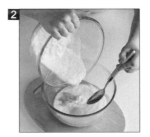

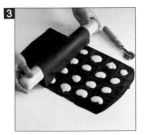

Chocolate Sponge with Rum

A warming way to end supper on a wintry evening, this steamed sponge is very easy to make.

🍶 15 mins   🕐 65–70 mins

SERVES 4

INGREDIENTS

4 tbsp sweet butter, plus 1 tsp extra for greasing

1¼ cups self-rising flour, plus 2 tsp extra for dusting

2 oz/55 g dark chocolate

¼ tsp vanilla extract

scant ⅔ cup superfine sugar

2 eggs, lightly beaten

5 tbsp milk

SAUCE

1¼ cups milk

2 tbsp cornstarch

2 tbsp superfine sugar

2 tbsp dark rum

1   Grease and flour a 5-cup ovenproof bowl. Put the butter, chocolate, and vanilla in the top of a double boiler or a heatproof bowl set over a pan of barely simmering water. Heat gently until the butter and sugar have melted, then remove from the heat and cool slightly. Stir the sugar into the chocolate mixture, then beat in the eggs. Strain in the flour, stir in the milk, and mix well. Pour the mixture into the prepared ovenproof bowl, cover the top with foil and tie with string. Steam the sponge for 1 hour, topping off with boiling water if necessary.

2   To make the sauce, pour the milk into a small pan set over a medium heat. Stir in the cornstarch, then stir in the sugar until dissolved. Bring to a boil, stirring constantly, then lower the heat and simmer until thickened and smooth. Remove from the heat and stir in the rum.

3   To serve, remove the sponge from the heat and discard the foil. Run a round-bladed knife around the side of the bowl, place a serving plate on top of the sponge and, holding them together, invert. Serve immediately, handing the sauce separately.

Chocolate Cranberry Sponge

The sharpness of the fruit contrasts deliciously with the sweetness of the chocolate in this wonderful, fluffy sponge pudding.

🕐 20 mins   🕐 1 hr

SERVES 4

I N G R E D I E N T S

4 tbsp sweet butter, plus 1 tsp extra for greasing

4 tbsp dark brown sugar, plus 2 tsp extra for sprinkling

¾ cup cranberries, thawed if frozen

1 large tart apple

2 eggs, lightly beaten

⅔ cup self-rising flour

3 tbsp unsweetened cocoa

S A U C E

6 oz/175 g dark chocolate, broken into pieces

1¾ cups evaporated milk

1 tsp vanilla extract

½ tsp almond extract

3 Meanwhile, to make the sauce, put the dark chocolate and milk in the top of a double boiler or a heatproof bowl set over a pan of barely simmering water. Stir until the chocolate has melted, then remove from the heat. Whisk in the vanilla and almond extracts and continue to beat until the sauce is thick and smooth.

4 To serve, remove the sponge from the heat and discard the foil. Run a round-bladed knife around the side of the bowl, place a serving plate on top of the sponge and, holding them together, invert. Serve immediately, handing the sauce separately.

1 Grease a 5-cup ovenproof bowl, sprinkle with brown sugar to coat the sides and tip out any excess. Put the cranberries in a bowl. Peel, core, and dice the apple and mix with the cranberries. Put the fruit in the prepared ovenproof bowl.

2 Place the butter, brown sugar, and eggs in a large bowl. Strain in the flour and cocoa and beat well until thoroughly mixed. Pour the mixture into the ovenproof bowl on top of the fruit, cover the top with foil and tie with string. Steam for about 1 hour, until risen, topping up with boiling water if necessary.

Stuffed Nectarines

This delectable combination of juicy fruit, crunchy amaretti cookies and continental chocolate is an irresistible summer treat.

15 mins   40–45 mins

SERVES 6

INGREDIENTS

3 oz/85 g dark continental chocolate, finely chopped

1 cup amaretti cookie crumbs

1 tsp finely grated lemon zest

1 large egg, separated

6 tbsp amaretto liqueur

6 nectarines, halved and pitted

1¼ cups white wine

2 oz/55 g light chocolate, grated

whipped cream or ice cream, to serve

1 In a large bowl, mix together the chocolate, amaretti crumbs, and lemon zest. Lightly beat the egg white and add it to the mixture with half the amaretto liqueur. (Use the yolk in another recipe.) Using a small sharp knife, slightly enlarge the cavities in the nectarines. Add the removed nectarine flesh to the chocolate and crumb mixture and mix together well.

2 Preheat the oven to 375°F/190°C. Place the nectarines, cut side up, in an ovenproof dish just large enough to hold them in a single layer. Pile the chocolate and crumb mixture into the cavities, dividing it equally among them. Mix the wine and remaining amaretto and pour it into the dish around the nectarines. Bake in the preheated oven for 40–45 minutes, until the nectarines are tender. Transfer 2 nectarine halves to each individual serving plate and spoon over a little of the cooking juices. Sprinkle over the grated light chocolate and serve immediately with whipped cream or ice cream.

Chocolate Castles

Covered in a rich chocolate sauce, these light-as-air individual desserts are a delicious treat on a cold day.

🍮 25 mins ⏲ 40 mins

SERVES 4

INGREDIENTS

3 tbsp butter, plus 2 tsp extra for greasing

3 tbsp superfine sugar

1 large egg, lightly beaten

⅔ cup self-rising flour

2 oz/55 g dark chocolate, melted

SAUCE

2 tbsp unsweetened cocoa

2 tbsp cornstarch

⅔ cup light cream

1¼ cups milk

1–2 tbsp dark brown sugar

1 Grease 4 muffin cups or small heatproof bowls with butter. In a mixing bowl, cream together the butter and sugar until pale and fluffy. Gradually add the egg, beating well after each addition.

2 In a separate bowl, sift the flour, fold it into the butter mixture with a metal spoon, then stir in the melted chocolate. Divide the mixture among the muffin cups, filling them to about two-thirds full to allow for expansion during cooking. Cover each cup with a circle of foil, and tie in place with string.

3 Bring a large pan of water to a boil and set a steamer over it. Place the muffin cups in the steamer and cook for 40 minutes. Check the water level from time to time and top up with boiling water when necessary.

4 To make the sauce, put the cocoa, cornstarch, cream, and milk in a heavy-based pan. Bring to the boil, then reduce the heat and simmer over a low heat, whisking constantly, until thick and smooth. Cook for a further 2–3 minutes, then stir in brown sugar to taste. Pour the sauce into a pitcher.

5 Lift the muffin cups out of the steamer and remove the foil circles from them. Run a knife blade around the sides of the cups and turn out the chocolate castles onto warmed individual plates. Serve immediately, handing the sauce separately.

Chocolate Fudge Sauce

This creamy white chocolate sauce adds a touch of luxury and sophistication to the dinner table.

 5 mins, plus 15–20 mins cooling

10–15 mins

MAKES SCANT 1 CUP

INGREDIENTS

⅔ cup heavy cream

4 tbsp sweet butter, diced

3 tbsp superfine sugar

6 oz/175 g white chocolate, broken into pieces

2 tbsp brandy

1 Pour the cream into the top of a double boiler or a heatproof bowl set over a pan of barely simmering water. Add the butter and sugar and stir until the mixture is smooth. Remove from the heat.

2 Stir in the chocolate, a few pieces at a time, waiting until each batch has melted before adding the next. Add the brandy and stir the sauce until smooth. Cool to room temperature before serving.

French Chocolate Sauce

This rich, warm—and alcoholic—sauce is superb with both hot and cold desserts and positively magical with ice cream.

5 hours   10–15 mins

MAKES ⅔ CUP

I N G R E D I E N T S

6 tbsp heavy cream

3 oz/85 g dark chocolate, broken into small pieces

2 tbsp orange liqueur

1 Bring the cream gently to a boil in a small, heavy-based pan over a low heat. Remove the pan from the heat, add the chocolate and stir until smooth.

2 Stir in the liqueur and serve immediately, or keep the sauce warm until required.

Glossy Chocolate Sauce

This simple sauce is a deliciously rich accompaniment to hot and cold desserts and is suitable for all the family.

 5 mins   10–15 mins

MAKES ⅔ CUP

INGREDIENTS

½ cup superfine sugar

4 tbsp water

6 oz/175 g dark chocolate, broken into pieces

2 tbsp diced sweet butter

2 tbsp orange juice

1 Put the sugar and water into a small, heavy-based pan set over a low heat and stir until the sugar has dissolved. Stir in the chocolate, a few pieces at a time, waiting until each batch has melted before adding the next. Stir in the butter, a few pieces at a time, waiting until each batch has been incorporated before adding the next. Do not allow the sauce to boil.

2 Stir in the orange juice and remove the pan from the heat. Serve immediately or keep warm until required. Alternatively, let cool, transfer to a freezerproof container and freeze for up to 3 months. Thaw at room temperature before re-heating to serve.

Savories

Chocolate may seem an unusual ingredient to use in savory dishes, but Mexican cooks have long known about its wonderful affinity for chilies and red bell peppers. It can be used to add a marvelous new flavor to dishes that you may have normally cooked in a more traditional way. Chilies, red bell peppers, and chocolate feature in two of

the recipes in this section, Mole Poblano and Mexican Beef Stew. For a lighter dish that is also suitable for vegetarians, try the Nut and Chocolate Pasta. Finally, the Veal in Chocolate Sauce is perfect for a dinner party, where the chocolate will add an interesting flavor to this meat stew to surprise and satisfy you and your guests.

Mole Poblano

This great Mexican celebration dish, ladled out at fiestas, baptisms, and weddings, is known for its combination of chilies and chocolate.

20 mins, plus 1–8 hrs soaking

15 mins

SERVES 4

INGREDIENTS

3 mulato chilies

3 mild ancho chilies

5–6 New Mexico or California chilies

1 onion, chopped

5 garlic cloves, chopped

1 lb/450 g ripe tomatoes

2 tortillas, preferably stale, cut into small pieces

pinch of cloves

pinch of fennel seeds

⅛ tsp each ground cinnamon, coriander, and cumin

3 tbsp lightly toasted sesame seeds or tahini

3 tbsp flaked or coarsely ground blanched almonds

2 tbsp raisins

1 tbsp peanut butter, optional

2 cups chicken bouillon

3–4 tbsp grated dark chocolate, plus extra for garnishing

2 tbsp mild chili powder

3 tbsp vegetable oil

about 1 tbsp lime juice

salt and pepper

1 Using metal tongs, toast each chili over an open flame for a few seconds until the color darkens. Alternatively, roast the chilies in an ungreased skillet over a medium heat, turning constantly, for about 30 seconds.

2 Place the toasted chilies in a bowl or a pan and pour boiling water over to cover. Cover with a lid and set aside to soften for at least 1 hour or overnight. Once or twice lift the lid and rearrange the chilies so that they soak evenly.

3 Remove the softened chilies with a slotted spoon. Discard the stems and seeds and cut the flesh into pieces. Place in a blender.

4 Add the onion, garlic, tomatoes, tortillas, cloves, fennel seeds, cinnamon, coriander, cumin, sesame seeds, almonds, raisins, and peanut butter if using, then process to combine. With the motor running, add enough bouillon through the feed tube to make a smooth paste. Stir in the remaining bouillon, chocolate, and chili powder.

5 Heat the oil in a heavy-based pan until it is smoking, then pour in the mole mixture. It will splatter and pop as it hits the hot oil. Cook for about 10 minutes, stirring occasionally to prevent it from burning.

6 Season with salt, pepper, and lime juice, garnish with grated chocolate, and serve.

Mexican Beef Stew

Colorful and richly-flavored, this stew is somewhat time-consuming, but well worth the effort.

15 mins   2–2¼ hrs

SERVES 4

INGREDIENTS

2 red bell peppers

1 beefsteak tomato

1 onion, cut into quarters

2 oz/55 g dark chocolate, broken into pieces

2 garlic cloves, coarsely chopped

3 tbsp red wine vinegar

3 tbsp vegetable oil

1 lb 12 oz/800 g lean braising steak, diced

1½ cups beef bouillon

2 cloves

1 inch/2.5 cm piece of cinnamon stick

2 large carrots, peeled and finely chopped

1 large potato, peeled and diced

salt and pepper

1 tbsp chopped fresh cilantro, to garnish

2 Meanwhile, cut a cross in the skin on the bottom of the tomato. Put it in a bowl, cover with boiling water and let stand for 1 minute. Remove the tomato from the water, then peel and seed it. Dice the tomato flesh, and put it into a food processor. When the peppers are cool enough to handle, peel and seed them, then chop the flesh. Add the peppers to the food processor together with the onion, chocolate, garlic, and vinegar. Process the ingredients to a paste.

3 Heat the oil in a flameproof casserole or large pan. Add the steak, in batches if necessary, and cook over a medium heat, stirring frequently, until browned all over. Season to taste with salt and pepper. Add the chocolate paste and beef bouillon. Tie the cloves and cinnamon in a small piece of cheesecloth and add to the pan. Bring to a boil, then lower the heat, cover, and simmer for 1–1¼ hours.

4 Add the carrots and potato to the pan, stir well and simmer for a further 30 minutes. Remove and discard the cloves and cinnamon. Taste the stew and adjust the seasoning if necessary. Garnish with the fresh cilantro and serve immediately with cooked green vegetables such as green beans.

1 Preheat the oven to 475°F/240°C. Arrange the red bell peppers on a cookie sheet and cook in the preheated oven for about 20 minutes, until the skins have blackened and are beginning to blister. Using tongs, transfer them to a plastic bag. Tie the top and set aside.

Nut and Chocolate Pasta

This is a popular main course dish in northern Europe, and makes a satisfying vegetarian supper.

🍲 20 mins   🕐 35–40 mins

SERVES 4

INGREDIENTS

salt

12 oz/350 g dried ribbon pasta, such as tagliatelle or fettucine

1 tsp butter, for greasing

2–3 tbsp fresh white breadcrumbs

SAUCE

6 tbsp butter

¾ cup confectioners' sugar

4 eggs, separated

¾ cup ground, roasted hazelnuts

3 oz/85 g dark chocolate, grated

4 tbsp fresh white breadcrumbs

½ tsp ground cinnamon

finely grated zest of ½ lemon

1 Bring a large pan of lightly salted water to a boil. Add the pasta and cook for 6 minutes or according to the instructions on the package, until tender, but still firm to the bite. Drain, rinse under cold running water and set aside.

2 To make the sauce, beat together the butter, half the sugar, and the egg yolks until frothy.

3 In a separate bowl, whisk the egg whites with the remaining sugar until stiff, then fold them into the butter mixture.

4 In another bowl, mix the hazelnuts, grated chocolate, breadcrumbs, cinnamon, and lemon zest, then stir into the egg mixture. Add the pasta and stir gently to mix.

5 Preheat the oven to 400°F/200°C. Grease an ovenproof dish with butter and sprinkle with breadcrumbs. Tap lightly to coat the bottom and sides, then tip out any excess. Spoon the pasta mixture into the dish and bake in the preheated oven for 25–30 minutes. Serve immediately, with roasted vine tomatoes (see Cook's Tip), if desired.

COOK'S TIP

To roast vine tomatoes, put 12 small tomatoes in an ovenproof dish, sprinkle with 2 tablespoons of olive oil, and season with salt and pepper to taste. Roast in an oven preheated to 400°F/200°C for 15–20 minutes, then remove from the oven and serve hot.

Veal in Chocolate Sauce

Chocolate can enrich stews based on a broad range of meats, including game, but it is important to be light-handed or it can become cloying.

20 mins   1¾ hrs

SERVES 4

INGREDIENTS

5 tbsp vegetable oil

1½ lb/675 g boneless veal (or pork if veal is unavailable), cut into 1 inch/2.5 cm cubes

1 onion, chopped

2 garlic cloves, chopped

2 carrots, chopped

2 celery stalks, chopped

2 fresh red chilies, seeded and chopped

1¼–1¾ cups red wine

½ cup beef bouillon

2 tsp chopped fresh thyme

1 bay leaf

4 juniper berries, lightly crushed

2 cloves

1 inch/2.5 cm piece of cinnamon stick

8 oz/225 g chestnuts

8 shallots, quartered

2 oz/55 g dark chocolate, grated

salt and pepper

GARNISH

2 tbsp chopped fresh parsley

2 fresh bay leaves, optional

2 Preheat the oven to 400°F/200°C. Stir in 1¼ cups of the wine and all of the bouillon, and return the meat to the casserole. Add the thyme, bay leaf, juniper berries, cloves, and cinnamon, and season with salt and pepper. Bring to a boil, stirring, then cook in the oven for 1 hour. Top up the casserole with more wine from time to time, if necessary.

3 Meanwhile, make a cross in the bottom of the chestnuts, put them on a cookie sheet, bake at 400°F/200°C for 20 minutes, then shell them.

4 While the chestnuts are cooking, place the shallots in a small roasting pan and coat them with the remaining oil. Roast at the same oven temperature for 15–20 minutes, until golden and tender.

5 Remove the casserole from the oven and lift out the meat with a draining spoon. Place it in a serving dish, add the chestnuts and shallots, and keep warm. Strain the cooking juices into a clean pan. Discard the contents of the strainer. Set the pan over a medium heat, bring to a boil and cook until slightly reduced. Stir in the chocolate until melted and adjust the seasoning, if necessary. Pour the sauce over the meat, sprinkle with the parsley, and bay leaves if using, and serve.

1 Heat 3 tablespoons of the oil in a large, flameproof casserole. Add the veal and cook over a medium heat, stirring, until lightly browned. Remove from the casserole with and set aside. Add the onion, garlic, carrots, celery, and chilies to the casserole and cook, stirring, for 5 minutes, until the onion is softened.

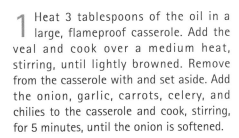

Cold Desserts

Cool, creamy, sumptuous, indulgent are just a few of the words that spring to mind when you think of cold chocolate desserts. The desserts contained in this chapter are a combination of all of these.

Some of the desserts are surprisingly quick and simple to make, while others are more elaborate. One of the best things about these desserts is they can all be made in advance, sometimes days in advance, making them perfect for entertaining. A quick decoration when necessary is all that is needed on the day. Even the Baked Chocolate Alaska can be assembled in advance and popped into the oven just before serving.

Chocolate Mint Swirl

The classic combination of chocolate and mint flavors makes an attractive dessert for special occasions.

45 mins   5 mins

SERVES 6

INGREDIENTS

1¼ cups heavy cream

⅔ cup mascarpone cheese

2 tbsp confectioners' sugar

1 tbsp crème de menthe

6 oz/175 g dark chocolate

chocolate, to decorate

1 Place the cream in a large mixing bowl and whisk until standing in soft peaks.

2 Fold in the mascarpone cheese and confectioners' sugar, then place about one-third of the mixture in a smaller bowl. Stir the crème de menthe into the smaller bowl. Melt the dark chocolate and stir it into the remaining mixture.

3 Place alternate spoonfuls of the 2 mixtures into serving glasses, then swirl the mixture together to give a decorative effect. Chill until required.

4 To make the piped chocolate decorations, melt a small amount of chocolate and place in a paper pastry bag.

5 Place a sheet of baking parchment on a board and pipe squiggles, stars, or flower shapes with the melted chocolate. Alternatively, to make curved decorations, pipe decorations on to a long strip of baking parchment, then carefully place the strip over a rolling pin, securing with sticky tape. Let the chocolate set, then carefully remove from the baking parchment.

6 Decorate each dessert with the piped chocolate decorations and serve. The desserts can be decorated and then chilled, if preferred.

2

5

5

COOK'S TIP
Pipe the patterns freehand or draw patterns on to baking parchment first, turn the parchment over and then pipe the chocolate, following the drawn outline.

Chocolate Rum Pots

Wickedly rich little pots, flavored with a hint of dark rum, are pure indulgence on any occasion!

2 hrs 20 mins | 5 mins

SERVES 6

INGREDIENTS

8 oz/225 g dark chocolate

4 eggs, separated

⅓ cup superfine sugar

4 tbsp dark rum

4 tbsp heavy cream

TO DECORATE

a little whipped cream

marbled chocolate shapes (see page 114)

1 Melt the chocolate and let cool slightly.

2 Whisk the egg yolks with the caster superfine sugar in a bowl until very pale and fluffy.

3 Drizzle the chocolate into the mixture and fold in together with the rum and the heavy cream.

4 Whisk the egg whites in a grease-free bowl until standing in soft peaks. Fold the egg whites into the chocolate mixture in 2 batches. Divide the mixture between 6 individual dishes, and let chill for at least 2 hours.

5 To serve, decorate with a little whipped cream and Marbled Chocolate Shapes.

COOK'S TIP

Make sure you use a perfectly clean, grease-free bowl for whisking the egg whites. They will not aerate if any grease is present as the smallest amount breaks down the bubbles in the whites, preventing them from trapping and holding air.

Chocolate & Vanilla Creams

These rich, creamy desserts are completely irresistible. Serve them with crisp dessert cookies.

🕐 40 mins   🕐 5–10 mins

SERVES 4

INGREDIENTS

scant 2 cups heavy cream

⅓ cup superfine sugar

1 vanilla bean

generous ¾ cup crème fraîche

2 tsp gelatin

3 tbsp water

1¾ oz/50 g dark chocolate

MARBLED CHOCOLATE SHAPES

a little melted white chocolate

a little melted dark chocolate

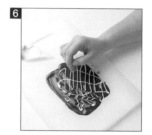

1 Place the cream and sugar in a pan. Cut the vanilla bean into 2 pieces and add to the cream. Heat gently, stirring until the sugar has dissolved, then bring to a boil. Reduce the heat and simmer for 2–3 minutes.

2 Remove the pan from the heat and take out the vanilla bean. Stir in the crème fraîche.

3 Sprinkle the gelatin over the water in a small heatproof bowl and let it go spongy, then place over a pan of hot water and stir until dissolved. Stir into the cream

mixture. Pour half of this mixture into another mixing bowl.

4 Melt the dark chocolate and stir it into one half of the cream mixture. Pour the chocolate mixture into 4 individual glass serving dishes and chill for 15–20 minutes until just set. While it is chilling, keep the vanilla mixture at room temperature.

5 Spoon the vanilla mixture on top of the chocolate mixture and chill until the vanilla is set.

6 Meanwhile, make the shapes for the decoration. Spoon the melted white chocolate into a paper pastry bag and snip off the tip. Spread some melted dark chocolate on a piece of baking parchment. Whilst still wet, pipe a fine line of white chocolate in a scribble over the top. Use the tip of a toothpick to marble the white chocolate into the dark. When firm but not too hard, cut into shapes with a small shaped cutter or a sharp knife. Chill the shapes until firm, then use to decorate the desserts.

Chocolate Hazelnut Pots

Chocoholics will adore these creamy desserts consisting of a rich baked chocolate custard with the delicious flavor of hazelnuts.

15 mins

35–40 mins

SERVES 6

INGREDIENTS

2 eggs

2 egg yolks

1 tbsp superfine sugar

1 tsp cornstarch

2½ cups milk

3 oz/85 g dark chocolate

4 tbsp chocolate and hazelnut spread

TO DECORATE

grated chocolate or quick chocolate curls
   (see page 15)

1 Beat together the eggs, egg yolks, superfine sugar, and cornstarch until well combined. Heat the milk until it is almost boiling.

2 Gradually pour the milk on to the eggs, whisking as you do so. Melt the chocolate and hazelnut spread in a bowl set over a pan of gently simmering water, then whisk the melted chocolate mixture into the eggs.

3 Pour into 6 small ovenproof dishes and cover the dishes with foil. Place them in a roasting pan. Fill the pan with boiling water until halfway up the sides of the dishes.

4 Bake in a preheated oven, 325°F/ 170°C, for 35–40 minutes, until the custard is just set. Remove from the pan and cool, then chill until required. Serve decorated with grated chocolate or chocolate curls.

COOK'S TIP
This dish is traditionally made in little pots called pots de crème, which are individual ovenproof dishes with a lid. Custard pots are fine. The dessert can also be made in one large dish: cook for about 1 hour or until set.

Mocha Creams

These creamy chocolate and coffee-flavored desserts make a perfect end to a fine meal.

30 mins   5 mins

SERVES 4

I N G R E D I E N T S

8 oz/225 g dark chocolate

1 tbsp instant coffee powder

1¼ cups boiling water

1 sachet gelatin

3 tbsp cold water

1 tsp vanilla extract

1 tbsp coffee-flavored liqueur, optional

1¼ cups double heavy cream

4 chocolate coffee beans

8 amaretti cookies

1   Break the chocolate into small pieces and place in a pan with the coffee. Stir in the boiling water and heat gently, stirring until the chocolate melts.

2   Sprinkle the gelatin over the cold water and let it go spongy, then whisk it into the hot chocolate mixture to dissolve it.

3   Stir in the vanilla extract and coffee-flavored liqueur, if using. Let stand in a cool place until just beginning to thicken; whisk from time to time.

4   Whisk the cream until it is standing in soft peaks, then reserve a little for decorating the desserts and fold the remainder into the chocolate mixture. Spoon into serving dishes and allow to set.

5   Decorate with the reserved cream and coffee beans and serve with the amaretti cookies.

VARIATION

To add a delicious almond flavor to the dessert, replace the coffee-flavored liqueur with amaretto liqueur.

Layered Chocolate Mousse

Three layers of rich mousse give this elegant dessert extra chocolate appeal. It is a little fiddly to prepare, but well worth the extra effort.

3 hrs   10 mins

SERVES 4

INGREDIENTS

3 eggs

1 tsp cornstarch

4 tbsp superfine sugar

1¼ cups milk

1 sachet gelatin

3 tbsp water

1¼ cups heavy cream

2¾ oz/75 g dark chocolate

2¾ oz/75 g white chocolate

2¾ oz/75 g light chocolate

chocolate caraque, to decorate
(see page 15)

1 Line a 1 lb/450 g loaf pan with baking parchment. Separate the eggs, putting each egg white in a separate bowl. Place the egg yolks and sugar in a large mixing bowl and whisk until well combined. Place the milk in a pan and heat gently, stirring until almost boiling. Pour the milk on to the egg yolks, whisking.

2 Set the bowl over a pan of gently simmering water and cook, stirring until the mixture thickens enough to thinly coat the back of a wooden spoon.

3 Sprinkle the gelatin over the water in a small heatproof bowl and let it go spongy. Place over a pan of hot water and stir until dissolved. Stir into the hot mixture. Let the mixture cool.

4 Whip the cream until just holding its shape. Fold into the egg custard, then divide the mixture into 3. Melt the 3 types of chocolate separately. Fold the dark chocolate into one egg custard portion. Whisk one egg white until standing in soft peaks and fold into the dark chocolate custard until combined. Pour into the

prepared pan and level the top. Chill in the coldest part of the refrigerator until just set. The remaining mixtures should stay at room temperature.

5 Fold the white chocolate into another portion of the egg custard. Whisk another egg white and fold in. Pour on top of the dark chocolate layer and chill quickly. Repeat with the remaining light chocolate and egg white. Chill for at least 2 hours, until set. To serve, carefully turn out on to a serving dish and decorate with chocolate caraque.

Chocolate Marquise

This classic French dish is part way between a mousse and a parfait. It is usually chilled in a large mold, but here it is made in individual molds.

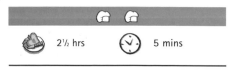

2½ hrs   5 mins

SERVES 6

INGREDIENTS

7 oz/200 g dark chocolate

generous ⅓ cup butter

3 egg yolks

⅓ cup superfine sugar

1 tsp chocolate extract or 1 tbsp chocolate-flavored liqueur

1¼ cups heavy cream

TO SERVE

crème fraîche

chocolate-dipped fruits

unsweetened cocoa, to dust

1 Break the chocolate into pieces. Place the chocolate and butter in a bowl over a pan of gently simmering water and stir until melted and well combined. Remove from the heat and let cool.

2 Place the egg yolks in a mixing bowl with the sugar and whisk until pale and fluffy. Using an electric whisk running on low speed, slowly whisk in the cool chocolate mixture. Stir in the chocolate extract or chocolate-flavored liqueur.

3 Whip the cream until just holding its shape. Fold into the chocolate mixture. Spoon into 6 small custard pots, or individual metal molds. Chill the desserts for at least 2 hours.

4 To serve, turn out the desserts on to individual serving dishes. If you have difficulty turning them out, dip the pots or molds into a bowl of warm water for a few seconds to help the marquise to slip out. Serve with chocolate-dipped fruit and crème fraîche and dust with cocoa.

COOK'S TIP
The slight tartness of the crème fraîche contrasts well with this very rich dessert. Dip the fruit in white chocolate to give a good color contrast.

Iced White Chocolate Terrine

This iced dessert is somewhere between a chocolate mousse and an ice cream. Serve it with a chocolate sauce or a fruit coulis and fresh fruit.

12 hrs 50 mins   5 mins

SERVES 8

INGREDIENTS

2 tbsp granulated sugar

5 tbsp water

10½ oz/300 g white chocolate

3 eggs, separated

1¼ cups heavy cream

1 Line a 1 lb/450 g loaf pan with foil or plastic wrap, pressing out as many creases as you can.

2 Place the granulated sugar and water in a heavy-based pan and heat gently, stirring until the sugar has dissolved. Bring to a boil and boil for 1–2 minutes until syrupy, then remove from the heat.

3 Break the white chocolate into small pieces and stir it into the syrup, continuing to stir until the chocolate has melted and combined with the syrup. Let the mixture cool slightly.

4 Beat the egg yolks into the chocolate mixture. Let cool completely.

5 Lightly whip the cream until just holding its shape, and fold it into the chocolate mixture.

6 Whisk the egg whites in a grease-free bowl until they are standing in soft peaks. Fold the whites into the chocolate

mixture. Pour into the prepared loaf pan and freeze overnight.

7 To serve, remove the terrine from the freezer about 10–15 minutes before serving. Turn out of the pan and cut into slices to serve.

COOK'S TIP

To make a coulis, place 8 oz/ 225 g soft fruit of your choice— strawberries, mangoes, or raspberries are ideal—in a food processor. Add 1–2 tablespoons of confectioners' sugar and blend to a paste. If the fruit contains seeds, push the paste through a sieve to remove them. Chill until required.

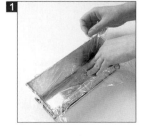

Chocolate Banana Sundae

A banana split in a glass! Choose the best vanilla ice cream you can find, or better still, make your own.

🍎 15 mins 🕐 5 mins

SERVES 4

INGREDIENTS

GLOSSY CHOCOLATE SAUCE

2 oz/60 g dark chocolate

4 tbsp light corn syrup

1 tbsp butter

1 tbsp brandy or rum, optional

SUNDAE

4 bananas

⅔ cup double heavy cream

8–12 scoops of good quality vanilla ice cream

¾ cup slivered or chopped almonds, toasted

grated or flaked chocolate, to sprinkle

4 fan wafer cookies

1 To make the chocolate sauce, break the chocolate into small pieces and place in a heatproof bowl with the syrup and butter. Heat over a pan of hot water until melted, stirring until well combined. Remove the bowl from the heat and stir in the brandy or rum, if using.

2 Slice the bananas and whip the cream until just holding its shape. Place a scoop of ice cream in the bottom of 4 tall sundae dishes. Top with slices of banana, some chocolate sauce, a spoonful of cream, and a good sprinkling of nuts.

3 Repeat the layers, finishing with a good dollop of cream, sprinkled with nuts, and a little grated or flaked chocolate. Serve with fan wafer cookies.

VARIATION

For a traditional banana split, halve the bananas lengthwise and place on a plate with two scoops of ice cream between. Top with cream and sprinkle with nuts. Serve with the glossy chocolate sauce poured over the top.

Rich Chocolate Ice Cream

A rich chocolate ice cream, delicious on its own or with chocolate sauce. For a special dessert, serve it in these attractive trellis cups.

🍰 4–5 hrs   🕐 12 mins

SERVES 6

INGREDIENTS

ICE CREAM

1 egg

3 egg yolks

scant ½ cup superfine sugar

1¼ cups full cream milk

9 oz/250 g dark chocolate

1¼ cups heavy cream

TRELLIS CUPS

3½ oz/100 g dark chocolate

1 Beat together the egg, egg yolks, and superfine sugar in a mixing bowl until well combined. Heat the milk until it is almost boiling.

2 Gradually pour the hot milk on to the eggs, whisking as you do so. Place the bowl over a pan of gently simmering water and cook, stirring until the mixture thickens sufficiently to thinly coat the back of a wooden spoon.

3 Break the dark chocolate into small pieces and add to the hot custard. Stir until the chocolate has melted. Cover with a sheet of dampened baking parchment and let cool.

4 Whip the cream until just holding its shape, then fold into the cooled chocolate custard. Transfer to a freezer container and freeze for 1–2 hours until the mixture is frozen 1 inch/2.5 cm from the sides.

5 Scrape the ice cream into a chilled bowl and beat again until smooth. Refreeze until firm.

6 To make the trellis cups, invert a muffin pan and cover 6 alternate mounds with plastic wrap. Melt the chocolate, place it in a paper pastry bag and snip off the end.

7 Pipe a circle around the bottom of the mound, then pipe chocolate back and forth over it to form a trellis; carefully pipe a double thickness. Pipe around the bottom again. Chill until set, then lift from the pan and remove the plastic wrap. Serve the ice cream in the trellis cups.

Baked Chocolate Alaska

A cool dessert that leaves the cook completely unflustered—assemble it in advance and keep it in the freezer until required.

🍳 50 mins   🕐 12 mins

SERVES 4

INGREDIENTS

2 eggs

4 tbsp superfine sugar

¼ cup all-purpose flour

2 tbsp unsweetened cocoa

3 egg whites

⅔ cup superfine sugar

4 cups good quality chocolate ice cream

1 Grease a 7 inch/18 cm round cake pan and line the bottom with baking parchment.

2 Whisk the egg and the 4 tablespoons of sugar in a mixing bowl until very thick and pale. Strain the flour and cocoa together and carefully fold in.

3 Pour into the prepared pan and bake in a preheated oven, 425°F/220°C, for 7 minutes or until springy to the touch. Transfer to a wire rack to cool completely.

4 Whisk the egg whites in a grease-free bowl until they are standing in soft peaks. Gradually add the sugar, whisking until you have a thick, glossy meringue.

5 Place the sponge on a cookie sheet and pile the ice cream on to the center in a heaped dome.

6 Pipe or spread the meringue over the ice cream, making sure the ice cream

is completely enclosed. (At this point the dessert can be frozen, if wished.)

7 Return it to the oven, for 5 minutes until the meringue is just golden. Serve immediately.

COOK'S TIP

This dessert is delicious served with a blackcurrant coulis. Cook a few blackcurrants in a little orange juice until soft, blend to a paste and push through a sieve, then sweeten to taste with a little confectioners' sugar.

White Chocolate Ice Cream

This white chocolate ice cream is served in a cookie cup. If desired, top with a chocolate sauce for a true chocolate addict's treat.

4–5 hrs   15 mins

SERVES 6

INGREDIENTS

ICE CREAM

1 egg

1 egg yolk

3 tbsp caster superfine sugar

5½ oz/150 g white chocolate

1¼ cups milk

⅔ cup heavy cream

COOKIE CUPS

1 egg white

4 tbsp superfine sugar

2 tbsp all-purpose flour, strained

2 tbsp unsweetened cocoa, strained

2 tbsp butter, melted

1 Place baking parchment on 2 cookie sheets. To make the ice cream, beat the egg, egg yolks, and sugar. Break the chocolate into pieces, place in a bowl with 3 tablespoons of milk and melt over a pan of hot water. Heat the milk until almost boiling and pour on to the eggs, whisking. Place over a pan of simmering water and cook, stirring until the mixture thickens enough to coat the back of a wooden spoon. Whisk in the chocolate. Cover with dampened baking parchment and let cool.

2 Whip the cream until just holding its shape and fold into the custard. Transfer to a freezer container and freeze the mixture for 1–2 hours until frozen 1 inch/2.5 cm from the sides. Scrape into a bowl and beat again until smooth. Re-freeze until firm.

3 To make the cups, beat the egg white and sugar together. Beat in the flour and cocoa, then the butter. Place 1 tablespoon of mixture on one cookie sheet and spread out into a 5 inch/12.5 cm circle.

Bake in a preheated oven, 400°F/200°C, for 4–5 minutes. Remove and mold over an upturned cup. Let the cookie cup set, then cool on a wire rack. Repeat to make 6 cookie cups. Serve the ice cream in the cups.

Cardamom Cream Horns

A crisp chocolate cookie cone encloses a fabulous cardamom-flavored cream, making this an unusual dessert.

30 mins   4–5 mins

SERVES 6

INGREDIENTS

1 egg white

4 tbsp superfine sugar

2 tbsp all-purpose flour

2 tbsp unsweetened cocoa

2 tbsp butter, melted

1¾ oz/50 g dark chocolate

CARDAMOM CREAM

⅔ cup heavy cream

1 tbsp confectioners' sugar

¼ tsp ground cardamom

pinch of ground ginger

1 oz/25 g preserved ginger, finely chopped

1 Place a sheet of baking parchment on 2 cookie sheets. Lightly grease 6 cream horn molds. To make the horns, beat the egg white and sugar in a mixing bowl until well combined. Strain the flour and cocoa together, then beat into the egg followed by the melted butter.

2 Place 1 tablespoon of the mixture on to 1 cookie sheet and spread out to form a 5 inch/12.5 cm circle. Bake in a preheated oven, 400°F/200°C, for 4–5 minutes.

3 Working quickly, remove the cookie with a spatula and wrap around the cream horn mold to form a cone. Let the cone set, then remove from the mold. Repeat with the remaining mixture to make 6 cones.

4 Melt the chocolate and dip the open edges of the horn in the chocolate.

Place on a piece of baking parchment and let the chocolate set.

5 To make the cardamom cream, place the cream in a bowl and strain the

confectioners' sugar and ground spices over the surface. Whisk the cream until standing in soft peaks. Fold in the chopped ginger and use to fill the chocolate cones.

Chocolate Charlotte

This chocolate dessert, consisting of a rich chocolate mousse-like filling enclosed in lady-fingers, is a variation of a popular classic.

5 hrs 40 mins | 5 mins

SERVES 8

INGREDIENTS

about 22 lady-fingers

4 tbsp orange-flavored liqueur

9 oz/250 g dark chocolate

⅔ cup heavy cream

4 eggs

⅔ cup superfine sugar

TO DECORATE

⅔ cup whipping cream

2 tbsp superfine sugar

½ tsp vanilla extract

quick dark chocolate curls
(see page 15)

chocolate decorations (see page 112),
optional

1 Line the base of a Charlotte mold or a deep 7 inch/18 cm round cake pan with a piece of baking parchment.

2 Place the lady-fingers on a tray and sprinkle with half of the orange-flavored liqueur. Use to line the sides of the mold or pan, trimming if necessary to make a tight fit.

3 Break the chocolate into small pieces, place in a bowl and melt over a pan of hot water. Remove from the heat and stir in the heavy cream.

4 Separate the eggs and place the whites in a large grease-free bowl. Beat the egg yolks into the chocolate mixture.

5 Whisk the egg whites until standing in stiff peaks, then gradually add the superfine sugar, whisking until stiff and glossy. Carefully fold the egg whites into the chocolate mixture in 2 batches, taking care not to knock out all of the air. Pour into the center of the mold. Trim the lady-fingers so that they are level with the chocolate mixture. Chill for at least 5 hours.

6 To decorate, whisk the cream, sugar, and vanilla extract until standing in soft peaks. Turn out the Charlotte on to a serving dish. Pipe cream rosettes around the bottom and decorate with chocolate curls and other decorations of your choice.

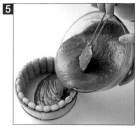

Marble Cheesecake

A dark and white chocolate cheesecake filling is marbled together to give an attractive finish to this rich and decadent dessert.

🍲 2 hrs 30 mins   🕐 5 mins

SERVES 10

I N G R E D I E N T S

BASE

8 oz/225 g toasted oat cereal

½ cup toasted hazelnuts, chopped

4 tbsp butter

1 oz/25 g dark chocolate

FILLING

12 oz/350 g full fat soft cheese

½ cup superfine sugar

generous ¾ cup thick yogurt

1¼ cups heavy cream

1 sachet gelatin

3 tbsp water

6 oz/175 g dark chocolate, melted

6 oz/175 g white chocolate, melted

1 Place the toasted oat cereal in a plastic bag and crush with a rolling pin. Pour the crushed cereal into a mixing bowl and stir in the hazelnuts.

2 Melt the butter and chocolate together over a low heat and stir into the cereal mixture, stirring until well coated.

3 Using the bottom of a glass, press the mixture into the bottom and up the sides of an 8 inch/20 cm springform pan.

4 Beat together the cheese and sugar with a wooden spoon until smooth. Beat in the yogurt. Whip the cream until just holding its shape and fold into the mixture. Sprinkle the gelatin over the water in a heatproof bowl and let it go

spongy. Place over a pan of hot water and stir until dissolved. Stir into the mixture.

5 Divide the mixture in half and beat the dark chocolate into one half and the white chocolate into the other half.

6 Place alternate spoonfuls of mixture on top of the cereal base. Swirl the filling together with the tip of a knife to give a marbled effect. Level the top with a scraper or a spatula. Chill for at least 2 hours, until set, before serving.

Banana Coconut Cheesecake

The exotic combination of banana and coconut goes well with chocolate. Fresh coconut gives a better flavor than shredded coconut.

2½ hrs   5 mins

SERVES 10

INGREDIENTS

8 oz/225 g chocolate chip cookies

4 tbsp butter

12 oz/350 g medium-fat soft cheese

⅓ cup superfine sugar

1¾ oz/50 g fresh coconut, grated

2 tbsp coconut-flavored liqueur

2 ripe bananas

4½ oz/125 g dark chocolate

1 sachet gelatin

3 tbsp water

⅔ cup heavy cream

TO DECORATE

1 banana

lemon juice

a little melted chocolate

1 Place the cookies in a plastic bag and crush with a rolling pin. Pour into a mixing bowl. Melt the butter and stir into the cookie crumbs until well coated. Firmly press the cookie mixture into the bottom and up the sides of an 8 inch/20 cm springform pan.

2 Beat together the soft cheese and superfine sugar until well combined, then beat in the grated coconut and coconut-flavored liqueur. Mash the 2 bananas and beat them in. Melt the dark chocolate and beat in until well combined.

3 Sprinkle the gelatin over the water in a heatproof bowl and let it go spongy. Place over a pan of hot water and stir until dissolved. Stir into the chocolate mixture. Whisk the cream until just holding its shape and stir into the chocolate mixture. Spoon over the biscuit shell and chill for 2 hours, until set.

4 To serve, carefully transfer to a serving plate. Slice the banana, toss in the lemon juice, and arrange around the edge of the cheesecake. Drizzle with melted chocolate and allow to set.

COOK'S TIP
To crack the coconut, pierce 2 of the 'eyes' and drain off the liquid. Tap hard around the center with a hammer until it cracks and lever it apart.

Chocolate Brandy Torte

A crumbly ginger chocolate shell topped with velvety smooth chocolate brandy cream makes this a blissful cake.

2 hrs 40 mins   5 mins

SERVES 12

I N G R E D I E N T S

BASE

9 oz/250 g gingersnaps

2¾ oz/75 g dark chocolate

generous ⅓ cup butter

FILLING

8 oz/225 g dark chocolate

9 oz/250 g mascarpone cheese

2 eggs, separated

3 tbsp brandy

1¼ cups heavy cream

4 tbsp superfine sugar

TO DECORATE

scant ½ cup heavy cream

chocolate coffee beans

1 Crush the gingersnaps in a bag with a rolling pin or in a food processor. Melt the chocolate and butter together and pour over the gingersnaps. Mix well, then use to line the bottom and sides of a 9 inch/23 cm loose-bottomed fluted flan pan or springform pan. Chill while preparing the filling.

2 To make the filling, melt the dark chocolate in a pan, remove from the heat and beat in the mascarpone cheese, egg yolks, and brandy.

3 Lightly whip the cream until just holding its shape and fold in the chocolate mixture.

4 Whisk the egg whites in a grease-free bowl until standing in soft peaks.

Add the superfine sugar a little at a time and whisk until thick and glossy. Fold into the chocolate mixture, in 2 batches, until just mixed.

5 Spoon the mixture into the prepared gingersnap shell and chill for at least 2 hours. Carefully transfer to a serving plate. To decorate, whip the cream and pipe on to the cheesecake and add the chocolate coffee beans.

VARIATION
If chocolate coffee beans are unavailable, use chocolate-coated raisins to decorate.

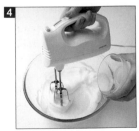

Chocolate Shortcake Towers

Stacks of crisp shortcake are sandwiched with chocolate-flavored cream and fresh raspberries, and served with a fresh raspberry coulis.

30 mins   10 mins

SERVES 6

INGREDIENTS

SHORTCAKE

1 cup butter

½ cup light brown sugar

1¾ oz/50 g dark chocolate, grated

scant 2½ cups all-purpose flour

TO FINISH

12 oz/350 g fresh raspberries

2 tbsp confectioners' sugar

3 tbsp milk

1¼ cups heavy cream

3½ oz/100 g white chocolate, melted

confectioners' sugar, to dust

1 Lightly grease a cookie sheet. To make the shortcake, beat together the butter and sugar until light and fluffy. Beat in the dark chocolate. Mix in the flour to form a stiff dough.

2 Roll out the dough on a lightly floured counter and stamp out 18 circles, 3 inches/7.5 cm across, with a fluted cookie cutter. Place the circles on the cookie sheet and bake in a preheated oven, 400°F/200°C, for 10 minutes, until crisp and golden. Let cool on the sheet.

3 To make the coulis, set aside about 3½ oz/100 g of the raspberries. Blend the remainder in a food processor with the confectioners' sugar, then push through a strainer to remove the seeds. Chill. Set aside 2 teaspoons of the cream. Whip the remainder until just holding its shape. Fold in the milk and the melted chocolate.

4 For each tower, spoon a little coulis on to a serving plate. Drop small dots of the reserved cream into the coulis around the edge of the plate and use a skewer to drag through the cream to make an attractive pattern.

5 Place a shortcake circle on the plate and spoon on a little of the chocolate cream. Top with 2 or 3 raspberries, top with another shortcake and repeat. Place a third biscuit on top. Dust with sugar.

Black Forest Trifle

Try all the delightful flavors of a Black Forest Gateau in this new guise— the results are stunning.

1½ hrs   10 mins

SERVES 6

INGREDIENTS

6 thin slices chocolate butter cream roll

1 lb 12 oz/800 g canned black cherries

2 tbsp kirsch

1 tbsp cornstarch

2 tbsp superfine sugar

generous 1¾ cups milk

3 egg yolks

1 egg

2¾ oz/75 g dark chocolate

1¼ cups heavy cream, lightly whipped

TO DECORATE

chocolate caraque (see page 15)

maraschino cherries (optional)

5 Place the bowl over a pan of hot water and cook over a low heat until the custard thickens, stirring. Add the chocolate and stir until melted.

6 Pour the chocolate custard over the cherries and cool. When cold, spread the cream over the custard, swirling with the back of a spoon. Chill before decorating.

7 Decorate with chocolate caraque and whole maraschino cherries, if using, before serving.

1 Place the slices of chocolate roll in the bottom of a glass serving bowl.

2 Drain the black cherries, reserving 6 tablespoons of the juice. Place the cherries and the reserved juice on top of the cake. Sprinkle with the kirsch.

3 In a bowl, mix the cornstarch and superfine sugar. Stir in enough of the milk to mix to a smooth paste. Beat in the egg yolks and the whole egg.

4 Heat the remaining milk in a small pan until almost boiling, then gradually pour it on to the egg mixture, whisking well until it is combined.

Champagne Mousse

Any dry sparkling wine made by the traditional method used for champagne can be used for this elegant dessert.

🥄 3¼ hrs   🕐 8 mins

SERVES 4

INGREDIENTS

SPONGE

4 eggs

½ cup superfine sugar

⅔ cup self-rising flour

2 tbsp unsweetened cocoa

2 tbsp butter, melted

MOUSSE

1 sachet gelatin

3 tbsp water

1¼ cups champagne

1¼ cups heavy cream

2 egg whites

⅓ cup superfine sugar

TO DECORATE

2 oz/50 g dark chocolate-flavored cake covering, melted

1 Line a 15 x 10 inch/37.5 x 25 cm jelly roll pan with greased baking parchment. Place the eggs and sugar in a bowl and beat, using an electric whisk if you have one, until the mixture is very thick and the whisk leaves a trail when lifted. If using a balloon whisk, stand the bowl over a pan of hot water whilst whisking. Strain the flour and cocoa together and fold into the egg mixture. Fold in the butter. Pour into the pan and bake in a preheated oven, 400°F/200°C, for 8 minutes or until springy to the touch. Cool for 5 minutes, then turn out on to a wire rack until cold. Meanwhile, line four 4 inch/10 cm baking rings with baking parchment. Line the sides with

1 inch/2.5 cm strips of cake and the bottom with circles.

2 For the mousse, sprinkle the gelatin over the water and let it go spongy. Place the bowl over a pan of hot water; stir until dissolved. Stir in the champagne.

3 Whip the cream until just holding its shape. Fold in the champagne mixture.

Stand in a cool place until on the point of setting, stirring. Whisk the egg whites until standing in soft peaks, add the sugar and whisk until glossy. Fold into the setting mixture. Spoon into the sponge cases, allowing the mixture to go above the sponge. Chill for 2 hours. Pipe the cake covering in squiggles on a piece of parchment, let them set, then use them to decorate the mousses.

Chocolate Freezer Cake

Hidden in a ring of chocolate sponge lies the secret of this freezer cake—a chocolate mint ice cream. Use orange or coffee ice cream if preferred.

🍞 3 hrs   🕐 30 mins

SERVES 8

INGREDIENTS

4 eggs

¾ cup superfine sugar

¾ cup self-rising flour

scant ⅓ cup unsweetened cocoa

2¼ cups chocolate and mint ice cream

Glossy Chocolate Sauce (see page 103)

1 Lightly grease a 9 inch/23 cm ring pan. Place the eggs and sugar in a large mixing bowl. Using an electric whisk if you have one, whisk the mixture until it is very thick and the whisk leaves a trail. If using a balloon whisk, stand the bowl over a pan of hot water whilst whisking.

2 Strain the flour and cocoa together and fold into the egg mixture. Pour into the prepared pan and bake in a preheated oven, 350°F/180°C, for 30 minutes or until springy to the touch. Let cool in the pan before turning out on to a wire rack to cool completely.

3 Rinse the cake pan and line with a strip of plastic wrap, overhanging slightly. Carefully cut off the top ½ inch/ 1 cm of the cake in one slice, and then set aside.

4 Return the cake to the pan. Using a spoon, scoop out the center of the cake, leaving a shell approximately 1 cm/½ inch thick.

5 Remove the ice cream from the freezer and let stand for a few minutes, then beat with a wooden spoon until softened a little. Fill the center of the cake with the ice cream, levelling the top. Replace the top of the cake.

6 Cover with the overhanging plastic wrap and freeze for at least 2 hours.

7 To serve, turn the cake out on to a serving dish and drizzle over some of the chocolate sauce in an attractive pattern, if you wish. Cut the cake into slices and then serve the remaining sauce separately.

Mississippi Mud Pie

An all-time favorite with chocoholics—the "mud" refers to the gooey, rich chocolate layer of the cake.

3½ hrs   1 hr 10 mins

SERVES 8

INGREDIENTS

2 cups all-purpose flour

¼ cup unsweetened cocoa

⅔ cup butter

2 tbsp superfine sugar

about 2 tbsp cold water

FILLING

¾ cup butter

2⅓ cups dark brown sugar

4 eggs, lightly beaten

4 tbsp unsweetened cocoa, strained

5½ oz/150 g dark chocolate

1¼ cups light cream

1 tsp chocolate extract

TO DECORATE

1¾ cups heavy cream, whipped

chocolate flakes and quick chocolate curls
(see page 15)

1 To make the pie dough, strain the flour and cocoa into a mixing bowl. Rub in the butter until the mixture resembles fine breadcrumbs. Stir in the sugar and enough cold water to mix to a soft dough. Chill for 15 minutes.

2 Roll out the dough on a lightly floured counter and use to line a deep 9 inch/23 cm loose-bottomed flan pan or ceramic flan dish. Line with foil or baking parchment and baking beans. Bake blind in a preheated oven, 375°F/190°C, for 15 minutes. Remove the beans and foil or parchment and cook for a further 10 minutes until crisp.

3 To make the filling, beat the butter and sugar in a bowl and gradually beat in the eggs with the cocoa. Melt the chocolate and beat it into the mixture with the light cream and the chocolate extract.

4 Pour the mixture into the cooked pie shell and bake at 325°F/170°C for 45 minutes or until the filling is set.

5 Let the mud pie cool completely, then transfer the pie to a serving plate, if preferred. Cover with the whipped cream and let chill.

6 Decorate the pie with quick chocolate curls and chocolate flakes and then let it chill.

Chocolate Fruit Tartlets

Chocolate pastry trimmed with nuts makes a perfect flan shell for fruit in these tasty individual tartlets. You can use fresh or canned fruit.

1½ hrs   20–25 mins

SERVES 6

INGREDIENTS

2¼ cups all-purpose flour

3 tbsp unsweetened cocoa

⅔ cup butter

3 tbsp superfine sugar

2–3 tbsp water

1¾ oz/50 g dark chocolate

½ cup chopped mixed nuts, toasted

12 oz/350 g prepared fruit

3 tbsp apricot jelly or redcurrant jelly

1 Strain the flour and cocoa into a mixing bowl. Cut the butter into small pieces and rub into the flour with your fingertips until the mixture resembles fine breadcrumbs.

2 Stir in the sugar. Add enough of the water to mix to a soft dough—about 1–2 tablespoons. Cover and chill for 15 minutes.

3 Roll out the pie dough on a lightly floured counter and use to line 6 tartlet pans, each 4 inches/10 cm across. Prick the shells with a fork and line with a little crumpled foil. Bake in a preheated oven, 375°F/190°C, for 10 minutes.

4 Remove the foil and bake for a further 5–10 minutes until the pie dough is crisp. Place the pans on a wire rack to cool completely.

5 Melt the chocolate. Spread out the chopped nuts on a plate. Remove the pie shells from the pans. Spread melted chocolate on the rims, then dip in the nuts. Let the chocolate set.

6 Arrange the fruit in the tartlet shells. Melt the apricot or redcurrant jelly with the remaining 1 tablespoon of water and brush it over the fruit. Chill the tartlets until required.

VARIATION

If liked, you can fill the cases with a little sweetened cream before topping with the fruit. For a chocolate-flavored filling, blend 8 oz/225 g chocolate hazelnut spread with 5 tablespoons of thick yogurt or whipped cream.

Banana Cream Profiteroles

Chocolate profiteroles are a popular choice. In this recipe they are filled with a delicious banana-flavored cream—the perfect combination!

45 mins   15–20 mins

SERVES 4

INGREDIENTS

DOUGH

⅔ cup water

5 tbsp butter

¾ cup strong all-purpose flour, strained

2 eggs

CHOCOLATE SAUCE

3½ oz/100 g dark chocolate, broken
   into pieces

2 tbsp water

4 tbsp confectioners' sugar

2 tbsp sweet butter

FILLING

1¼ cups heavy cream

1 banana

2 tbsp confectioners' sugar

2 tbsp banana-flavored liqueur

1 Lightly grease a cookie sheet and sprinkle with a little water. To make the dough, place the water in a pan. Cut the butter into small pieces and add to the pan. Heat gently until the butter melts, then bring to a rolling boil. Remove the pan from the heat and add the flour in one go, beating well until the mixture leaves the sides of the pan and forms a ball. Let cool slightly, then gradually beat in the eggs to form a smooth, glossy mixture. Spoon the paste into a large pastry bag fitted with a ½ inch/1 cm plain tip.

2 Pipe about 18 small balls of the paste on to the cookie sheet, allowing enough room for them to expand during cooking. Bake in a preheated oven, 425°F/220°C, for 15–20 minutes, until crisp and golden. Remove from the oven and make a small slit in each one for steam to escape. Cool on a wire rack.

3 To make the sauce, place all the ingredients in a heatproof bowl, set over a pan of simmering water and heat until combined to make a smooth sauce, stirring constantly.

4 To make the filling, whip the cream until standing in soft peaks. Mash the banana with the sugar and liqueur. Fold into the cream. Place in a pastry bag fitted with a ½ inch/1 cm plain tip and pipe into the profiteroles. Serve with the sauce poured over.

Tiramisu Layers

This is a modern version of the well-known and very traditional chocolate dessert from Italy.

🕐 1 hr 25 mins   ⏱ 5 mins

SERVES 6

INGREDIENTS

⅔ cup heavy cream

10½ oz/300 g dark chocolate

14 oz/400 g mascarpone cheese

14 fl oz/400 ml black coffee with
   ¼ cup superfine sugar, cooled

6 tbsp dark rum or brandy

36 lady-fingers, about 400 g/14 oz

unsweetened cocoa, to dust

1 Whip the cream until it just holds its shape. Melt the chocolate in a bowl set over a pan of simmering water, stirring occasionally. Let the chocolate cool slightly, then stir it into the mascarpone and cream.

2 Mix the coffee and rum together in a bowl. Dip the lady-fingers into the mixture briefly so that they absorb the coffee and rum mixture but do not become soggy.

3 Place 3 lady-fingers on 3 serving plates.

4 Spoon a layer of the chocolate, mascarpone, and cream mixture over the lady-fingers.

5 Place 3 more lady-fingers on top of the chocolate and mascarpone mixture. Spread another layer of chocolate and mascarpone and place 3 more lady-fingers on top.

6 Let the tiramisu chill in the refrigerator for at least 1 hour. Dust with a little cocoa just before serving.

VARIATION
Try adding ⅓ cup toasted, chopped hazelnuts to the chocolate and mascarpone mixture in Step 1, if you prefer.

Rich Chocolate Loaf

Another rich chocolate dessert, this loaf is very simple to make and can be served as a coffee-time treat as well.

 1 hr 20 mins   5 mins

MAKES 16 SLICES

I N G R E D I E N T S

5½ oz/150 g dark chocolate

6 tbsp sweet butter

scant 1 cup condensed milk

2 tsp cinnamon

2¾ oz/75 g almonds

2¾ oz/75 g amaretti cookies, broken

1¾ oz/50 g dried no-soak apricots, coarsely chopped

1 Line a 1½ lb/675 g loaf pan with a sheet of kitchen foil.

2 Using a sharp knife, roughly chop the almonds.

3 Place the chocolate, butter, milk, and cinnamon in a heavy-based pan.

4 Heat the chocolate mixture over a low heat for 3–4 minutes, stirring with a wooden spoon, or until the chocolate has melted. Beat the mixture well.

COOK'S TIP

To melt chocolate, first break it into manageable pieces. The smaller the pieces, the quicker it will melt.

5 Stir the almonds, cookies, and apricots into the chocolate mixture, stirring with a wooden spoon, until well mixed.

6 Pour the mixture into the prepared pan and chill in the refrigerator for about 1 hour or until set.

7 Cut the rich chocolate loaf into slices to serve.

Chocolate Mousse

This is a light and fluffy mousse with a subtle hint of orange. It is wickedly delicious served with a fresh fruit sauce.

 2¼ hours   ⏱ 5 mins

SERVES 8

INGREDIENTS

3½ oz/100 g dark chocolate, melted

1¼ cups unsweetened yogurt

⅔ cup Quark

4 tbsp superfine sugar

1 tbsp orange juice

1 tbsp brandy

1½ tsp gelozone (vegetarian gelatin)

9 tbsp cold water

2 large egg whites

coarsely grated dark and white chocolate and orange zest, to decorate

1 Put the melted chocolate, yogurt, Quark, sugar, orange juice, and brandy in a food processor and process for 30 seconds. Transfer the mixture to a large bowl.

2 Sprinkle the gelozone over the water and stir until dissolved.

3 In a pan, bring the gelozone and water to the boil for 2 minutes. Cool slightly, then stir into the chocolate.

4 Whisk the egg whites until stiff peaks form and fold into the chocolate mixture using a metal spoon.

5 Line a 1 lb 2 oz/500 g loaf pan with plastic wrap. Spoon the mousse into the pan. Chill in the refrigerator for 2 hours, until set. Turn the mousse out on to a serving plate, decorate and serve.

Chocolate Cheesecake

This cheesecake takes a little time to prepare and cook but is well worth the effort. It is quite rich and is good served with a little fresh fruit.

🕐 15 mins   ⏱ 1–1¼ hours

SERVES 12

INGREDIENTS

¾ cup all-purpose flour

¾ cup ground almonds

1⅓ cups raw brown sugar

⅔ cup margarine

1½ lb/675 g firm bean curd

¾ cup vegetable oil

½ cup orange juice

¾ cup brandy

½ cup unsweetened cocoa, plus extra to decorate

2 tsp almond extract

TO DECORATE

confectioners' sugar

ground cherries

1 Put the flour, ground almonds, and 1 tablespoon of the sugar in a bowl and mix well. Rub the margarine into the mixture to form a dough.

2 Lightly grease and line the bottom of a 9 inch/23 cm springform pan. Press the dough into the bottom of the pan to cover, pushing the dough right up to the edge of the pan.

3 Roughly chop the bean curd and put in a food processor with the vegetable oil, orange juice, brandy, cocoa, almond essence, and remaining sugar, and process until smooth and creamy. Pour over the dough in the pan and cook in a preheated oven, 325 /160 C, for 1–1¼ hours, or until set.

4 Leave to cool in the pan for 5 minutes, then remove from the pan and chill in the refrigerator. Dust with confectioners' sugar and cocoa. Decorate with ground cherries and serve.

COOK'S TIP
Ground cherries make an attractive decoration for many desserts. Peel open the papery husks to expose the bright orange fruits.

Chocolate Cheese Pots

These super-light desserts are just the thing if you have a craving for chocolate. Serve them on their own or with a selection of fruits.

40 mins   0 mins

SERVES 4

INGREDIENTS

1¼ cups low-fat ricotta cheese, drained

⅔ cup low-fat unsweetened yogurt

2 tbsp confectioners' sugar

4 tsp low-fat drinking chocolate powder

4 tsp unsweetened cocoa

1 tsp vanilla extract

2 tbsp dark rum, optional

2 medium egg whites

4 chocolate cake decorations

TO SERVE

pieces of kiwi fruit, orange, and banana

strawberries and raspberries

COOK'S TIP

This chocolate mixture can also be used as a cheesecake filling. Make the base out of crushed amaretti cookies and egg white, and set the filling with 2 teaspoons of powdered gelatin dissolved in 2 tablespoons of boiling water.

1 Mix the mascarpone and low-fat yogurt together in a bowl. Sift in the sugar, drinking chocolate, and cocoa and mix well.

2 Add the vanilla extract, and rum (if using).

3 In another bowl, whisk the egg whites until stiff. Using a metal spoon, fold the egg whites into the chocolate mixture.

4 Spoon the yogurt and chocolate mixture into 4 small china dessert pots and chill for about 30 minutes.

5 Decorate each chocolate cheese pot with a chocolate cake decoration and serve with an assortment of fresh fruit, such as pieces of kiwi fruit, orange, and banana, and a few whole strawberries and raspberries.

Mocha Swirl Mousse

A combination of feather-light yet rich chocolate and coffee mousses, whipped and attractively presented in serving glasses.

1¼ hours   0 mins

SERVES 4

INGREDIENTS

1 tbsp coffee and chicory extract

2 tsp unsweetened cocoa, plus extra for dusting

1 tsp low-fat drinking chocolate powder

⅔ cup low-fat crème fraîche, plus 4 tsp to serve

2 tsp powdered gelatin

2 tbsp boiling water

2 large egg whites

2 tbsp superfine sugar

4 chocolate coffee beans, to serve

1 Place the coffee and chicory extract in one bowl, and 2 teaspoons of cocoa and the drinking chocolate in another bowl. Divide the crème fraîche between the 2 bowls and mix both well.

2 Dissolve the gelatin in the boiling water and set aside. In a grease-free bowl, whisk the egg whites and sugar until stiff and divide this evenly between the two mixtures.

3 Divide the dissolved gelatin between the 2 mixtures and, using a large metal spoon, gently fold until well mixed.

4 Spoon small amounts of the 2 mousses alternately into 4 serving glasses and swirl together gently. Chill for 1 hour or until set.

5 To serve, top each mousse with a teaspoon of crème fraîche, a chocolate coffee bean and a light dusting of cocoa. Serve immediately.

COOK'S TIP

Vegetarians should not be denied this delicious chocolate dessert. Instead of gelatin, use the vegetarian equivalent, gelozone, available from health-food shops. Be sure to read the instructions on the package first, because it is prepared differently from gelatin.

Panforte di Siena

This famous Tuscan honey and nut cake is a Christmas speciality. In Italy it is sold in pretty boxes, and served in very thin slices.

10 mins   1¼ hours

SERVES 12

INGREDIENTS

1 cup split whole almonds

¾ cup hazelnuts

½ cup cut candied peel

2 oz/55 g no-soak dried apricots

2 oz/55 g candied pineapple

grated zest of 1 large orange

½ cup all-purpose flour

2 tbsp unsweetened cocoa

2 tsp ground cinnamon

½ cup superfine sugar

½ cup honey

confectioners' sugar, for dredging

1 Toast the almonds under the broiler until lightly browned, and place them in a bowl.

2 Toast the hazelnuts until the skins split. Place on a dry dish towel and rub off the skins. Roughly chop the hazelnuts and add to the almonds with the candied peel.

3 Chop the apricots and pineapple fairly finely, add to the nuts with the orange zest, and mix well.

4 Sift together the flour, cocoa, and cinnamon; mix into the nut mixture.

5 Line a round 8 inch/20 cm cake tin or deep loose-bottomed flan pan with baking parchment.

6 Put the superfine sugar and honey into a pan and heat until the sugar dissolves, then boil gently for about 5 minutes or until the mixture thickens and begins to turn a deeper shade of brown. Quickly add to the chocolate nut mixture and mix together evenly. Turn into the prepared pan and level the top using the back of a damp spoon.

7 Cook in a preheated oven, 300°F/ 150°C, for 1 hour. Remove from the oven and let cool completely in the pan. Take out of the pan and carefully peel off the paper. Before serving, dredge the cake heavily with sifted confectioners' sugar. Serve in very thin slices.

Chocolate & Almond Tart

This is a variation on the classic pecan pie recipe—here, nuts and chocolate are encased in a thick syrup filling.

🕐 1½ hrs   🕐 1 hr

SERVES 8

INGREDIENTS

PIE DOUGH

1 ¼ cups all-purpose flour

2 tbsp superfine sugar

½ cup butter, cut into small pieces

1 tbsp water

FILLING

½ cup light corn syrup

4 tbsp butter

½ cup soft brown sugar

3 eggs, lightly beaten

½ cup whole blanched almonds, coarsely chopped

3½ oz/100 g white chocolate, coarsely chopped

cream, to serve (optional)

VARIATION

You can use a mixture of white and dark chocolate for this tart, if preferred.

1 To make the tart shell, place the flour and sugar in a mixing bowl and rub in the butter with your fingers. Add the water and work the mixture together until a soft dough has formed. Wrap and let chill for 30 minutes.

2 On a lightly floured surface, roll out the dough and line a 9½ inch/24 cm loose-bottomed flan pan. Prick the tart shell with a fork and let chill for 30 minutes. Line the shell with foil and baking beans and bake in a preheated oven, 375°F/190°C, for 15 minutes.

Remove the foil and baking beans and cook for a further 15 minutes.

3 To make the filling, gently melt the syrup, butter, and sugar together in a pan. Remove from the heat and let cool slightly. Stir in the beaten eggs, almonds, and chocolate.

4 Pour the chocolate and nut filling into the prepared tart shell and cook in the oven for 30–35 minutes or until just set. Let cool before removing the tart from the pan. Serve with cream, if wished.

Chocolate & Pear Sponge

What could be better than the lovely combination used in this cake of chocolate and fresh pears in a moist sponge?

 1¼ hrs   🕐 1 hr

SERVES 6

INGREDIENTS

¾ cup butter, softened

generous 1 cup soft brown sugar

3 eggs, beaten

1¼ cups self-rising flour

2 tbsp unsweetened cocoa

2 tbsp milk

2 small pears, peeled, cored, and sliced

1 Grease an 8 inch/23 cm loose-bottomed cake pan and line the bottom with baking parchment.

2 In a bowl, cream together the butter and soft brown sugar until the mixture is pale and fluffy.

3 Gradually add the beaten eggs to the creamed mixture, beating well after each addition.

4 Strain the self-rising flour and cocoa into the creamed mixture and fold in gently until all of the ingredients are well combined.

5 Stir in the milk, then spoon the chocolate mixture into the prepared pan. Level the surface with the back of a spoon or a spatula.

6 Place the pear slices on top of the chocolate mixture, arranging them in a radiating pattern.

7 Bake in a preheated oven, 350°F/180°C, for about 1 hour, until the cake is just firm to the touch.

8 Let the sponge cake cool in the pan, then transfer to a wire rack until completely cold before serving.

COOK'S TIP
Serve the cake with melted chocolate drizzled over the top for a delicious dessert.

Mint-Chocolate Gelato

Rich, creamy gelati, or ice creams, are one of the great Italian culinary contributions to the world. This version is made with fresh mint.

5–6 hrs   20 mins

SERVES 4

INGREDIENTS

6 large eggs

¾ cup superfine sugar

1¼ cups milk

⅔ cup heavy cream

large handful of fresh mint leaves, rinsed and dried

2 drops green food coloring, optional

2 oz/55 g dark chocolate, finely chopped

1 Put the eggs and sugar in a heatproof bowl that will sit over a pan with plenty of room underneath. Using an electric mixer, beat the eggs and sugar together until thick and creamy.

2 Put the milk and cream in the pan and bring to a simmer, where small bubbles appear all around the edge, stirring. Pour on to the eggs, whisking constantly. Rinse the pan and put 1 inch/2.5 cm water in the bottom. Place the bowl on top, making sure the bottom does not touch the water. Turn the heat to medium–high.

3 Transfer the mixture to a pan and cook the mixture, stirring constantly, until it is thick enough to coat the back of the spoon and leave a mark when you pull your finger across it.

4 Tear the mint leaves and stir them into the custard. Remove the custard from the heat. Let cool, then cover and set aside to infuse for at least 2 hours, chilling for the last 30 minutes.

5 Strain the mixture through a small nylon strainer to remove the pieces of mint. Stir in the food coloring, if using. Transfer to a freezer container and freeze the mixture for 1–2 hours until frozen 1 inch/2.5 cm from the sides.

6 Scrape into a bowl and beat again until smooth. Stir in the chocolate pieces, smooth the top and cover with plastic wrap or foil. Freeze until set, for up to 3 months. Soften in the refrigerator for 20 minutes before serving.

Chocolate Rice Dessert

What could be more delicious than creamy tender rice cooked in a rich chocolate sauce? This dessert is almost like a dense chocolate mousse.

2 hrs 5 mins   1 hr 10 mins

SERVES 8

INGREDIENTS

½ cup long-grain white rice

pinch of salt

2½ cups milk

½ cup granulated sugar

7 oz/200 g bitter or dark chocolate, chopped

4 tbsp butter, diced

1 tsp vanilla extract

2 tbsp brandy or Cognac

¾ cup heavy cream

whipped cream, for piping (optional)

chocolate curls (see page 15), to decorate (optional)

1 Bring a pan of water to the boil. Sprinkle in the rice and add the salt; reduce the heat and simmer gently for 15–20 minutes until the rice is just tender. Drain, rinse, and drain again.

2 Heat the milk and the sugar in a large heavy-based pan over a medium heat until the sugar dissolves, stirring frequently. Add the chocolate and butter and stir until melted and smooth.

3 Stir in the cooked rice and reduce the heat to low. Cover and simmer, stirring occasionally, for 30 minutes until the milk is absorbed and the mixture thickened. Stir in the vanilla extract and brandy. Remove from the heat and allow to cool to room temperature.

4 Using an electric mixer, beat the cream until soft peaks form. Stir one heaped spoonful of the cream into the chocolate rice mixture to lighten it; then fold in the remaining cream.

5 Spoon into glass serving dishes, cover, and chill for about 2 hours. If wished, decorate with piped whipped cream and top with chocolate curls. Serve cold.

VARIATION

To mold the chocolate rice, soften 1 sachet gelatin in about ¼ cup cold water and heat gently until dissolved. Stir into the chocolate just before folding in the cream. Pour into a rinsed mold, allow to set, then unmold.

Quick Chocolate Desserts

This rich creamy dessert takes hardly any time to prepare, but you will need to allow time for chilling.

8 mins, plus 2 hrs chilling

8 mins

SERVES 4

INGREDIENTS

½ cup water

4 tbsp superfine sugar

6 oz/175 g dark chocolate, broken into pieces

3 egg yolks

1¼ cups heavy cream

sweet cookies, to serve

1 Pour the water into a pan and add the sugar. Stir over a low heat until the sugar has dissolved. Bring to a boil and continue to boil, without stirring, for 3 minutes. Remove the pan from the heat and let cool slightly.

2 Put the chocolate in a food processor and add the hot syrup. Process until the chocolate has melted, then add the egg yolks and process briefly until smooth. Finally, add the cream and process until fully incorporated.

3 Pour the mixture into 4 glasses or individual bowls, cover with plastic wrap and chill in the refrigerator for 2 hours, until set. Serve with sweet cookies.

Chocolate Marshmallow Ice

Richly flavored and with a wonderful texture, this home-made ice cream really couldn't be simpler.

10 mins, plus 2½ hrs cooling/freezing

5–10 mins

SERVES 4

INGREDIENTS

3 oz/85 g dark chocolate, broken into pieces

6 oz/175 g white marshmallows

⅔ cup milk

1¼ cups heavy cream

1 Put the chocolate and marshmallows in a pan and pour in the milk. Warm over a very low heat until the chocolate and marshmallows have melted. Remove from the heat and let cool completely.

2 Whisk the cream until thick, then fold it into the cold chocolate mixture with a metal spoon. Pour into a 1 lb/450 g loaf pan and freeze for at least 2 hours, until firm (it will keep for 1 month in the freezer). Serve with fresh fruit.

Chocolate Sorbet

This is a truly special sorbet and it is worth buying the best possible quality chocolate for it.

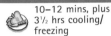

10–12 mins, plus
3½ hrs cooling/
freezing

7–10 mins

SERVES 6

INGREDIENTS

5 oz/140 g bitter continental chocolate, coarsely chopped

5 oz/140 g dark continental chocolate, coarsely chopped

scant 2 cups water

1 cup superfine sugar

langues de chats cookies, to serve

1 Put both types of chocolate into a food processor and process briefly until very finely chopped.

2 Pour the water into a heavy-based pan and add the sugar. Stir over a medium heat to dissolve, then bring to a boil. Boil for 2 minutes, without stirring, then remove the pan from the heat.

3 With the motor of the food processor running, pour the hot syrup on to the chocolate. Process for about 2 minutes, until all the chocolate has melted and the mixture is smooth. Scrape down the sides of the food processor, if necessary. Strain the chocolate mixture into a freezerproof container and let cool.

4 When the mixture is cool, place it in the freezer for about 1 hour until

slushy, but beginning to become firm around the edges. Tip the mixture into the food processor and process until smooth. Return to the container and freeze for at least 2 hours until firm.

5 Remove the sorbet from the freezer about 10 minutes before serving and let stand at room temperature to allow it to soften slightly. Serve in scoops with langues de chats cookies.

Chocolate & Orange Trifle

The slight tartness of mandarin oranges beautifully counterbalances the richness of the trifle, but you could use clementines, if preferred.

25 mins, plus 1½ hrs cooling/chilling

15–20 mins

SERVES 6

INGREDIENTS

4 trifle sponges

2 large chocolate coconut macaroons, crumbled

4 tbsp sweet sherry

8 satsumas

7 oz/200 g dark chocolate, broken into pieces

2 egg yolks

2 tbsp superfine sugar

2 tbsp cornstarch

scant 1 cup milk

generous 1 cup mascarpone cheese

1 cup heavy cream

TO DECORATE

Marbled Chocolate Shapes (see page 114)

10–12 satsuma segments

2 Put the chocolate in a double boiler or a heatproof bowl set over a pan of barely simmering water. Stir over a low heat until melted and smooth. Remove from the heat and let cool completely.

3 In a separate bowl, mix together the egg yolks, sugar, and cornstarch to make a smooth paste. Bring the milk to just below boiling point in a small pan. Remove from the heat and pour it into the egg yolk mixture, stirring constantly. Return the custard to a clean pan and

cook over a low heat, stirring constantly, until thickened and smooth. Return to the bowl, then stir in the mascarpone until thoroughly combined. Stir in the cooled chocolate. Spread the chocolate custard evenly over the mandarin oranges and then chill in the refrigerator for 1 hour until set.

4 Whip the cream until thick, then spread it over the top of the trifle. Decorate with Marbled Chocolate Shapes and satsuma segments.

1 Break up the trifle sponges and place them in a large glass serving dish. Sprinkle the crumbled macaroons on top, then sprinkle with the sherry. Squeeze the juice from two of the satsumas and sprinkle it over the crumbled macaroons. Peel and segment the remaining satsumas and arrange them in the dish.

Strawberry Petits Choux

These little chocolate puffs are filled with a melting mixture of strawberry mousse and fresh fruit.

35–40 mins, plus 2 hrs chilling/cooling

40–45 mins

SERVES 6

INGREDIENTS

2 tbsp water

2 tsp gelatin

3 cups strawberries

1 cup ricotta cheese

1 tbsp superfine sugar

2 tsp crème de fraises de bois or strawberry brandy

PETITS CHOUX

¾ cup all-purpose flour

2 tbsp unsweetened cocoa

6 tbsp sweet butter

1 cup water

2 eggs, plus 1 egg white

pinch of salt

confectioners' sugar, for dusting

1 Sprinkle the gelatin over the water in a heatproof bowl. Let it soften for 2–3 minutes. Place the bowl over a pan of barely simmering water and stir until the gelatin dissolves. Remove from the heat.

2 Place 8 oz/225 g of the strawberries in a blender with the ricotta, sugar, and liqueur. Process until blended. Add the gelatin and process briefly. Transfer the mousse to a bowl, cover with plastic wrap and chill for 1–1½ hours, until set.

3 Meanwhile, to make the petits choux, line a cookie sheet with baking paper. Sieve the flour, cocoa, and salt on to a sheet of waxed paper. Put the butter and water into a heavy-based pan and heat gently until the butter has melted.

4 Preheat the oven to 425°F/220°C. Remove the pan from the heat and add the flour mixture all in one go, beating vigorously with a wooden spoon. Return the pan to the heat and beat vigorously until the mixture comes away from the sides of the pan. Remove from the heat and cool slightly.

5 In a separate bowl, beat the eggs with the extra egg white, then gradually add them to the chocolate mixture, beating vigorously until a glossy paste forms. Drop 12 rounded spoonfuls of the mixture onto the prepared cookie sheet and bake for 20–25 minutes, until puffed up and firm.

6 Remove from the oven and make a slit in the side of each petits choux. Return the petits choux to the oven for 5 minutes to dry out. Transfer to a wire rack to cool.

7 Slice the remaining strawberries. Slice the petits choux in half, removing any uncooked dough from the centers, and divide the set strawberry mousse among them. Add a layer of strawberry slices and replace the tops. Dust lightly with confectioners' sugar and place in the refrigerator. Serve within 1½ hours.

Triple Stripe Cream

Layers of chocolate, vanilla, and coffee, topped with a swirl of whipped cream, make a simple but elegant dessert.

15 mins, plus 2 hrs chilling

20 mins

SERVES 6

INGREDIENTS

1½ cups superfine sugar

6 tbsp cornstarch

3¼ cups milk

3 egg yolks

6 tbsp sweet butter, diced

1 heaping tbsp instant coffee powder

2 tsp vanilla extract

2 tbsp unsweetened cocoa

⅔ cup whipped cream, to decorate

1 Put ½ cup of the superfine sugar and 2 tablespoons of the cornstarch in a small, heavy-based pan. Gradually, whisk in one-third of the milk. Set the pan over a low heat and whisk in one of the egg yolks. Bring to a boil, whisking constantly, and boil for 1 minute. Remove the pan from the heat and stir in 1 tablespoon of the butter, and all the coffee powder. Set aside to cool slightly, then divide among 6 wine goblets and smooth the surfaces.

2 Place ½ cup of the remaining sugar and 2 tablespoons of the remaining cornstarch in a small heavy-based pan. Gradually, whisk in 1¼ cups of the remaining milk. Set the pan over a low heat and whisk in one of the remaining egg yolks. Bring to a boil, whisking constantly, and boil for 1 minute. Remove the pan from the heat and stir in 2 tablespoons of the remaining butter, and all the vanilla. Set aside to cool slightly, then divide among the goblets and smooth the surfaces.

3 Put the remaining sugar and cornstarch into a small heavy-based pan. Gradually, whisk in the remaining milk. Set the pan over a low heat and whisk in the last egg yolk. Bring to a boil, whisking constantly, and boil for 1 minute. Remove from the heat and stir in the remaining butter, and all the cocoa. Set the mixture aside to cool slightly, then divide among the goblets. Cover with plastic wrap and chill in the refrigerator for 2 hours, until set.

4 Whip the cream until thick, then pipe a swirl on top of each of the desserts. Serve immediately.

Strawberry Cheesecake

Sweet strawberries are teamed with creamy mascarpone cheese and luxurious white chocolate to make this mouthwatering cheesecake.

1 hr, plus 2 hrs cooling   1½ hrs

SERVES 8

INGREDIENTS

BASE

¼ cup sweet butter

2⅔ cups crushed graham crackers

½ cup chopped walnuts

FILLING

2 cups mascarpone cheese

2 eggs, beaten

3 tbsp superfine sugar

9 oz/250 g white chocolate, broken into pieces

2 cups strawberries, hulled and quartered

TOPPING

¾ cup mascarpone cheese

chocolate caraque (see page 15)

16 whole strawberries

1 Melt the butter over a low heat and stir in the crushed crackers and the nuts. Spoon the mixture into a 9 inch/ 23 cm loose-bottomed cake pan and press evenly over the bottom with the back of a spoon. Set aside.

2 Preheat the oven to 300°F/150°C. To make the filling, beat the cheese until smooth, then beat in the eggs and sugar. Put the chocolate in the top of a double boiler or in a heatproof bowl set over a pan of barely simmering water. Stir over a low heat until melted and smooth. Remove from the heat and cool slightly, then stir into the cheese mixture. Finally, stir in the strawberries.

3 Spoon the mixture into the cake pan, spread out evenly and smooth the surface. Bake in the preheated oven for 1 hour, until the filling is just firm. Turn off the oven but and let the cheesecake cool inside it until completely cold.

4 Transfer the cheesecake to a serving plate and spread the mascarpone on top. Decorate with chocolate caraque and whole strawberries.

Chocolate Cloud

This unbelievably easy but delicious dessert can be made in a matter of a few minutes.

20 mins, plus 1 hr chilling/ cooling

5 mins

SERVES 6

I N G R E D I E N T S

4 oz/115 g dark chocolate, broken into pieces

4 eggs, separated

2¼ cups heavy cream

toasted slivered almonds, to decorate

1 Put the chocolate in the top of a double boiler or in a heatproof bowl set over a pan of barely simmering water. Stir over a low heat until melted. Remove from the heat and cool slightly, then beat in the egg yolks.

2 In a separate bowl, whisk the egg whites until they are stiff, then fold them into the chocolate mixture. Set aside for 30 minutes until beginning to set.

3 Whip half the cream until thick, then fold ⅔ cup of it into the chocolate mixture. Spoon half the chocolate mixture into 6 sundae glasses. Divide another ⅔ cup of whipped cream between the glasses in a layer over the chocolate mixture, then top with the remaining chocolate mixture. Cover with plastic wrap and chill in the refrigerator for 30 minutes.

4 Just before serving, whip the remaining cream until it is thick. Pipe a swirl of cream on the top of each dessert and sprinkle with the almonds.

Chocolate Pecan Pie

This classic American dessert is packed with deliciously contrasting flavors and textures and is simply irresistible.

 40 mins, plus 2 hrs chilling/cooling

1¼ hrs

MAKES 1 X 25 CM/10 INCH PIE

INGREDIENTS

PIE DOUGH

2½ cups all-purpose flour, plus extra for dusting

½ cup unsweetened cocoa

1 cup confectioners' sugar

scant 1 cup sweet butter, diced

1 egg yolk

pinch of salt

FILLING

3 oz/85 g dark chocolate, broken into small pieces

3 cups shelled pecan nuts

6 tbsp sweet butter

generous 1 cup brown sugar

3 eggs

2 tbsp heavy cream

¼ cup all-purpose flour

1 tbsp confectioners' sugar, for dusting

1 To make the pie dough, strain the flour, cocoa, sugar, and salt into a mixing bowl and make a well in the center. Put the butter and egg yolk in the well and gradually mix in the dry ingredients. Knead lightly into a ball. Cover with plastic wrap and chill in the refrigerator for 1 hour.

2 Unwrap the dough and roll it out on a lightly floured counter. Use it to line a 10 inch/25 cm nonstick springform pie pan and prick the shell with a fork. Preheat the oven to 350°F/180°C. Line the pie shell with baking parchment and fill with baking

beans. Bake in the preheated oven for 15 minutes. Remove from the oven, discard the beans and paper and let cool.

3 To make the filling, put the chocolate in a heatproof bowl set over a pan of barely simmering water. Stir until melted. Remove from the heat and set aside. Roughly chop 2 cups of the pecans and set aside. Mix the butter with ⅓ cup of the brown sugar. Beat in the eggs, one at a time, then add the remaining brown sugar and mix well. Stir in the cream, flour, melted chocolate, and chopped pecans.

4 Spoon the filling into the pie shell and smooth the surface. Cut the remaining pecan nuts in half and arrange in concentric circles over the pie.

5 Bake in the preheated oven at the same temperature for 30 minutes, then remove the pie and cover the top with foil to prevent it from burning. Bake for a further 25 minutes. Remove the pie from the oven and let cool slightly before removing from the pan and transferring to a wire rack to cool completely. Dust with confectioners' sugar.

Chocolate Ice Cream Roll

This is a family favorite—spiral slices of moist sponge cake and ice cream never fail to please.

35 mins, plus 35–40 standing | 20–25 mins

SERVES 8

INGREDIENTS

butter, for greasing

generous ¾ cup all-purpose flour, plus extra for dusting

4 eggs

generous ½ cup superfine sugar

3 tbsp unsweetened cocoa

confectioners' sugar, for dusting

2½ cups chocolate ice cream

dark chocolate quick curls, to decorate (see page 00)

1 cup Chocolate Fudge Sauce, to serve (see page 101)

1 Line a 15 x 10 inch/38 x 25 cm jelly roll pan with waxed paper. Grease the bottom and dust with flour. Put the eggs and superfine sugar into the top of a double boiler or in a heatproof bowl set over a pan of barely simmering water. Beat over a low heat for 5–10 minutes until the mixture is pale and fluffy. Remove from the heat and continue beating for 10 minutes until the mixture is cool and the whisk leaves a ribbon trail when lifted. Strain the flour and cocoa over the surface and gently fold it in.

2 Preheat the oven to 375°F/190°C. Pour the mixture into the prepared pan and spread out evenly with a spatula. Bake in the preheated oven for 15 minutes, until firm to the touch and beginning to shrink from the sides of the pan.

3 Spread out a clean dish towel and cover with a sheet of baking parchment. Lightly dust it with confectioners' sugar. Turn out the cake on to the baking parchment and carefully peel off the lining paper. Trim off any crusty edges. Starting from a short side, pick up the cake and the baking parchment and roll them up together. Wrap the dish towel around the rolled cake and place on a wire rack to cool.

4 Remove the ice cream from the freezer and put it in the refrigerator for 15–20 minutes to soften slightly. Remove the dish towel and unroll the cake. Spread the ice cream evenly over the cake, then roll it up again without the baking parchment. Wrap the cake in foil and place in the freezer.

5 Remove the cake from the freezer about 20 minutes before serving. Unwrap, place on a serving plate, and dust with confectioners' sugar. Make the chocolate quick curls and arrange them on top. Place the cake in the refrigerator until required. Serve in slices with Chocolate Fudge Sauce.

Blackberry Chocolate Tart

This richly flavored tart looks superb and tastes wonderful—a perfect choice for a special occasion.

30 mins, plus 2 hrs chilling/cooling

15 mins

SERVES 6

INGREDIENTS

2 cups all-purpose flour, plus extra for dusting

½ cup unsweetened cocoa

1 cup confectioners' sugar

pinch of salt

scant 1 cup diced sweet butter

1 egg yolk

4 cups blackberries

1 tbsp lemon juice

2 tbsp superfine sugar

2 tbsp crème de cassis

FILLING

1¼ cups heavy cream

⅔ cup blackberry jelly

8 oz/225 g dark chocolate, broken into pieces

¼ cup diced sweet butter

1 First, make the pie dough. Strain the flour, cocoa, confectioners' sugar, and salt into a mixing bowl and make a well in the center. Put the butter and egg yolk in the well and gradually mix in the dry ingredients, using a pie dough blender or two forks. Knead lightly and form into a ball. Cover with plastic wrap and chill in the refrigerator for 1 hour.

2 When chilled, unwrap the dough. Preheat the oven to 350°F/180°C. Roll out the dough on a lightly floured counter. Use it to line a 12 x 4 inch/30 x 10 cm rectangular tart pan and prick the pie shell with a fork. Line the shell with baking parchment and fill with baking beans.

Bake in the preheated oven for 15 minutes. Remove from the oven, remove the beans and baking parchment and set aside to cool.

3 To make the filling, put the cream and jelly into a pan and bring to a boil over a low heat. Remove the pan from the heat and stir in the chocolate until melted and smooth. Stir in the butter until melted and smooth. Pour the mixture into the pie shell and set aside to cool.

4 Put 1⅓ cups of the blackberries, the lemon juice and superfine sugar into a food processor and process until smooth. Transfer to a bowl and stir in the crème de cassis. Set aside.

5 Remove the tart from the pan and place on a serving plate. Arrange the remaining blackberries on top and brush with a little of the blackberry and liqueur sauce. Serve the tart and hand the sauce separately.

Zuccotto

This famous Italian ice cream bombe is so named because its shape resembles a pumpkin, or *zucca*.

30 mins, plus
2 hrs chilling

0 mins

SERVES 8

INGREDIENTS

2½ cups heavy cream

¼ cup confectioners' sugar

½ cup hazelnuts, toasted

8 oz/225 g cherries, halved and pitted

4 oz/115 g dark chocolate, finely chopped

2 x 20 cm/8 inch round chocolate
   sponge cakes

4 tbsp brandy

4 tbsp amaretto liqueur

TO DECORATE

2 tbsp confectioners' sugar

2 tbsp unsweetened cocoa

1 In a large bowl, whisk the cream until it is stiff, then fold in the sugar, followed by the hazelnuts, cherries, and chocolate. Cover with plastic wrap and chill in the refrigerator until required.

2 Meanwhile, cut the sponge cakes in half horizontally and then cut the pieces to fit a 5 cup bowl, so that the base and sides are completely lined. Reserve the remaining sponge cake. Mix together the brandy and amaretto in a small bowl and sprinkle the mixture over the sponge cake lining.

3 Remove the cream filling from the refrigerator and spoon it into the lined bowl. Cover the top with the remaining sponge cake, cut to fit. Cover with plastic wrap and chill the bombe in the refrigerator for 2 hours, or until it is ready to serve.

4 For the decoration, strain the confectioners' sugar into a bowl and the cocoa into another bowl. To serve, remove the bombe from the refrigerator and run a round-bladed knife around the sides to loosen it. Place a serving plate on top of the bowl and, holding them firmly together, invert. Dust two opposite quarters with confectioners' sugar and the other opposite quarters with cocoa to make alternating sections of color.

Zuccherini

Italians, especially Sicilians and Sardinians, are famous for having a sweet tooth—and for their superb desserts.

30 mins, plus 8½ hrs chilling

10 mins

SERVES 6

INGREDIENTS

6 oz/175 g dark chocolate, broken into pieces

10 amaretti cookies, crushed

MOUSSE

2 oz/55 g dark chocolate, broken into pieces

1 tbsp cold, strong, black coffee

2 eggs, separated

2 tsp orange-flavored liqueur

TO DECORATE

⅔ cup heavy cream

2 tbsp unsweetened cocoa

6 chocolate-covered coffee beans

1 To make the chocolate cups, put the 6 oz/175 g dark chocolate in the top of a double boiler or in a heatproof bowl set over a pan of barely simmering water. Stir until melted and smooth, but not too runny, then remove from the heat. Coat the inside of 12 double paper cake cases with chocolate, using a small brush. Stand them on a plate and chill for at least 8 hours or overnight in the refrigerator.

2 To make the mousse, put the chocolate and coffee in the top of a double boiler or in a heatproof bowl set over a pan of barely simmering water. Stir over a low heat until the chocolate has melted and the mixture is smooth, then remove from the heat. Cool slightly, then stir in the egg yolks and liqueur.

3 Whisk the egg whites in a separate bowl until they form stiff peaks. Fold the whites into the chocolate mixture with a metal spoon, then set aside to cool.

4 Remove the chocolate cups from the refrigerator and carefully peel off the paper cases. Divide the crushed amaretti cookies equally among the chocolate cups and top with the chocolate mousse. Return to the refrigerator for at least 30 minutes. Just before serving, whip the cream and pipe a star on the top of each chocolate cup. Dust half of the zuccherini with cocoa and decorate the other half with the chocolate-covered coffee beans.

Chocolate & Orange Slices

Contrasting flavors, textures, and colors are combined to create this delectable masterpiece.

30–40 mins, plus 3–4 hrs chilling

10 mins

SERVES 8

INGREDIENTS

2 tsp butter, for greasing

1 lb/450 g dark chocolate, broken into pieces

3 small, loose-skinned oranges, such as tangerines, mandarins, or satsumas

4 egg yolks

scant 1 cup crème fraîche

2 tbsp raisins

1¼ cups whipped cream, to serve

1 Grease a 1 lb/450 g loaf pan and line it with plastic wrap. Put 14 oz/400 g of the chocolate in the top of a double boiler or into a heatproof bowl set over a pan of barely simmering water. Stir over a low heat until melted. Remove from the heat and cool slightly.

2 Meanwhile, peel the oranges, removing all traces of pith. Cut the zest into very thin sticks. Beat the egg yolks into the chocolate, one at a time, then add most of the orange zest (reserve the rest for decoration), and all the crème fraîche and raisins, and beat until smooth and thoroughly combined. Spoon the mixture into the prepared pan, cover with plastic wrap and chill in the refrigerator for 3–4 hours, until set.

3 While the chocolate mixture is chilling, put the remaining chocolate in the top of a double boiler or into a heatproof bowl set over a pan of barely simmering water. Stir over a low heat until melted. Remove the pan from the heat and cool slightly.

Meanwhile, segment the oranges. Dip each segment into the melted chocolate and spread out on a sheet of baking parchment for about 30 minutes until set.

4 To serve, remove the pan from the refrigerator and turn out the chocolate mold. Remove the plastic wrap and cut the mold into slices. Place a slice on each of 8 individual serving plates and decorate with the chocolate-coated orange segments and the remaining orange zest. Serve immediately with whipped cream.

Crispy Chocolate Pie

The rich, whisky-flavored chocolate filling makes this delicious chocolate pie very moreish.

25 mins, plus 30 mins cooling

35–40 mins

MAKES 6

INGREDIENTS

2 tsp butter, for greasing

2 egg whites

1 cup ground almonds

¼ cup ground rice

⅔ cup superfine sugar

¼ tsp almond extract

8 oz/225 g dark chocolate, broken into small pieces

4 egg yolks

4 tbsp confectioners' sugar

4 tbsp whisky

4 tbsp heavy cream

TO DECORATE

⅔ cup whipped cream

2 oz/55 g dark chocolate, grated

1 Preheat the oven to 325°F/160°C. Grease an 8 in/20 cm tart pan and line the bottom with baking parchment. Whisk the egg whites until they form stiff peaks. Gently fold in the ground almonds, ground rice, superfine sugar, and almond extract. Spread the mixture over the base and sides of the prepared pan. Bake in the preheated oven for 15 minutes.

2 Meanwhile, put the chocolate in the top of a double boiler or into a heatproof bowl set over a pan of barely simmering water. Stir over a low heat until melted. Remove from the heat and cool slightly, then beat in the egg yolks, confectioners' sugar, whisky, and the 4 tablespoons of cream until thoroughly incorporated.

3 Remove the tart pan from the oven and pour in the chocolate mixture. Cover with foil, return to the oven and bake at the same temperature for 20–25 minutes, until set. Remove from the oven and let cool completely.

4 Mix together the whipped cream and 1 oz/25 g of the grated chocolate, then spread over the cake. Top with the remaining grated chocolate, and serve immediately.

Chocolate Salami

Don't be alarmed—this Italian dish gets its name from its appearance, not because it contains pork.

25mins, plus 6–8 hrs standing/freezing

5–7 mins

SERVES 10

INGREDIENTS

350 g/12 oz dark chocolate, broken into small pieces

4 tbsp amaretto liqueur or brandy

1 cup sweet butter, cut into small pieces

24 plain sweet cookies, such as Petit Beurre, coarsely crushed

2 egg yolks

½ cup toasted slivered almonds, chopped

¼ cup ground almonds

1 tsp vegetable oil or olive oil, for greasing

1 Put the chocolate in the top of a double boiler or in a heatproof bowl set over a pan of barely simmering water. Add the liqueur or brandy and 2 tablespoons of the butter. Stir over a low heat until melted and smooth. Remove from the heat and cool slightly.

2 Stir in the egg yolks, then stir in the remaining butter, a little at a time, making sure each addition is fully incorporated before adding more. Stir in about three-quarters of the crushed cookies and all the toasted almonds. Cover with plastic wrap then set aside for 45–60 minutes, until beginning to set. Meanwhile, put the remaining crushed cookies into a food processor and process until finely crushed. Transfer them to a bowl and stir in the ground almonds. Set aside.

3 Lightly oil a sheet of baking parchment and turn out the chocolate mixture on to it. Using a spatula, shape the mixture into a salami about 35 cm/ 14 inches long. Wrap the salami in the parchment and place in the freezer for 4–6 hours, until set.

4 About 1¼ hours before serving, spread out the ground almond mixture on a sheet of baking parchment. Remove the salami from the freezer and unwrap. Roll it over the ground almond mixture until thoroughly and evenly coated. Cover with plastic wrap then set aside for 1 hour at room temperature. Cut into slices and serve.

Chocolate Loaf

Full of flavor and contrasting textures, this classic Italian dessert is very quick and easy to prepare.

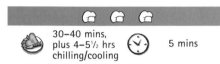

30–40 mins, plus 4–5½ hrs chilling/cooling

5 mins

SERVES 8

INGREDIENTS

vegetable oil, for brushing

8 oz/225 g dark chocolate, broken into pieces

4 tbsp dark rum

/1 cup sweet butter

⅔ cup superfine sugar

2 eggs, separated

1½ cups ground almonds

2 cups crushed amaretti cookies or macaroons

2 tbsp confectioners' sugar

pinch of salt

TO DECORATE

2¾ oz/75 g dark chocolate

8 chocolate-covered cherries

8 chocolate leaves (see page 15)

1 Line a 2 lb/1 kg loaf pan with baking parchment, allowing it to overlap the sides. Brush with oil. Put the chocolate in the top of a double boiler or in a heatproof bowl set over a pan of barely simmering water. Stir over a low heat until melted. Remove the pan from the heat, stir in the rum and set aside to cool.

2 Cream together the butter and superfine sugar until pale and fluffy, then beat in the egg yolks, one at a time. Add the almonds and then beat in the cooled chocolate.

3 Whisk the egg whites with a pinch of salt until they form stiff peaks. Gently fold the whites into the chocolate mixture, then fold in the cookie crumbs. Spoon the mixture into the prepared pan, spread it out evenly and smooth the top. Cover with plastic wrap and chill in the refrigerator for 4–5 hours, until firm.

4 To serve, uncover the pan and run a round-bladed knife around the sides. Dip the bottom in hot water. Place a serving plate on top of the pan, then, holding them firmly together, invert. Remove the baking parchment. Dust with the confectioners' sugar.

5 To decorate, melt the 2¾ oz/75 g dark chocolate as before, and put spoonfuls along the top of the cake. Top with chocolate-covered cherries and chocolate leaves.

Raspberry Chocolate Boxes

Mocha mousse, fresh raspberries, and sponge cake, all presented in neat little chocolate boxes—almost too good to eat.

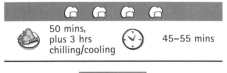

50 mins, plus 3 hrs chilling/cooling

45–55 mins

SERVES 12

INGREDIENTS

7 oz/200 g dark chocolate, broken into pieces

1½ tsp cold, strong, black coffee

1 egg yolk

1½ tsp coffee liqueur

2 egg whites

2 tsp butter, for greasing

7 oz/200g raspberries

SPONGE CAKE

2 tsp butter, for greasing

1 egg, plus 1 egg white

¼ cup superfine sugar

scant ½ cup all-purpose flour

1 To make the mocha mousse, melt 2 oz/55 g of the chocolate in a heatproof bowl set over a pan of barely simmering water. Add the coffee and stir over a low heat until smooth, then remove from the heat and cool slightly. Stir in the egg yolk and the coffee liqueur.

2 Whisk the egg whites in a separate bowl into stiff peaks. Fold into the chocolate mixture, cover with plastic wrap and chill in for about 2 hours, until set.

3 For the sponge cake, lightly grease an 8 inch/20 cm square cake pan and line the bottom with baking parchment. Put the egg and extra white with the sugar in a heatproof bowl set over a pan of barely simmering water. Whisk over a low heat for 5–10 minutes until pale and thick. Remove from the heat and continue whisking for 10 minutes until cold and the whisk leaves a ribbon trail when lifted.

4 Preheat the oven to 350°F/180°C. Strain the flour over the egg mixture and gently fold it in. Pour the mixture into the prepared pan and spread evenly. Bake in the preheated oven for 20–25 minutes, until firm to the touch and slightly shrunk from the sides of the tin. Turn out on to a wire rack to cool, then invert the cake, keeping the baking parchment in place.

5 To make the chocolate boxes, grease a 12 x 9 inch/30 x 23 cm jelly roll pan and line with waxed paper. Place the remaining chocolate in a heatproof bowl set over a pan of barely simmering water. Stir over a low heat until melted, but not too runny. Pour it into the pan and spread evenly with a spatula. Set aside in a cool place for about 30 minutes, until set.

6 Turn out the set chocolate onto a clean counter. Using a ruler and sharp knife, cut it into 36 rectangles, measuring 3 x 1 inches/7.5 x 2.5 cm. Cut 12 of these rectangles in half to make 24 rectangles measuring 1½ x 1 inches/3.75 x 2.5 cm.

7 Trim the crusty edges off the sponge cake, then cut it into 12 slices, measuring 3 x 1¼ inches/7.5 x 3 cm. Spread a little of the set mocha mousse along the sides of each sponge rectangle and gently press 2 long and 2 short chocolate rectangles in place on each side to make boxes. Divide the remaining mousse among the boxes and top with the raspberries. Refrigerate until ready to use.

Phyllo Nests

Green and black grapes decorate the creamy chocolate filling in these crisp little phyllo pastry nests.

25 mins, plus 20 mins cooling | 15–18 mins

SERVES 4

INGREDIENTS

1 tbsp sweet butter

6 sheets phyllo pastry, about 12 x 6 inches/30 x 15 cm each

1½ oz/40 g dark chocolate, broken into pieces

½ cup ricotta cheese

16 seedless green grapes, halved

24 seedless black grapes, halved

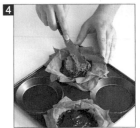

1 Put the butter into a small pan and set over a low heat until melted. Remove from the heat. Preheat the oven to 375°F/190°C. Cut each sheet of phyllo pastry into four, to give 24 rectangles, each measuring about 6 x 3 inches/15 x 7.5 cm, then stack them all on top of each other. Brush 4 shallow muffin pans with melted butter. Line 1 pan with a rectangle of phyllo pastry, brush with melted butter and place another rectangle on top at an angle to the first, and brush it with melted butter. Continue in this way, lining each pan with 6 rectangles, each brushed with melted butter. Brush the top layers with melted butter.

2 Bake in the preheated oven for 7–8 minutes, until golden and crisp. Remove from the oven and set aside to cool in the pans.

3 Put the chocolate in the top of a double boiler or into a heatproof bowl set over a pan of barely simmering water. Stir over a low heat until melted. Remove from the heat and cool slightly. Brush the insides of the pastry shells with about half the melted chocolate. Beat the ricotta until smooth, then beat in the remaining melted chocolate.

4 Divide the chocolate ricotta among the pastry shells and arrange the grapes alternately around the edges. Carefully lift the shells out of the pans and serve immediately.

Chocolate Pear Tart

The classic partnership of chocolate and pears appears in many forms, both hot and cold. This tart will soon become a family favorite.

25 mins, plus 50–55 mins cooling

30 mins

SERVES 8

INGREDIENTS

DOUGH

scant 1 cup all-purpose flour, plus 1 tbsp extra for dusting

2 tbsp superfine sugar

½ cup diced sweet butter

1 egg yolk

1 tbsp lemon juice

pinch of salt

TOPPING

4 oz/115 g dark chocolate, grated

4 pears

½ cup light cream

1 egg, plus 1 egg yolk

½ tsp almond extract

3 tbsp superfine sugar

1 To make the dough, strain the flour and a pinch of salt into a mixing bowl. Add the sugar and butter and mix well with a dough blender or two forks until thoroughly incorporated. Stir in the egg yolk and the lemon juice to form a dough. Form the dough into a ball, wrap in plastic wrap and chill in the refrigerator for 30 minutes.

2 Preheat the oven to 400°F/200°C. Roll out the dough on a lightly floured counter and use it to line a 10 inch/25 cm loose-bottomed tart pan. Sprinkle the grated dark chocolate over the bottom of the tart shell. Peel the pears, cut them in half lengthwise and remove the cores. Thinly slice each pear half and fan out slightly. Using a fish slice or spatula, scoop up each sliced pear half and arrange in the tart shell.

3 Beat together the cream, egg, extra yolk, and almond extract, and spoon the mixture over the pears. Sprinkle the sugar over the tart.

4 Bake in the preheated oven for 10 minutes, then lower the temperature to 350°F/180°C and bake for a further 20 minutes, until the pears are beginning to caramelize and the filling is just set. Remove from the oven and cool to room temperature before serving.

Oeufs à la Neige au Chocolat

In this dessert, poached meringues float on a richly flavored chocolate custard like little snowballs.

15 mins, plus 2 hrs chilling

15–20 mins

SERVES 6

INGREDIENTS

2½ cups milk

1 tsp vanilla extract

scant 1 cup superfine sugar

2 egg whites

CUSTARD

¼ cup superfine sugar

3 tbsp unsweetened cocoa

4 egg yolks

1 Put the milk, vanilla, and 5 tablespoons of the superfine sugar into a heavy-based pan and stir over a low heat until the sugar has dissolved. Simmer gently.

2 Whisk the egg whites until they form stiff peaks. Whisk in 2 teaspoons of the remaining sugar and continue to whisk until glossy. Gently fold in the rest of the superfine sugar.

3 Drop large spoonfuls of the meringue mixture onto the simmering milk mixture and cook, stirring once, for 4–5 minutes, until the meringues are firm. Remove with a slotted spoon and set aside on paper towels to drain. Poach the remaining meringues in the same way, then reserve the milk mixture.

4 To make the custard, mix the sugar, cocoa, and egg yolks in the top of a double boiler or in a heatproof bowl. Gradually stir in the reserved milk mixture. Place over barely simmering water and cook for 5–10 minutes, stirring constantly, until thickened. Remove from the heat and cool slightly. Divide the chocolate custard among individual serving glasses and top with the meringues. Cover with plastic wrap and chill in the refrigerator for at least 2 hours before serving.

Chocolate & Pernod Creams

This unusual combination of flavors makes a sophisticated and tempting dessert to serve at a dinner party.

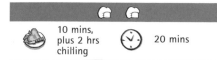

10 mins, plus 2 hrs chilling

20 mins

SERVES 4

INGREDIENTS

2 oz/55 g dark chocolate, broken into pieces

scant 1 cup milk

1¼ cup heavy cream

2 tbsp superfine sugar

1 tbsp arrowroot dissolved in 2 tbsp milk

3 tbsp Pernod

langues de chats cookies, or chocolate-tipped rolled wafers, to serve

1 Put the chocolate in the top of a double boiler or in a heatproof bowl set over a pan of barely simmering water. Stir over a low heat until melted. Remove the pan from the heat and cool slightly.

2 Pour the milk and cream into a pan over a low heat and bring to just below boiling point, stirring occasionally. Remove the pan from the heat and then set aside.

3 Beat the sugar and the arrowroot mixture into the melted chocolate. Gradually stir in the hot milk and cream mixture, then stir in the Pernod. Return the double boiler to the heat or set the bowl over a pan of barely simmering water and cook, over a low heat, for 10 minutes, stirring constantly, until thick and smooth. Remove from the heat and let cool.

4 Pour the chocolate and Pernod mixture into 4 individual serving glasses. Cover with plastic wrap and chill in the refrigerator for 2 hours before serving with langues de chats cookies or chocolate-tipped rolled wafers.

White Chocolate Molds

These pretty, colorful desserts are deliciously refreshing and would make a good finale to an *al fresco* meal.

20 mins, plus 2½ hrs chilling/standing   10–15 mins

SERVES 6

INGREDIENTS

4½ oz/125 g white chocolate, broken into pieces

scant 1 cup heavy cream

3 tbsp crème fraîche

2 eggs, separated

3 tbsp water

1½ tsp gelatin

1 tsp oil, for brushing

1 cup sliced strawberries

scant 1 cup raspberries

1¼ cups blackcurrants

5 tbsp superfine sugar

½ cup crème de framboise

12 blackcurrant leaves, if available

1 Put the chocolate in the top of a double boiler or in a heatproof bowl set over a pan of barely simmering water. Stir over a low heat until melted and smooth. Remove from the heat and set aside.

2 Meanwhile, pour the cream into a pan and bring to just below boiling point over a low heat. Remove from the heat, then stir the cream and crème fraîche into the chocolate and cool slightly. Beat in the egg yolks, one at a time.

3 Pour the water into a small, heatproof bowl and sprinkle the gelatin on the surface. Let stand for 2–3 minutes to soften, then set over a pan of barely simmering water until completely dissolved. Stir the gelatin into the chocolate mixture and let stand until nearly set.

4 Brush the inside of 6 timbales, dariole molds, or small cups with oil, and line the bottoms with baking parchment. Whisk the egg whites until soft peaks form, then fold them into the chocolate mixture. Divide the mixture evenly among the prepared molds and smooth the surface. Cover with plastic wrap and chill in the refrigerator for 2 hours, until set.

5 Put the strawberries, raspberries, and blackcurrants in a bowl and sprinkle with the superfine sugar. Pour in the liqueur and stir gently to mix. Cover with plastic wrap and chill in the refrigerator for 2 hours.

6 To serve, run a round-bladed knife around the sides of the molds and turn out on to individual serving plates. Divide the fruit among the plates and serve immediately, garnished with blackcurrant leaves, if available.

Chocolate Orange Sherbet

Elegant and sophisticated, dark chocolate encloses liqueur-flavored sherbet to provide this perfect dinner party dessert.

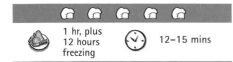

1 hr, plus 12 hours freezing

12–15 mins

SERVES 4

INGREDIENTS

2 tsp vegetable oil, for brushing

8 oz/225 g dark chocolate, broken into small pieces

4 cups crushed ice

2¼ cups freshly squeezed orange juice

⅔ cup water

¼ cup superfine sugar

finely grated zest of 1 orange

juice and finely grated zest of 1 lemon

1 tsp gelatin

3 tbsp orange-flavored liqueur

3 Reserve 3 tablespoons of the orange juice in a small, heatproof bowl. Pour the remainder into a pan and add the water, sugar, orange zest, and lemon juice and zest. Stir over a low heat until the sugar has dissolved, then increase the heat and bring the mixture to a boil. Remove the pan from the heat.

4 Meanwhile, sprinkle the gelatin on the surface of the orange juice in the bowl. Set aside for 2 minutes to soften, then set over a pan of barely simmering water until dissolved. Stir the dissolved gelatin and the liqueur into the orange juice mixture. Pour into a freezerproof container and place in the freezer for 30 minutes, until slushy.

5 Remove the sherbet from the freezer, transfer to a bowl and beat thoroughly to break up the ice crystals. Return it to the freezerproof container and put it back in the freezer for 1 hour. Repeat this process 3 more times.

6 Remove the sherbet from the freezer, transfer to a bowl and beat well once more. Remove the mold from the refrigerator and spoon the sherbet into it. Smooth the surface with a spatula. Put the mold in the freezer overnight.

7 Remove the mold from the freezer shortly before serving. Place a chilled serving plate on top and, holding them firmly together, invert. Serve immediately.

1 Brush an 3¼ cup mold with oil, drain well, then chill in the refrigerator. Put the chocolate in the top of a double boiler or into a heatproof bowl set over a pan of barely simmering water. Stir over a low heat until melted, then remove from the heat.

2 Remove the mold from the refrigerator and pour in the melted chocolate. Tip and turn the mold to coat the interior. Place the mold on a bed of crushed ice and continue tipping and turning until the chocolate has set. Return the mold to the refrigerator.

Chocolate & Hazelnut Parfait

Richly flavored, molded ice creams make a scrumptious summertime dessert for all the family.

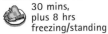 

30 mins, plus 8 hrs freezing/standing

10 mins

SERVES 6

INGREDIENTS

1½ cups blanched hazelnuts

6 oz/175 g dark chocolate, broken into small pieces

2½ cups heavy cream

3 eggs, separated

2½ cups confectioners' sugar

1 tbsp unsweetened cocoa, for dusting

6 small fresh mint sprigs, to decorate

wafer cookies, to serve

1 Spread out the hazelnuts on a cookie sheet and toast under a broiler preheated to medium, shaking the sheet from time to time, for about 5 minutes, until golden all over. Set aside to cool.

2 Put the chocolate in the top of a double boiler or in a heatproof bowl set over a pan of barely simmering water. Stir over a low heat until melted, then remove from the heat and cool. Put the toasted hazelnuts in a food processor and process until finely ground.

3 Whisk the cream until it is stiff, then fold in the ground hazelnuts and set aside. Beat the egg yolks with 3 tablespoons of the sugar for 10 minutes until pale and thick.

4 Whisk the egg whites in a separate bowl until soft peaks form. Whisk in the remaining sugar, a little at a time, until the whites are stiff and glossy. Stir the cooled chocolate into the egg yolk mixture, then fold in the cream and finally, fold in the egg whites. Divide the mixture among six freezerproof timbales or molds, cover with plastic wrap and freeze for at least 8 hours or overnight until firm.

5 Transfer the parfaits to the refrigerator about 10 minutes before serving to soften slightly. Turn out on to individual serving plates, dust the tops lightly with cocoa, decorate with mint sprigs and serve with wafers.

Chocolate Smoothie

Use your favorite fresh fruit in season and dip the pieces in this wonderful malted chocolate mixture.

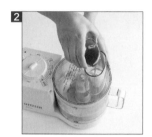

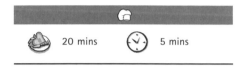

20 mins   5 mins

SERVES 4

I N G R E D I E N T S

2 oz/55 g dark chocolate, broken
    into pieces

2 large bananas

1 tbsp malt extract

selection of fresh fruit, cut into chunks or
    slices, as necessary

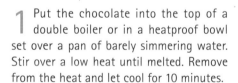

1 Put the chocolate into the top of a double boiler or in a heatproof bowl set over a pan of barely simmering water. Stir over a low heat until melted. Remove from the heat and let cool for 10 minutes.

2 Peel and slice the bananas. Place them in a food processor and process until smooth. With the motor still running, pour the malt extract through the feeder tube. Continue to process until fully incorporated, and thick and frothy. With the motor still running, pour the melted chocolate through the feeder tube in a slow, steady stream. Continue to process until thoroughly combined.

3 Scrape the smoothie into a small serving bowl and stand on a large serving plate. Arrange the fruit around the bowl and serve immediately.

Chocolate Chiffon Pie

The nutty crust of this delectable pie contrasts with the tempting, creamy chocolate filling.

35mins,
plus 4¼–4½ hrs
chilling/cooling

12–15 mins

SERVES 8

INGREDIENTS

5 oz/140 g shelled Brazil nuts

2 tbsp granulated sugar

2 tsp melted butter

scant 1 cup milk

2 tsp gelatin

generous ½ cup superfine sugar

2 eggs separated

8 oz/225 g dark chocolate,
    coarsely chopped

1 tsp vanilla extract

⅔ cup heavy cream

2 tbsp chopped Brazil nuts

1 Preheat the oven to 400°F/200°C. Put the Brazil nuts into a food processor and process until finely ground. Add the granulated sugar and melted butter and process briefly to combine. Tip the mixture into a 9 inch/23 cm round pie pan or dish and press it on to the bottom and sides with a spoon or your fingertips. Bake in the preheated oven for 8–10 minutes, until light golden brown. Set aside to cool.

2 Pour the milk into the top of a double boiler or into a heatproof bowl and sprinkle the gelatin over the surface. Let it soften for 2 minutes, then place over a pan of barely simmering water. Stir in half the superfine sugar, both the egg yolks and all the chocolate. Stir constantly over a low heat for 4–5 minutes until the gelatin has dissolved and the chocolate has melted. Remove from the heat and beat until the mixture is smooth and thoroughly blended. Stir in the vanilla extract, cover with plastic wrap and chill in the refrigerator for 45–60 minutes, until just beginning to set.

3 Whip the cream until it is stiff, then fold all but about 3 tablespoons into the chocolate mixture. Whisk the egg whites in another bowl until soft peaks form. Add 2 teaspoons of the remaining sugar and whisk until stiff peaks form. Fold in the remaining sugar, then fold the egg whites into the chocolate mixture. Pour the filling into the pie dish and chill in the refrigerator for 3 hours, or until set. Decorate the pie with the remaining whipped cream and the chopped nuts before serving.

Pineapple Chocolate Rings

These pretty fruit desserts make a perfect end to a summertime supper, but can also be served with morning coffee.

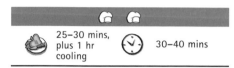

25–30 mins, plus 1 hr cooling

30–40 mins

SERVES 10

INGREDIENTS

⅔ cup sweet butter

¼ cup superfine sugar

1¼ cups all-purpose flour, plus extra for dusting

3 tbsp ground almonds

½ tsp almond extract

7 oz/200 g dark chocolate, broken into small pieces

10 canned pineapple rings, drained and can juice reserved

10 maraschino cherries

1 tsp cornstarch

1 Line a cookie sheet with baking parchment. Cream ½ cup of the butter with all the sugar until pale and fluffy. Strain in the flour, add the ground almonds and almond extract, and knead the mixture thoroughly until it forms a soft dough.

2 Preheat the oven to 375°F/190°C. Turn out the dough onto a lightly floured board and roll out to ¼ inch/5 mm thick. Stamp out 20 circles with a 3 inch/7.5 cm round cutter and place them on the prepared cookie sheet. Prick the surface of each almond circle with a fork, then bake in the preheated oven for 20 minutes, until lightly browned. Using a spatula, transfer the circles to a wire rack to cool.

3 Place the remaining butter and the chocolate in the top of a double boiler or in a heatproof bowl set over a pan of barely simmering water. Stir over a low heat until melted and smooth. Remove the pan from the heat. Sandwich the almond circles together in pairs, while still moist, with the chocolate mixture spread between them. Place a pineapple ring on top of each pair of circles before the chocolate sets and place a cherry in the center of each ring.

4 Put 4 tablespoons of the reserved can juice into a small pan and stir in the cornstarch. Bring to a boil over a moderate heat, stirring constantly and cook for 5–7 minutes until thickened. Remove the pan from the heat and let it cool to room temperature. Brush the glaze over the pineapple rings and let stand for 10 minutes to set before serving.

Chocolate & Honey Ice Cream

Ice cream is always a popular summer dessert—try this rather different recipe for a change.

30 mins, plus
5 hrs freezing/
cooling

15 mins

SERVES 6

INGREDIENTS

2 cups milk

7 oz/200 g dark chocolate, broken
   into pieces

4 eggs, separated

scant ½ cup superfine sugar

2 tbsp clear honey

pinch of salt

12 fresh strawberries, washed and hulled

1 Pour the milk into a pan, add 5½ oz/ 150 g of the chocolate and stir over a medium heat for 3–5 minutes until melted. Remove the pan from the heat and set aside.

2 In a separate bowl, beat the egg yolks with all but 1 tablespoon of the sugar until pale and thickened. Gradually beat in the milk mixture, a little at a time. Return the mixture to a clean pan and cook over a low heat, whisking constantly, until smooth and thickened. Remove from the heat and set aside to cool completely. Cover with plastic wrap and chill in the refrigerator for 30 minutes.

3 Whisk the egg whites with a pinch of salt until soft peaks form. Gradually whisk in the remaining sugar and continue whisking until stiff and glossy. Remove the chocolate mixture from the refrigerator and stir in the honey, then gently fold in the egg whites.

4 Divide the mixture among 6 individual freezerproof molds and place in the freezer for at least 4 hours, until frozen. Meanwhile, put the remaining chocolate in the top of a double boiler or in a heatproof bowl set over a pan of barely simmering water. Stir over a low heat until melted and smooth, then dip the strawberries in the melted chocolate so that they are half-coated. Place on a sheet of baking parchment to set. Transfer the ice cream to the refrigerator for 10 minutes before serving. Turn out onto serving plates and decorate with the strawberries.

Small Cakes & Cookies

This chapter contains everyday delights for chocolate fans. You are sure to be tempted by our wonderful array of cookies and small cakes. Make any day special with a home-made chocolate cookie to be served with coffee, as a snack, or to accompany a special dessert. Although some take a little longer to make, most are quick and easy to prepare and

decoration is often simple, although you can get carried away if you like!

You'll find recipes for old favorites such as Chocolate Chip Muffins and Chocolate Chip Cookies, Chocolate Butterfly Cakes and Sticky Chocolate Brownies. There are also some new cookies and small cakes, such as Chocolate & Coconut Squares or Malted Chocolate Wedges. Finally, we have given the chocolate treatment to some traditional recipes—try Chocolate Scones or Chocolate Chip Flapjacks.

Chocolate Boxes

Guests will think you have spent hours creating these little boxes, but a few tricks (such as ready-made cake) make them quick to put together.

20 mins   5 mins

SERVES 4

INGREDIENTS

8 oz/225 g dark chocolate

about 8 oz/225 g bought or ready-made plain or chocolate sponge cake

2 tbsp apricot jelly

⅔ cup heavy cream

1 tbsp maple syrup

3½ oz/100 g prepared fresh fruit, such as small strawberries, raspberries, kiwi fruit or redcurrants

1 Melt the dark chocolate and spread it evenly over a large sheet of baking parchment. Let harden in a cool room.

2 When just set, cut the chocolate into 2 inch/5 cm squares and remove from the parchment. Make sure that your hands are as cool as possible and handle the chocolate as little as possible.

3 Cut the cake into 2 cubes, 2 inches/ 5 cm across, then cut each cube in half. Warm the apricot jelly and brush it over the sides of the cake cubes. Carefully press a chocolate square on to each side of the cake cubes to make 4 chocolate boxes with cake at the bottom. Chill in the refrigerator for 20 minutes.

4 Whip the heavy cream with the maple syrup until just holding its shape. Spoon or pipe a little of the mixture into each chocolate box.

5 Decorate the top of each box with the prepared fruit. If liked, the fruit can be partially dipped into melted chocolate and allowed to harden before being placed into the boxes.

COOK'S TIP

For the best results, keep the boxes well chilled and fill and decorate them just before you want to serve them.

Chocolate Dairy Wraps

Light chocolate sponge is wrapped around a dairy cream filling. These individual cakes can be served for dessert, if desired.

🍰 40 mins   🕐 6–8 mins

SERVES 6

INGREDIENTS

2 eggs

4 tbsp superfine sugar

⅓ cup all-purpose flour

1½ tbsp unsweetened cocoa

4 tbsp apricot jelly

⅔ cup heavy cream, whipped

confectioners' sugar, to dust

1 Line 2 cookie sheets with pieces of baking parchment. Whisk the eggs and sugar together until the mixture is very light and fluffy and the whisk leaves a trail when lifted.

2 Sift together the flour and cocoa. Using a metal spoon or a spatula, gently fold it into the eggs and sugar in a figure of eight movement.

3 Drop rounded tablespoonfuls of the mixture on to the lined cookie sheets and spread them into oval shapes. Make sure they are well spaced as they will spread during cooking.

4 Bake in a preheated oven, 425°F/ 220°C, for about 6–8 minutes or until springy to the touch. Let cool on the cookie sheets.

5 When cold, slide the cakes on to a damp dish towel and allow to stand until cold. Carefully remove them from the dampened parchment. Spread the flat side of the cakes with apricot jelly, then spoon or pipe the whipped cream down the center of each one.

6 Fold the cakes in half and place them on a serving plate. Sprinkle with a little confectioners' sugar and serve.

VARIATION
Fold 4 teaspoons of crème de menthe or 2 oz/50 g melted chocolate into the cream for fabulous alternatives to plain cream.

Chocolate Cup Cakes

A variation on an old favorite, these sumptuous little cakes will appeal to both kids and grown-ups.

1¼ hrs ⏱ 20 mins

MAKES 18

I N G R E D I E N T S

generous ⅓ cup butter, softened

½ cup superfine sugar

2 eggs, lightly beaten

⅓ cup dark chocolate chips

2 tbsp milk

1¼ cups self-rising flour

¼ cup unsweetened cocoa

I C I N G

8 oz/225 g white chocolate

5½ oz/150 g low-fat soft cheese

1 Line an 18-hole shallow muffin pan with individual paper cases.

2 Beat together the butter and sugar until pale and fluffy. Gradually add the eggs, beating well after each addition. Add a little of the flour if the mixture begins to curdle. Add the milk, then fold in the chocolate chips.

3 Sift together the flour and cocoa and fold into the mixture with a metal spoon or spatula. Divide the mixture

equally between the paper cases and level the tops.

4 Bake in a preheated oven, 350°F/180°C, for 20 minutes, or until well risen and springy to the touch. Let the cakes cool on a wire rack.

5 To make the icing, melt the chocolate, then let cool slightly. Beat the cream cheese until softened slightly, then beat in the melted chocolate. Spread a little of the icing over each cake and chill for 1 hour before serving.

VARIATION

Add white chocolate chips or chopped pecan nuts to the mixture instead of the dark chocolate chips, if you prefer. You can also add the finely grated zest of 1 orange for a chocolate and orange flavor.

Chocolate Rum Babas

A little bit fiddly to make but well worth the effort. Indulge in these tasty cakes with coffee, or serve them as a dessert with summer fruits.

🍰 3 hrs   🕐 15 mins

SERVES 4

INGREDIENTS

¾ cup strong all-purpose flour

¼ cup unsweetened cocoa

6 g sachet active dry yeast

pinch of salt

1 tbsp superfine sugar

1½ oz/40 g dark chocolate, grated

2 eggs

3 tbsp lukewarm milk

4 tbsp butter, melted

SYRUP

4 tbsp clear honey

2 tbsp water

4 tbsp rum

TO SERVE

whipped cream

unsweetened cocoa, to dust

fresh fruit, optional

1 Lightly oil 4 individual ring pans. In a large warmed mixing bowl, strain the flour and cocoa together. Stir in the yeast, salt, sugar, and grated chocolate. In a separate bowl, beat the eggs together, add the milk and butter, and continue beating until mixed.

2 Make a well in the center of the dry ingredients and pour in the egg mixture, beating to mix to a batter. Beat for 10 minutes, ideally in a electric mixer with a dough hook. Divide the mixture between the pans—it should come halfway up the sides.

3 Place on a cookie sheet and cover with a damp dish towel. Let stand in a warm place until the mixture rises almost to the tops of the pans. Bake in a preheated oven, 400°F/200°C, for 15 minutes.

4 To make the syrup, gently heat all of the ingredients in a small pan. Turn out the babas and place on rack placed above a tray to catch the syrup. Drizzle the syrup over the babas and let stand for at least 2 hours for the syrup to soak in. Once or twice, spoon the syrup that has dripped on to the tray over the babas.

5 Fill the center of the babas with whipped cream and sprinkle a little cocoa over the top. Serve the babas with fresh fruit, if desired.

No-Bake Chocolate Squares

Children will enjoy making these as an introduction to chocolate cooking, and they keep well in the refrigerator.

2¼ hrs   5 mins

MAKES 16

INGREDIENTS

9½ oz/275 g dark chocolate

¾ cup butter

4 tbsp light corn syrup

2 tbsp dark rum, optional

6 oz/175 g plain cookies

1 oz/25 g toasted rice cereal

½ cup chopped walnuts or pecan nuts

½ cup candied cherries,
   coarsely chopped

1 oz/25 g white chocolate, to decorate

1 Place the dark chocolate in a large mixing bowl with the butter, syrup, and rum, if using, and set over a pan of gently simmering water until melted, stirring until blended.

2 Break the cookies into small pieces and stir into the chocolate mixture along with the toasted rice cereal, nuts, and cherries.

VARIATION
Brandy or an orange-flavored liqueur can be used instead of the rum, if you prefer. Cherry brandy also works well.

3 Line a 7 inch/18 cm square cake pan with baking parchment. Pour the mixture into the pan and level the top, pressing down well with the back of a spoon. Chill for 2 hours.

4 To decorate, melt the white chocolate and drizzle it over the top of the cake randomly. Let it set. To serve, carefully turn out of the pan and remove the baking parchment. Cut the cake into 16 squares.

Chocolate Butterfly Cakes

Filled with a tangy lemon cream, these appealing cakes will be a favorite with adults and children alike.

30 mins   15 mins

MAKES 12

INGREDIENTS

½ cup soft margarine

½ cup superfine sugar

1¼ cups self-rising flour

2 large eggs

2 tbsp unsweetened cocoa

1 oz/25 g dark chocolate, melted

LEMON BUTTER CREAM

generous ⅓ cup sweet butter, softened

1⅓ cups confectioners' sugar, strained

grated zest of ½ lemon

1 tbsp lemon juice

confectioners' sugar, to dust

1 Place 12 individual paper cases in a shallow muffin pan. Place all of the ingredients for the cakes, except for the melted chocolate, in a large mixing bowl, and beat with an electric whisk until the mixture is just smooth. Beat in the melted chocolate.

2 Spoon equal amounts of the mixture into each paper case, filling them three-quarters full. Bake in a preheated oven, 350°F/180°C, for 15 minutes or until springy to the touch. Transfer to a wire rack and let cool.

3 Meanwhile, make the lemon butter cream. Place the butter in a mixing bowl and beat until fluffy, then gradually beat in the confectioners' sugar. Beat in the lemon zest and gradually add the lemon juice, beating well.

4 When cold, cut the top off each cake, using a serrated knife. Cut each cake top in half.

5 Spread or pipe the butter cream icing over the cut surface of each cake and push the 2 cut pieces of cake top into the icing to form wings. Sprinkle with confectioners' sugar.

VARIATION

For a chocolate butter cream, beat the butter and confectioners' sugar together, then beat in 1 oz/25 g melted dark chocolate.

Sticky Chocolate Brownies

Everyone loves chocolate brownies and these are so gooey and delicious they are impossible to resist!

1 hr 20 mins   25 mins

MAKES 9

INGREDIENTS

generous ⅓ cup sweet butter

¾ cup superfine sugar

½ cup dark brown sugar

4½ oz/125 g dark chocolate

1 tbsp light corn syrup

2 eggs

1 tsp chocolate or vanilla extract

¾ cup all-purpose flour

2 tbsp unsweetened cocoa

½ tsp baking powder

1 Lightly grease an 8 inch/20 cm shallow square cake pan and line the bottom with baking parchment.

2 Place the butter, sugars, chocolate, and light corn syrup in a heavy-based pan and heat gently, stirring until the mixture is well blended and smooth. Remove from the heat and let cool.

3 Beat together the eggs and chocolate or vanilla extract. Whisk in the cooled chocolate mixture.

4 Strain together the flour, cocoa, and baking powder, and fold carefully into the egg and chocolate mixture using a metal spoon or spatula.

5 Spoon the mixture into the prepared pan and bake in a preheated oven, 350°F/180°C, for 25 minutes, until the top is crisp and the edge of the cake is beginning to shrink away from the pan. The inside of the cake mixture will still be quite stodgy and soft to the touch.

6 Let the cake cool completely in the pan, then cut it into squares to serve.

COOK'S TIP

This cake can be well wrapped and frozen for up to 2 months. Thaw at room temperature for about 2 hours or overnight in the refrigerator.

Chocolate Fudge Brownies

Here, a traditional brownie mixture has a cream cheese ribbon through the center and is topped with a delicious chocolate fudge icing.

1 hr 20 mins 🕐 40–45 mins

MAKES 16

INGREDIENTS

7 oz/200 g low-fat soft cheese

½ tsp vanilla extract

2 eggs

generous 1 cup superfine sugar

generous ⅓ cup butter

3 tbsp unsweetened cocoa

¾ cup self-rising flour, strained

⅓ cup chopped pecan nuts

FUDGE ICING

4 tbsp butter

1 tbsp milk

⅔ cup icing confectioners' sugar

2 tbsp unsweetened cocoa

pecan nuts, to decorate (optional)

1 Lightly grease an 8 inch/20 cm square shallow cake pan and line the bottom.

2 Beat together the cheese, vanilla extract, and 5 teaspoons of superfine sugar until smooth, then set aside.

VARIATION
Omit the cheese layer if preferred. Use walnuts in place of the pecan nuts.

3 Beat the eggs and remaining superfine sugar together until light and fluffy. Place the butter and cocoa in a small pan and heat gently, stirring until the butter melts and the mixture combines, then stir it into the egg mixture. Fold in the flour and nuts.

4 Pour half of the brownie mixture into the pan and level the top. Carefully spread the soft cheese over it, then cover it with the remaining brownie mixture. Bake in a preheated oven, 350°F/180°C, for 40–45 minutes. Cool in the pan.

5 To make the icing, melt the butter in the milk. Stir in the confectioners' sugar and cocoa. Spread the icing over the brownies and decorate with pecan nuts, if using. Let the icing set, then cut into squares to serve.

Chocolate Chip Muffins

Muffins are always popular and are so simple to make. Mini muffins are fabulous bite-sized treats for young children—and perfect for parties.

45 mins   25 mins

MAKES 12

I N G R E D I E N T S

generous ⅓ cup soft margarine

1 cup superfine sugar

2 large eggs

⅔ cup whole milk unsweetened yogurt

5 tbsp milk

2 cups all-purpose flour

1 tsp baking soda

6 oz/175 g dark chocolate chips

1 Line 12 muffin pans with paper cases.

2 Place the margarine and sugar in a mixing bowl and beat with a wooden spoon until light and fluffy. Beat in the eggs, yogurt, and milk until combined.

3 Strain the flour and baking soda together and add to the mixture. Stir until just blended.

4 Stir in the chocolate chips, then spoon the mixture into the paper cases and

VARIATION

The mixture can also be used to make 6 large or 24 mini muffins. Bake mini muffins for 10 minutes or until springy to the touch.

bake in a preheated oven, 375°F/190°C, for 25 minutes or until a fine skewer inserted into the center comes out clean.

Let the muffins cool in the pan for 5 minutes, then turn them out on to a wire rack to cool completely.

Chocolate Scones

A plain scone mixture is transformed into a chocoholics' treat by the simple addition of chocolate chips.

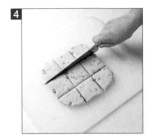

10 mins

10–12 mins

MAKES 4

INGREDIENTS

2 cups self-rising flour, strained

5 tbsp butter

1 tbsp superfine sugar

⅓ cup chocolate chips

about ⅔ cup milk

1 Lightly grease a cookie sheet. Place the flour in a mixing bowl. Cut the butter into small pieces and rub it into the flour with your fingertips until the scone mixture resembles fine breadcrumbs.

2 Stir in the superfine sugar and chocolate chips.

3 Mix in enough of the milk to form a soft dough.

4 On a lightly floured counter, roll out the dough to form a 4 x 6 inch/ 10 x 15 cm rectangle, about 1 inch/2.5 cm thick. Cut the dough into 9 squares.

5 Place the scones spaced well apart on the prepared cookie sheet.

6 Brush with a little milk and bake in a preheated oven, 425°F/220°C, for 10–12 minutes, until risen and golden.

COOK'S TIP
To be at their best, all scones should be freshly baked and served warm. Split the warm scones and spread them with a little chocolate and hazelnut spread or a good dollop of whipped cream.

Pain au Chocolat

These croissants can be a bit fiddly to make, but the flaky pie dough enclosing a fabulous rich chocolate filling make them worth the effort.

3¼ hrs   20–25 mins

MAKES 12

INGREDIENTS

4 cups strong all-purpose flour

½ tsp salt

6 g sachet of active dry yeast

2 tbsp shortening

1 egg, beaten lightly

1 cup lukewarm water

¾ cup butter, softened

3½ oz/100 g dark chocolate, broken into 12 squares

beaten egg, to glaze

confectioners' sugar, to dust

1 Lightly grease a cookie sheet. Strain the flour and salt into a mixing bowl and stir in the yeast. Rub in the fat with your fingertips. Add the egg and enough of the water to mix to a soft dough. Knead for about 10 minutes to make a smooth elastic dough.

2 Roll out to form a 15 x 8 inch/ 37.5 x 20 cm rectangle. Divide the butter into 3 portions and dot one portion over two-thirds of the rectangle, leaving a small border around the edge.

3 Fold the rectangle into 3 by first folding the plain part of the dough over and then the other side. Seal the edges of the dough by pressing with a rolling pin. Give the dough a quarter turn so the sealed edges are at the top and bottom. Re-roll and fold (without adding butter), then wrap the dough and chill for 30 minutes.

4 Repeat steps 2 and 3 until all of the butter has been used, chilling the dough each time. Re-roll and fold twice more without butter. Chill for a final 30 minutes.

5 Roll the dough to a 18 x 12 inch/ 45 x 30 cm rectangle, trim and halve, lengthwise. Cut each half into 6 rectangles and brush with beaten egg.

Place a chocolate square at one end of each rectangle and roll up to form a sausage. Press the ends together and place, seam-side down, on the cookie sheet. Cover and let rise for 40 minutes in a warm place. Brush with egg and bake in a preheated oven, 425°F/220°C, for 20–25 minutes until golden. Cool on a wire rack. Serve warm or cold.

Chocolate Chip Tartlets

These tasty little tartlets will be a big hit with the kids. Serve as a dessert or a special treat.

1 hr   20 mins

MAKES 6

INGREDIENTS

1¾ oz/50 g toasted hazelnuts

1¼ cups all-purpose flour

1 tbsp confectioners' sugar

⅓ cup soft margarine

FILLING

2 tbsp cornstarch

1 tbsp unsweetened cocoa

1 tbsp superfine sugar

1¼ cups semi-skim milk

3 tbsp chocolate and hazelnut spread

2½ tbsp dark chocolate chips

2½ tbsp milk chocolate chips

2½ tbsp white chocolate chips

1 Finely chop the nuts in a food processor. Add the flour, the 1 tablespoon of confectioners' sugar and the margarine. Process for a few seconds until the mixture resembles breadcrumbs. Add 2–3 tablespoons of water and process to form a soft dough. Cover and chill in the freezer for 10 minutes.

2 Roll out the dough and use it to line six 4 inch/10 cm loose-bottomed tartlet pans. Prick the bottom of the tartlet shells with a fork and line them with loosely crumpled foil. Bake in a preheated oven, 400°F/200°C, for 15 minutes. Remove the foil and bake for a further 5 minutes until the tartlet shells are crisp and golden. Remove from the oven and let cool.

3 Mix together the cornstarch, cocoa, and sugar with enough milk to make a smooth paste. Stir in the remaining milk. Pour into a pan and cook gently over a low heat, stirring until thickened. Stir in the hazelnut and chocolate spread.

4 Mix together the chocolate chips and reserve a quarter. Stir half of the remaining chips into the custard. Cover with damp waxed paper, let stand until almost cold, then stir in the second half of the chocolate chips. Spoon the mixture into the tartlet shells and let cool. Decorate with the reserved chips, scattering them over the top.

Chocolate Eclairs

Patisserie cream is the traditional filling for éclairs, but if time is short you can fill them with whipped cream.

1 hr   30–35 mins

MAKES 10

INGREDIENTS

DOUGH

⅔ cup water

5 tbsp butter, cut into small pieces

¾ cup strong all-purpose flour, strained

2 eggs

PATISSERIE CREAM

2 eggs, lightly beaten

¼ cup superfine sugar

2 tbsp cornstarch

1¼ cups milk

¼ tsp vanilla extract

ICING

2 tbsp butter

1 tbsp milk

1 tbsp unsweetened cocoa

½ cup confectioners' sugar

a little white chocolate, melted

1 Lightly grease a cookie sheet. Place the water in a pan, add the butter, and heat gently until the butter melts. Bring to a rolling boil, then remove the pan from the heat and add the flour in one go, beating well until the mixture leaves the sides of the pan and forms a ball. Let cool slightly, then gradually beat in the eggs to form a smooth, glossy mixture. Spoon into a large pastry bag fitted with a ½ inch/1 cm plain tip.

2 Sprinkle the cookie sheet with a little water. Pipe éclairs 3 inches/7.5 cm long, spaced well apart. Bake in a preheated oven, 400°F/200°C, for 30–35

minutes or until crisp and golden. Make a small slit in each one to let the steam escape. Cool on a wire rack.

3 Meanwhile, make the patisserie cream. Whisk the eggs and sugar until thick and creamy, then fold in the cornstarch. Heat the milk until almost boiling and pour on to the eggs, whisking. Transfer to the pan and cook over a low heat, stirring until thick. Remove the pan

from the heat and stir in the vanilla extract. Cover with baking parchment and let cool.

4 To make the icing, melt the butter with the milk in a pan, remove from the heat and stir in the cocoa and sugar. Split the éclairs lengthwise and pipe in the patisserie cream. Spread the icing over the top of the éclair. Spoon over the white chocolate, swirl in, and allow to set.

Chocolate Meringues

These melt-in-the-mouth meringues are ideal for a buffet dessert—pile them high in a pyramid for pure, bite-size magic.

 1 hr 25 mins 🕐 1 hr

MAKES 8

INGREDIENTS

4 egg whites

1 cup superfine sugar

1 tsp cornstarch

1½ oz/40 g dark chocolate, grated

TO COMPLETE

3½ oz/100 g dark chocolate

⅔ cup heavy cream

1 tbsp confectioners' sugar

1 tbsp brandy, optional

3 Spoon the mixture into a pastry bag fitted with a large star or plain tip. Pipe 16 large rosettes or mounds on the lined cookie sheets.

4 Bake in a preheated oven, 275°F/140°C, for about 1 hour, changing the position of the cookie sheets halfway through cooking. Without opening the oven door, turn off the oven and let the meringues cool in the oven.

Once they are cold, carefully peel away the baking parchment.

5 Melt the dark chocolate and spread it over the bottom of the meringues. Stand them upside down on a wire rack until the chocolate has set. Whip the cream, confectioners' sugar and brandy (if using), until the cream holds its shape. Spoon into a pastry bag and use to sandwich the meringues together in pairs. Serve.

1 Line 2 cookie sheets with baking parchment. Whisk the egg whites until standing in soft peaks, then gradually whisk in half of the sugar. Continue whisking until the mixture is very stiff and glossy.

2 Carefully fold in the remaining sugar, cornstarch, and grated chocolate with a metal spoon or spatula.

VARIATION
To make mini meringues, use a star shaped tip and pipe about 24 small rosettes. Bake for about 40 minutes until crisp.

Mexican Chocolate Meringues

The Mexican name for these delicate meringues is *suspiros*, meaning "sighs"—supposedly the contented sighs of the nuns who created them.

1¼ hrs   2 hrs

MAKES 25

I N G R E D I E N T S

4–5 egg whites, at room temperature

a pinch of salt

¼ tsp cream of tartar

¼–½ tsp vanilla extract

¾–1 cup superfine sugar

⅛–¼ tsp ground cinnamon

4 oz/115 g dark or bitter chocolate, grated

T O   S E R V E

ground cinnamon

4 oz/115 g strawberries

chocolate-flavored cream (see Cook's Tip)

1 Whisk the egg whites until they are foamy, then add the salt and cream of tartar and beat until very stiff. Whisk in the vanilla, then slowly whisk in the sugar, a small amount at a time, until the meringue is shiny and stiff. This should take about 3 minutes by hand, and under a minute with an electric whisk.

COOK'S TIP

To make the flavored cream, simply stir half-melted chocolate pieces into stiffly whipped cream, then chill until solid.

2 Whisk in the cinnamon and grated chocolate. Spoon mounds of about 2 tablespoons, on to an ungreased, non-stick cookie sheet. Space the mounds well.

3 Place in a preheated oven, 300°F/ 150°C, and cook for 2 hours until set.

4 Carefully remove from the cookie sheet. If the meringues are too moist and soft, return them to the oven to firm up and dry out more. Let them cool completely.

5 Serve the meringues dusted with cinnamon and accompanied by strawberries and the chocolate-flavored cream (see Cook's Tip).

Rice Tartlets

These delicious little tartlets have a soft dark chocolate layer covered with creamy rice pudding for a delicious special occasion dessert.

30 mins, plus 8 hrs defrosting

50 mins

SERVES 6

INGREDIENTS

1 packet frozen unsweetened pastry

4 cups milk

pinch of salt

1 vanilla bean, split, seeds removed and reserved

½ cup risotto or long-grain white rice

1 tbsp cornstarch

2 tbsp sugar

unsweetened cocoa, to dust

melted chocolate, to decorate

CHOCOLATE GANACHE

generous ¾ cup heavy cream

1 tbsp light corn syrup

6 oz/175 g dark or bitter chocolate, chopped

1 tbsp sweet butter

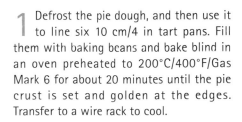

1 Defrost the pie dough, and then use it to line six 10 cm/4 in tart pans. Fill them with baking beans and bake blind in an oven preheated to 200°C/400°F/Gas Mark 6 for about 20 minutes until the pie crust is set and golden at the edges. Transfer to a wire rack to cool.

2 To make the chocolate ganache, bring the heavy cream and corn syrup to a boil. Remove from the heat and immediately stir in the chopped chocolate. Continue stirring until melted and smooth, then beat in the butter until well combined. Spoon a 1 inch/2.5 cm thick layer into each tartlet. Set aside.

3 Bring the milk and salt to a boil in a pan. Sprinkle in the rice and return to a boil. Add the vanilla bean and seeds. Reduce the heat and simmer until the rice is tender and the milk creamy.

4 Blend the cornstarch and sugar in a small bowl and add about 2 tablespoons of water to make a paste. Stir in a few spoonfuls of the rice mixture, then stir the cornstarch mixture into the rice. Bring to a boil and cook for about 1 minute until thickened. Cool the pan in iced water, stirring until thick.

5 Spoon into the tartlets, filling each to the brim. Allow to set at room temperature. To serve, dust with cocoa and pipe or drizzle with melted chocolate.

Chocolate Hazelnut Palmiers

These delicious chocolate and hazelnut cookies are very simple to make, yet so effective. For very young children, leave out the chopped nuts.

5 mins   10–15 mins

MAKES 26

INGREDIENTS

TOPPING

13 oz/375 g ready-made puff pie dough

8 tbsp chocolate hazelnut spread

½ cup chopped toasted hazelnuts

2 tbsp superfine sugar

1 Lightly grease a cookie sheet. On a lightly floured counter, roll out the puff pie dough to a rectangle about 15 x 9 inches/37.5 x 23 cm in size.

2 Spread the chocolate hazelnut spread over the pie dough using a spatula, then scatter the chopped hazelnuts over the top.

3 Roll up one long side of the pie dough to the center, then roll up the other side so that they meet in the middle. Where the pieces meet, dampen the edges with a little water to join them. Using a sharp knife, cut into thin slices. Place each slice on to the prepared cookie sheet and flatten slightly with a spatula. Sprinkle the slices with the superfine sugar.

4 Bake in a preheated oven, 425°F/ 220°C, for about 10–15 minutes until golden. Transfer to a wire rack to cool.

VARIATION

For an extra chocolate flavor, dip the palmiers in melted dark chocolate to half-cover each biscuit.

Chocolate Coconut Squares

These cookies consist of a chewy coconut layer resting on a crisp chocolate cookie base, cut into squares to serve.

🍰 1¼ hrs   🕐 30 mins

MAKES 9

INGREDIENTS

8 oz/225 g dark chocolate graham crackers

⅓ cup butter or margarine

¾ cup canned evaporated milk

1 egg, beaten

1 tsp vanilla extract

2 tbsp superfine sugar

⅓ cup self-rising flour, strained

1⅓ cups shredded coconut

1¾ oz/50 g dark chocolate, optional

1 Grease a shallow 8 inch/20 cm square cake pan and line the bottom.

2 Crush the crackers in a polythene bag with a rolling pin or process them in a food processor.

3 Melt the butter or margarine in a pan and stir in the crushed crackers until well combined.

4 Press the mixture into the bottom of the cake pan.

VARIATION
Store the squares in an airtight container for up to 4 days. They can be frozen, undecorated, for up to 2 months. Thaw at room temperature.

5 Beat together the evaporated milk, egg, vanilla, and sugar until smooth. Stir in the flour and shredded coconut. Pour over the cracker layer and use a spatula to level the top.

6 Bake in a preheated oven, 375°F/190°C, for 30 minutes or until the coconut topping has become firm and just golden.

7 Let cool in the cake pan for about 5 minutes, then cut into squares. Let cool completely in the pan.

8 Carefully remove the squares from the pan and place them on a board. Melt the dark chocolate (if using) and drizzle it over the squares to decorate them. Let the chocolate set before serving.

Chocolate & Coconut Cookies

These delicious, melt-in-the-mouth cookies are finished off with a simple gooey icing and a generous sprinkling of coconut.

🥧 40 mins   🕐 12–15 mins

MAKES 24

INGREDIENTS

½ cup soft margarine

1 tsp vanilla extract

½ cup confectioners' sugar, strained

1 cup all-purpose flour

2 tbsp unsweetened cocoa

⅔ cup shredded coconut

2 tbsp butter

3½ oz/100 g white marshmallows

⅓ cup shredded coconut

a little white chocolate, grated

1 Lightly grease a cookie sheet. Beat together the margarine, vanilla, and confectioners' sugar in a mixing bowl until fluffy. Sift together the flour and cocoa and beat it into the mixture with the coconut.

2 Roll rounded teaspoons of the mixture into balls and place on the prepared cookie sheet, allowing room for the cookies to spread during cooking.

3 Flatten the balls slightly and bake in a preheated oven, 350°F/180°C, for 12–15 minutes until just firm.

4 Let cool on the cookie sheet for a few minutes before transferring to a wire rack to cool completely.

5 Place the butter and marshmallows in a small pan and heat gently, stirring until melted. Spread a little of the icing mixture over each cookie and dip in the coconut. Let them set. Decorate with grated white chocolate before serving.

Chocolate Crispy Bites

A favorite with children, this version of crispy bites has been given a new twist which is sure to be popular.

🍰 45 mins 🕐 5–10 mins

MAKES 16

INGREDIENTS

WHITE LAYER

4 tbsp butter

1 tbsp light corn syrup

5½ oz/150 g white chocolate

1¾ oz/50 g toasted rice cereal

DARK LAYER

4 tbsp butter

2 tbsp light corn syrup

4½ oz/125 g dark chocolate, broken into small pieces

2¾ oz/75 g toasted rice cereal

1 Grease an 8 inch/20 cm square cake pan and line with baking parchment.

2 To make the white chocolate layer, melt the butter, light corn syrup, and chocolate in a bowl set over a pan of gently simmering water.

3 Remove from the heat and stir in the rice cereal until it is well combined.

4 Press into the prepared pan and level the surface.

5 To make the dark chocolate layer, melt the butter, light corn syrup, and dark chocolate in a bowl set over a pan of gently simmering water.

6 Remove from the heat and stir in the rice cereal. Pour the dark chocolate over the hardened white chocolate layer, cool, and chill until hardened.

7 Turn out of the cake pan and cut into small squares, using a sharp knife.

Dutch Macaroons

These unusual cookie treats are delicious served with coffee. They also make an ideal dessert cookie to serve with ice cream.

40 mins   15–20 mins

MAKES 20

INGREDIENTS

rice paper

2 egg whites

1 cup superfine sugar

1⅔ cups ground almonds

8 oz/225 g dark chocolate

1 Cover 2 cookie sheets with rice paper. Whisk the egg whites in a large mixing bowl until stiff, then fold in the sugar and ground almonds.

2 Place the mixture in a large pastry bag fitted with a ½ inch/1 cm plain tip and pipe fingers, about 3 inches/ 7.5 cm long, allowing space for the mixture to spread during cooking.

3 Bake in a preheated oven, 350°F/ 180°C, for 15–20 minutes, until golden. Transfer to a wire rack and let cool. Remove the excess rice paper from around the edges.

COOK'S TIP

Rice paper is edible so you can just break off the excess from around the edge of the cookies. Remove it completely before dipping in the chocolate, if you prefer.

4 Melt the chocolate and dip the bottom of each cookie into the chocolate. Place the macaroons on a sheet of baking parchment and allow to set.

5 Drizzle any remaining chocolate over the top of the cookies (you may need to reheat the chocolate in order to do this). Let it set before serving.

Chocolate Orange Cookies

These delicious chocolate cookies have a tangy orange icing. Children love them, especially if different shaped cutters are used.

55 mins   10–12 mins

SERVES 30

INGREDIENTS

⅓ cup butter, softened

⅓ cup superfine sugar

1 egg

1 tbsp milk

2 cups all-purpose flour

¼ cup unsweetened cocoa

ICING

1 cup confectioners' sugar, strained

3 tbsp orange juice

a little dark chocolate, melted

1 Line 2 cookie sheets with baking parchment.

2 Beat together the butter and sugar until light and fluffy. Beat in the egg and milk until well combined. Strain the flour and cocoa into the mixture and gradually mix to form a soft dough. Use your fingers to incorporate the last of the flour and bring the dough together.

3 Roll out the dough on to a lightly floured counter until ¼ inch/6 mm thick. Using a 2 inch/5 cm fluted round cutter, cut out as many cookies as you can. Re-roll the dough trimmings and cut out more cookies.

4 Place the cookies on the prepared cookie sheet and bake in a preheated oven, 350°F/180°C, for 10–12 minutes or until golden.

5 Let the cookies cool on the cookie sheet for a few minutes, then transfer to a wire rack to cool completely.

6 For the icing, place the confectioners' sugar in a bowl and stir in enough orange juice to form a thin icing that will coat the back of a spoon. Spread the icing over the cookies and allow to set. Drizzle with melted chocolate. Let the chocolate set before serving.

Chocolate Caramel Squares

It is difficult to say "No" to these wonderfully rich cookies, which consist of a crunchy oat layer, a creamy caramel filling, and a chocolate top.

   40 mins   25 mins

MAKES 16

INGREDIENTS

generous ⅓ cup soft margarine

⅓ cup light brown sugar

1 cup all-purpose flour

½ cup rolled oats

CARAMEL FILLING

2 tbsp butter

2 tbsp light brown sugar

generous ¾ cup condensed milk

TOPPING

100 g/3½ oz dark chocolate

25 g/1 oz white chocolate, optional

1 Beat together the margarine and brown sugar in a bowl until light and fluffy. Beat in the flour and the rolled oats. Use your fingertips to bring the mixture together, if necessary.

2 Press the oat mixture into the bottom of a shallow 8 inch/20 cm square cake pan.

3 Bake in a preheated oven, 350°F/ 180°C, for 25 minutes or until just golden and firm. Cool in the pan.

4 Place the ingredients for the caramel filling in a pan and heat gently, stirring until the sugar has dissolved and the ingredients combine. Bring slowly to a boil over a very low heat, then boil very gently for 3–4 minutes, stirring constantly, until thickened.

5 Pour the caramel filling over the oat layer in the pan and allow to set.

6 Melt the dark chocolate and spread it over the caramel. If using the white chocolate, melt it and pipe lines of white chocolate over the dark chocolate. Using a toothpick or skewer, feather the white chocolate into the dark chocolate. Allow to set. Cut into squares to serve.

COOK'S TIP

If liked, you can line the pan with baking parchment so that the oat layer can be lifted out before cutting into pieces.

Chocolate Chip Flapjacks

Turn ordinary flapjacks into something special with the addition of some chocolate chips. Use white rather than dark chocolate chips, if preferred.

🍰 40 mins   🕐 30 mins

MAKES 12

INGREDIENTS

½ cup butter

⅓ cup superfine sugar

1 tbsp light corn syrup

4 cups rolled oats

½ cup dark chocolate chips

⅓ cup golden raisins

1 Lightly grease a shallow 8 inch/20 cm square cake pan.

2 Place the butter, superfine sugar, and light corn syrup in a pan and cook over a low heat, stirring until the butter and sugar melt and the mixture is well combined.

3 Remove the pan from the heat and stir in the rolled oats until they are well coated. Add the chocolate chips and the golden raisins and mix well to combine everything.

COOK'S TIP

The flapjacks will keep in an airtight container for up to 1 week, but they are so delicious they are unlikely to last that long!

4 Turn into the prepared pan and press down well.

5 Bake in a preheated oven, 350°F/ 180°C, for 30 minutes. Cool slightly,

then mark into fingers. When almost cold cut into bars or squares and transfer to a wire rack until cold.

Chocolate Chip Cookies

No chocolate cook's repertoire would be complete without a chocolate chip cookie recipe. This recipe can be used to make several variations.

35 mins   10–12 mins

MAKES 18

INGREDIENTS

1½ cups all-purpose flour

1 tsp baking powder

½ cup soft margarine

scant ⅔ cup light brown sugar

¼ cup superfine sugar

½ tsp vanilla extract

1 egg

⅔ cup dark chocolate chips

1 Place all of the ingredients in a large mixing bowl and beat until they are thoroughly combined.

2 Lightly grease 2 cookie sheets. Place tablespoonfuls of the mixture on to the cookie sheets, spacing them well apart to allow for spreading during cooking.

3 Bake in a preheated oven, 375°F/190°C, for 10–12 minutes or until the cookies are golden brown.

4 Using a spatula, transfer the cookies to a wire rack to cool completely.

VARIATION

For Choc & Nut Cookies, add ½ cup chopped hazelnuts to the basic mixture.

For Double Choc Cookies, beat in 1½ oz/40 g melted dark chocolate.

For White Chocolate Chip Cookies, use white chocolate chips instead of the dark chocolate chips.

Chocolate Shortbread

This buttery chocolate shortbread is the perfect addition to the cookie jar of any chocoholic.

 40 mins   40 mins

MAKES 12

INGREDIENTS

1½ cups all-purpose flour

1 tbsp unsweetened cocoa

4 tbsp superfine sugar

⅔ cup butter, softened

1¾ oz/50 g dark chocolate, finely chopped

1 Place all of the ingredients in a large mixing bowl and then beat together until they form a dough. Knead the dough lightly.

2 Lightly grease a cookie sheet. Place the dough on the cookie sheet and roll out to form a 8 inch/20 cm circle.

3 Pinch the edges of the dough with your fingertips to form a decorative edge. Prick the dough all over with a fork and mark into 12 wedges, using a sharp knife.

4 Bake in a preheated oven, 325°F/160°C, for 40 minutes until firm and golden. Let cool slightly before cutting into wedges. Transfer to a wire rack to cool completely.

VARIATION

For round shortbread cookies, roll out the dough on a lightly floured counter to ¾ inch/8 mm thick. Cut out 3 inch/7.5 cm circles with a cookie cutter. Transfer to a greased cookie sheet and bake as above. If liked, coat half the biscuit in melted chocolate.

 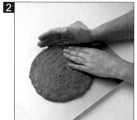 

Malted Chocolate Wedges

These are perfect with a bedtime drink, although you can enjoy these tasty cookie wedges at any time of the day.

45 mins

5 mins

MAKES 16

INGREDIENTS

generous ⅓ cup butter

2 tbsp light corn syrup

2 tbsp malted chocolate drink

8 oz/225 g malted milk cookies

2¾ oz/75 g light or dark chocolate, broken into pieces

2 tbsp confectioners' sugar

2 tbsp milk

1 Grease a shallow 7 inch/18 cm round cake pan or tart pan and then line the bottom.

2 Place the butter, light corn syrup, and malted chocolate drink in a small pan and heat gently, stirring all the time until the butter has melted and the mixture is well combined.

3 Crush the cookies in a plastic bag with a rolling pin, or process them in a food processor. Stir the cookie crumbs into the chocolate mixture and mix well.

VARIATION
Add chopped pecan nuts
to the cookie crumb mixture
in Step 3, if liked.

4 Press the mixture into the prepared pan and then chill in the refrigerator until firm.

5 Place the chocolate pieces in a small heatproof bowl with the confectioners' sugar and the milk. Place the bowl over a pan of gently simmering water and stir until the chocolate melts and the mixture is combined.

6 Spread the chocolate icing over the cookie base and let the icing set in the pan. Using a sharp knife, cut into wedges to serve.

Checkerboard Cookies

Children will love these two-tone chocolate cookies. If you do not mind a little mess, let them help to form the cookies.

1 hr 20 mins · 10 mins

SERVES 18

INGREDIENTS

¾ cup butter, softened

6 tbsp confectioners' sugar

1 teaspoon vanilla extract or grated zest of ½ orange

2¼ cups all-purpose flour

1 oz/25 g dark chocolate, melted

a little beaten egg white

1 Lightly grease a cookie sheet. Beat the butter and confectioners' sugar in a mixing bowl until light and fluffy. Beat in the vanilla extract or grated orange zest.

2 Gradually beat in the flour to form a soft dough. Use your fingers to incorporate the last of the flour and bring the dough together.

3 Divide the dough in half and beat the melted chocolate into one half. Keeping each half of the dough separate, cover, and let chill for about 30 minutes.

4 Roll out each piece of dough to a rectangle measuring 3 x 8 inches/ 7.5 x 20 cm and 3 cm/1½ inches thick. Brush one piece of dough with a little egg white and place the other on top.

5 Cut the block of dough in half lengthwise and turn over one half. Brush the side of one strip with egg white and butt the other up to it, so that it resembles a checkerboard.

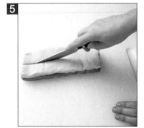
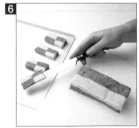

6 Cut the block into thin slices and place each slice flat on the cookie sheet, allowing enough room for them to spread a little during cooking.

7 Bake in a preheated oven, 350°F/ 180°C, for about 10 minutes until just firm. Let cool on the cookie sheets for a few minutes, before carefully transferring to a wire rack with a spatula. Allow to cool completely.

Viennese Chocolate Fingers

These cookies have a fabulously light, melting texture. You can leave them plain, but for real indulgence dip them in chocolate to decorate.

🥗 1 hr   🕐 12–15 mins

MAKES 18

INGREDIENTS

½ cup unsalted butter

6 tbsp confectioners' sugar

1½ cups self-rising flour, strained

3 tbsp cornstarch

7 oz/200 g dark chocolate

1 Lightly grease 2 cookie sheets. Beat the butter and sugar in a mixing bowl until light and fluffy. Gradually beat in the flour and cornstarch.

2 Melt 2¾ oz/75 g of the dark chocolate and beat into the cookie dough.

3 Place in a pastry bag fitted with a large star tip and pipe fingers about 2 inches/5 cm long on the cookie sheets, spaced apart to allow for spreading.

4 Bake in a preheated oven, 375°F/ 190°C, for 12–15 minutes. Let cool slightly on the cookie sheets, then transfer with a spatula to a wire rack and let cool completely.

5 Melt the remaining chocolate and dip one end of each cookie in the chocolate, allowing the excess to drip back into the bowl.

6 Place the cookies on a sheet of baking parchment and let the chocolate set before serving.

COOK'S TIP

If the cookie dough is too thick to pipe, beat in a little milk to thin it out.

Chocolate Pretzels

If you thought of pretzels as savories, then think again. These are fun to make and prove that pretzels come in a sweet variety, too.

1½ hrs   8–12 mins

SERVES 30

INGREDIENTS

generous ⅓ cup sweet butter

½ cup superfine sugar

1 egg

2 cups all-purpose flour

¼ cup unsweetened cocoa

TO FINISH

1 tbsp butter

3½ oz/100 g dark chocolate

confectioners' sugar, to dust

1 Lightly grease a cookie sheet. Beat together the butter and sugar in a mixing bowl until light and fluffy. Beat in the egg.

2 Sift together the flour and cocoa and gradually beat in to form a soft dough. Use your fingers to incorporate the last of the flour and bring the dough together. Chill for 15 minutes.

3 Break pieces from the dough and roll into thin sausage shapes about 4 inches/10 cm long and ¼ inch/6 mm thick. Twist into pretzel shapes by making a circle, then twist the ends through each other to form a letter "B."

4 Place on the prepared cookie sheet, slightly spaced apart to allow for spreading during cooking.

5 Bake in a preheated oven, 375°F/ 190°C, for 8–12 minutes. Let the pretzels cool slightly on the cookie sheet, then transfer them to a wire rack to cool completely.

6 Melt the butter and chocolate in a bowl set over a pan of gently simmering water, stirring to combine.

7 Dip half of each pretzel into the chocolate and allow the excess chocolate to drip back into the bowl. Place the pretzels on a sheet of baking parchment and allow to set.

8 When set, dust the non-chocolate-coated side of each pretzel with confectioners' sugar before serving.

Chocolate Wheatmeals

A good everyday cookie, these wheatmeals will keep well in an airtight container for at least 1 week. Dip them in white, light, or dark chocolate.

1 hr   15–20 mins

MAKES 20

INGREDIENTS

⅓ cup butter

⅔ cup raw brown sugar

1 egg

1 oz/25 g wheatgerm

1 cup whole-wheat self-rising flour

½ cup self-rising flour, strained

4½ oz/125 g chocolate

1 Lightly grease a cookie sheet. Beat the butter and sugar until fluffy. Add the egg and beat well. Stir in the wheatgerm and flours. Bring the mixture together with your hands.

2 Roll rounded teaspoonfuls of the mixture into balls and place on the prepared cookie sheet, allowing room for the cookies to spread during cooking.

3 Flatten the cookies slightly with the prongs of a fork. Bake in a preheated oven, 350°F/180°C, for 15–20 minutes,

COOK'S TIP
These cookies can be frozen very successfully. Freeze them at the end of Step 3 for up to 3 months. Thaw and then dip them in melted chocolate.

until golden. Let cool on the cookie sheet for a few minutes before transferring to a wire rack to cool completely.

4 Melt the chocolate, then dip each cookie in the chocolate to cover the flat side and come a little way around the

edges. Let the excess chocolate drip back into the bowl.

5 Place the cookies on a sheet of baking parchment and let the chocolate set in a cool place before serving.

Chocolate Brownies

You really can have a low-fat chocolate treat. These moist bars contain a dried fruit paste, which enables you to bake without adding any fat.

1¼ hrs   35–40 mins

MAKES 12

INGREDIENTS

2 oz/55 g unsweetened pitted dates, chopped

2 oz/55 g no-soak dried prunes, chopped

6 tbsp unsweetened apple juice

4 medium eggs, beaten

2 cups dark brown sugar

1 tsp vanilla extract

4 tbsp low-fat drinking chocolate powder, plus extra for dusting

2 tbsp unsweetened cocoa

1½ cups all-purpose flour

2 oz/55 g dark chocolate chips

ICING

¾ cup confectioners' sugar

1–2 tsp water

1 tsp vanilla extract

1 Preheat the oven to 350°F/180°C. Grease and line a 7 x 11 inch/18 x 28 cm cake pan with baking parchment. Place the dates and prunes in a small pan and add the apple juice. Bring to a boil, cover, and simmer for 10 minutes until soft. Beat to form a smooth paste, then set aside to cool.

2 Place the cooled fruit in a mixing bowl and stir in the eggs, sugar, and vanilla extract. Sift in 4 tablespoons of drinking chocolate, the cocoa, and the flour, and fold in along with the chocolate chips until well incorporated.

3 Spoon the mixture into the prepared pan and smooth over the top. Bake for 25–30 minutes until firm to the touch or until a skewer inserted into the center comes out clean. Cut into 12 bars and let cool in the tin for 10 minutes. Transfer to a wire rack to cool completely.

4 To make the icing, sift the sugar into a bowl and mix with sufficient water and the vanilla extract to form a soft, but not too runny, icing.

5 Drizzle the icing over the chocolate brownies and allow to set. Dust with the extra chocolate powder before serving.

COOK'S TIP

Make double the amount, cut one of the cakes into bars and open freeze, then store in plastic bags. Take out pieces of cake as and when you need them—they'll take no time at all to thaw.

Cannoli

No Sicilian celebration is complete without cannoli. If you can't find the molds, use large dried pasta tubes covered with foil, shiny side out.

🍰 1¾ hrs   ⏱ 15–20 mins

MAKES 20

INGREDIENTS

3 tbsp lemon juice

3 tbsp water

1 large egg

1¾ cups all-purpose flour

1 tbsp superfine sugar

1 tsp ground allspice

pinch of salt

2 tbsp butter, softened

sunflower oil, for deep-frying

1 small egg white, lightly beaten

confectioners' sugar

FILLING

3¼ cups ricotta cheese, drained

4 tbsp confectioners' sugar

1 tsp vanilla extract

finely grated zest of 1 large orange

4 tbsp very finely chopped candied fruit

1¾ oz/50 g dark chocolate, grated

pinch of ground cinnamon

2 tbsp Marsala wine or orange juice

1 Combine the lemon juice, water, and egg. Put the flour, sugar, spice, and salt in a food processor and quickly process. Add the butter, then, with the motor running, pour the egg mixture through the feed tube. Process until the mixture just forms a dough.

2 Turn the dough out on to a lightly floured counter and knead lightly. Wrap and chill for at least 1 hour.

3 Meanwhile, make the filling. Beat the ricotta cheese until smooth. Sift in the confectioners' sugar, then beat in the remaining ingredients. Cover and chill until required.

4 Roll out the dough on a floured counter until ¹⁄₁₆ inch/1.5 mm thick. Using a ruler, cut out 3 ½ x 3 inch/ 8.5 x 7.5 cm pieces, re-rolling and cutting the trimmings; the dough should make about 20 pieces.

5 Heat 2 inches/5 cm oil in a pan to 375°F/190°C. Roll a piece of dough around a greased cannoli mold, to just

6 Remove with a slotted spoon and drain on paper towels. Let cool, then carefully slide off the molds. Repeat with the remaining cannoli.

overlap the edge. Seal with egg white, pressing firmly. Repeat with all the molds you have. Fry 2 or 3 molds until the cannoli are golden, crisp, and bubbly.

7 Store unfilled in an airtight container for up to 2 days. Pipe in the filling no more than 30 minutes before serving to prevent the cannoli becoming soggy. Sift confectioners' sugar over the top and serve.

Chocolate Peanut Cookies

These delicious cookies contain two popular ingredients, peanuts and chocolate; the rice flour gives them an original twist.

🕐 1 hr 5 mins   ⏰ 20 mins

MAKES 50

INGREDIENTS

1½ cups all-purpose flour

2¼ cups rice flour

¼ cup unsweetened cocoa

1 tsp baking powder

pinch salt

¾ cup shortening

1 cup superfine sugar

1 tsp vanilla extract

1 cup raisins, chopped

1 cup unsalted peanuts, finely chopped

6 oz/175 g bitter or dark chocolate, melted

1 Sift the flours, cocoa, baking powder, and salt into a bowl, then stir well to combine.

2 Using an electric mixer, beat the fat and sugar in a large bowl for about 2 minutes until very light and creamy. Beat in the vanilla extract. Gradually blend in the flour mixture to form a soft dough. Stir in the raisins.

3 Put the chopped peanuts in a small bowl. Pinch off walnut-sized pieces of the dough and roll into balls. Drop into the peanuts and roll to coat, pressing them lightly to stick. Place the balls about 3 inches/7.5 cm apart on 2 large, greased, non-stick cookie sheets.

4 Using the flat bottom of a drinking glass dipped in flour, gently flatten each ball to a circle about ¼ inch/5 mm thick.

5 Bake in a preheated oven, 350°F/180°C, for about 10 minutes, until golden and lightly set; do not over-bake. Cool on the sheets for about 1 minute, then, using a thin spatula, transfer to a wire rack to cool. Continue with the remaining dough and peanuts.

6 Arrange the cooled cookies close together on the wire rack and drizzle the tops with the melted chocolate. Allow to set before transferring to an airtight container with waxed paper between the layers.

Pine Nut Tartlets

Pine nuts and orange zest are popular ingredients in Mediterranean dishes—here they add a twist of flavor to luscious chocolate tartlets.

🕐 1 hr 40 mins ⏱ 45 mins

SERVES 8

INGREDIENTS

2 oz/55 g dark chocolate with at least 70% cocoa solids

4 tbsp unsalted butter

¾ cup plus 2 tbsp superfine sugar

5 tbsp light brown sugar

6 tbsp milk

3½ tbsp light corn syrup

finely grated zest of 2 large oranges and 2 tbsp freshly squeezed juice

1 tsp vanilla extract

3 large eggs, lightly beaten

3½ oz/100 g pine nuts

TARTLET SHELLS

1¾ cups all-purpose flour

pinch of salt

generous ⅓ cup butter

1 cup confectioners' sugar

1 large egg and 2 large egg yolks

1 To make the pastry, sift the flour and a pinch of salt into a bowl. Make a well in the center and add the butter, confectioners' sugar, whole egg, and egg yolks. Using your fingertips, mix the ingredients in the well into a paste.

2 Gradually incorporate the surrounding flour to make a soft dough. Quickly and lightly knead the dough. Shape into a ball, wrap in plastic wrap, and chill for at least 1 hour.

3 Roll the pastry into 8 circles, 6 inches/15 cm across. Use to line 8 loose-bottomed 4 inch/10 cm tartlet pans. Line each with baking parchment to fit and top with baking beans. Chill for 10 minutes.

4 Bake in a preheated oven, 400°F/200°C, for 5 minutes. Remove the paper and beans and bake for a further 8 minutes. Let cool on a wire rack. Reduce the oven temperature to 350°F/180°C.

5 Meanwhile, break the chocolate into a pan over a medium heat. Add the butter and stir until blended.

6 Stir in the remaining ingredients. Spoon the filling into the tartlet shells on a cookie sheet. Bake for 25–30 minutes, or until the tops puff up and crack and feel set. Cover with baking parchment for the final 5 minutes if the shells are browning too much. Transfer to a wire rack and let cool for at least 15 minutes before unmolding. Serve warm or at room temperature.

Lemon Chocolate Pinwheels

These stunning cookies will have your guests guessing as to what the mystery ingredients are that give the pinwheels their exotic flavor!

1¼ hrs   10–12 mins

MAKES 40

INGREDIENTS

¾ cup butter, softened

1⅓ cups superfine sugar

1 egg, beaten

3 cups all-purpose flour

1 oz/25 g dark chocolate, melted and cooled slightly

grated zest of 1 lemon

1 Grease and flour several cookie sheets.

2 In a large mixing bowl, cream together the butter and sugar until light and fluffy.

3 Gradually add the beaten egg to the creamed mixture, beating well after each addition.

4 Strain the flour into the creamed mixture and mix thoroughly until a soft dough forms.

5 Transfer half of the dough to another bowl and then beat in the cooled melted chocolate.

6 Stir the grated lemon zest into the other half of the plain dough.

7 On a lightly floured surface, roll out the 2 pieces of dough to form rectangles of the same size.

8 Lay the lemon dough on top of the chocolate dough. Roll up the dough tightly into a sausage shape, using a sheet of baking parchment to guide you. Let the dough chill in the refrigerator.

9 Cut the roll into about 40 slices, place them on the cookie sheets and bake in a preheated oven, 375°F/190°C, for 10–12 minutes or until lightly golden. Transfer the pinwheels to a wire rack and let cool completely before serving.

COOK'S TIP

To make rolling out easier, place each piece of dough between 2 sheets of baking parchment.

White Chocolate Cookies

These chunky cookies melt in the mouth and the white chocolate gives them a deliciously rich flavor.

40 mins

10–12 mins

MAKES 24

INGREDIENTS

½ cup butter, softened

¾ cup soft brown sugar

1 egg, beaten

1¾ cups self-rising flour

pinch of salt

4½ oz/125 g white chocolate, coarsely chopped

⅓ cup chopped brazil nuts

1 Lightly grease several cookie sheets.

2 In a large mixing bowl, cream together the butter and sugar until light and fluffy.

3 Gradually add the beaten egg to the creamed mixture, beating well after each addition.

4 Strain the flour and salt into the creamed mixture and blend well.

5 Stir in the white chocolate chunks and brazil nuts.

6 Place heaped teaspoons of the white chocolate mixture on to the prepared cookie sheets. Do not put more than 6 teaspoons of the mixture on to each cookie sheet, as the cookies will spread considerably during cooking.

7 Bake in a preheated oven, 375°F/190°C, for 10–12 minutes or until just golden brown.

8 Transfer the cookies to wire racks and let stand until completely cold before serving.

VARIATION

Use dark or light chocolate instead of white chocolate, if you prefer.

Millionaire's Shortbread

These rich squares of shortbread are topped with caramel and finished with chocolate to make a very special treat!

55 mins   30 mins

MAKES 4

INGREDIENTS

1½ cups all-purpose flour

½ cup butter, cut into small pieces

⅓ cup soft brown sugar, strained

TOPPING

4 tbsp butter

⅓ cup soft brown sugar

1¾ cups condensed milk

5½ oz/150 g milk chocolate

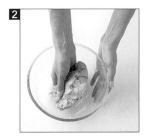

1 Grease a 9 inch/23 cm square cake pan.

2 Strain the flour into a mixing bowl and rub in the butter with your fingers until the mixture resembles fine breadcrumbs. Add the sugar and mix to form a firm dough.

3 Press the dough into the bottom of the prepared pan and prick the bottom with a fork.

4 Bake in a preheated oven, 375°F/190°C, for 20 minutes until lightly golden. Let cool in the pan.

COOK'S TIP

Ensure the caramel layer is completely cool and set before coating it with the melted chocolate, otherwise they will mix together.

5 To make the topping, place the butter, sugar, and condensed milk in a non-stick pan and cook over a gentle heat, stirring constantly, until the mixture comes to a boil.

6 Reduce the heat and cook for 4–5 minutes until the caramel is pale golden and thick and is coming away from the sides of the pan. Pour the topping over the shortbread layer and let cool.

7 When the caramel topping is firm, melt the milk chocolate in a heatproof bowl set over a pan of simmering water. Spread the melted chocolate over the topping, allow to set in a cool place, then cut the shortbread into squares or fingers to serve.

Chocolate Chip Brownies

Choose a good quality chocolate for these chocolate chip brownies to give them a rich flavor that is not too sweet.

45 mins   30–35 mins

MAKES 12

INGREDIENTS

5½ oz/150 g dark chocolate, broken into pieces

1 cup butter, softened

2 cups self-rising flour

½ cup superfine sugar

4 eggs, beaten

½ cup chopped pistachio nuts

3½ oz/100 g white chocolate, coarsely chopped

confectioners' sugar, for dusting

1 Lightly grease a 9 inch/23 cm baking pan and line with greaseproof paper.

2 Melt the dark chocolate and butter in a heatproof bowl set over a pan of simmering water. Let cool slightly.

3 Strain the flour into a separate mixing bowl and stir in the superfine sugar.

4 Stir the eggs into the melted chocolate mixture, then pour this mixture into the flour and sugar mixture, beating well. Stir in

the pistachio nuts and white chocolate, then pour the mixture into the pan, spreading it evenly into the corners.

5 Bake in a preheated oven, 350°/180°C, for 30–35 minutes until firm to the

touch. Let cool in the pan for 20 minutes, then turn out on to a wire rack.

6 Dust the brownie with confectioners' sugar, allow to cool completely, then cut into 12 pieces.

COOK'S TIP

The brownie won't be completely firm in the middle when it is removed from the oven, but it will set when it has cooled.

Chocolate Biscotti

These dry cookies are delicious served with black coffee after your evening meal.

🍰 55 mins 🕐 30–40 mins

MAKES 16

INGREDIENTS

1 egg

⅓ cup superfine sugar

1 tsp vanilla extract

1 cup all-purpose flour

½ tsp baking powder

1 tsp ground cinnamon

1¾ oz/50 g dark chocolate, coarsely chopped

½ cup toasted slivered almonds

⅓ cup pine nuts

1 Lightly grease a large cookie sheet.

2 Whisk the egg, sugar, and vanilla extract in a mixing bowl with an electric mixer until thick and pale—ribbons of mixture should trail from the whisk as you lift it.

3 Strain the flour, baking powder, and cinnamon into a separate bowl, then strain into the egg mixture and fold in gently. Stir in the chocolate, almonds, and pine nuts.

4 Turn on to a lightly floured counter and shape into a flat log, 9 inches/ 23 cm long and ¾ inch/1.5 cm wide. Transfer to the cookie sheet.

5 Bake in a preheated oven, 350°F/ 180°C, for 20–25 minutes or until golden. Remove from the oven and let cool for 5 minutes or until firm.

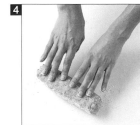

6 Transfer the log to a cutting board. Using a serrated bread knife, cut the log on the diagonal into slices about ½ inch/1 cm thick and arrange them on the cookie sheet. Cook for 10–15 minutes, turning halfway through the cooking time.

7 Let cool for about 5 minutes, then transfer to a wire rack to cool completely.

Chocolate Macaroons

Classic gooey macaroons are always a favorite for coffee-time: they are made even better by the addition of rich dark chocolate.

🏠 🏠 🏠

🍲 1 hr   🕐 25 mins

MAKES 18

INGREDIENTS

2¾ oz/75 g dark chocolate, broken into pieces

2 egg whites

pinch of salt

1 cup superfine sugar

1¼ cups ground almonds

shredded coconut, for sprinkling (optional)

1 Grease 2 cookie sheets and line with baking parchment or rice paper.

2 Melt the dark chocolate in a small heatproof bowl set over a pan of simmering water. Leave to cool slightly.

3 In a mixing bowl, whisk the egg whites with the salt until they form soft peaks.

4 Gradually whisk the superfine sugar into the egg whites, then fold in the almonds and cooled melted chocolate.

5 Place heaped teaspoons of the mixture spaced well apart on the prepared cookie sheets and spread into circles about 2½ inches/6 cm across. Sprinkle with shredded coconut, if using.

6 Bake in a preheated oven, 300°F/ 150°C, for about 25 minutes or until they are firm.

7 Let cool before carefully lifting from the cookie sheets. Transfer the macaroons to a wire rack and let cool completely before serving.

VARIATION
For a traditional finish, top each macaroon with half a candied cherry before baking.

Florentines

These luxury cookies will be popular at any time of the year, but they make a particularly wonderful treat at Christmas.

50 mins 　 10 mins

MAKES 10

INGREDIENTS

4 tbsp butter

¼ cup superfine sugar

scant ¼ cup all-purpose flour, strained

⅓ cup almonds, chopped

⅓ cup chopped candied peel

¼ cup raisins, chopped

2 tbsp chopped candied cherries

finely grated zest of ½ lemon

4½ oz/125 g dark chocolate, melted

1 Line 2 large cookie sheets with baking parchment.

2 Heat the butter and superfine sugar in a small pan until the butter has just melted and the sugar dissolved. Remove the pan from the heat.

3 Stir in the flour and mix well. Stir in the chopped almonds, mixed peel, raisins, cherries, and lemon zest. Place teaspoonfuls of the mixture well apart on the cookie sheets.

4 Bake in a preheated oven, 350°F/ 180°C, for 10 minutes or until they are lightly golden.

5 As soon as the florentines are removed from the oven, press the edges into neat shapes while still on the cookie sheets, using a cookie cutter. Let cool on the cookie sheets until firm, then transfer to a wire rack to cool completely.

6 Spread the melted chocolate over the smooth side of each florentine. As the

chocolate begins to set, mark wavy lines in it with a fork. Let the florentines set, chocolate side up.

VARIATION
Replace the dark chocolate with white chocolate or, for a dramatic effect, cover half of the florentines in dark chocolate and half in white.

Chocolate Fingers

Tasty bread fingers flavored with sherry and coated with chocolate and sugar are surprisingly tasty and very popular.

 15 mins   30 mins

MAKES 24

INGREDIENTS

4 eggs, lightly beaten

2½ cups milk

5 tbsp sherry

8 slices of day-old white bread,
  ½ inch/1 cm thick

4 tbsp sunflower oil

generous ½ cup superfine sugar

8 oz/225 g dark chocolate, grated

vanilla ice cream, to serve (optional)

1 Pour the beaten eggs, milk, and sherry into a shallow dish and beat lightly to mix. Cut each slice of bread lengthwise into three fingers. Soak the bread fingers in the egg mixture until soft, then drain on paper towels.

2 Heat the oil in a large, heavy-based skillet. Carefully add the bread fingers to the pan, in batches, and cook over a medium heat for 12 minutes on each side, until golden. Using tongs, transfer the fingers to paper towels to drain.

3 When all the fingers are cooked and thoroughly drained, roll them first in the sugar and then in the grated chocolate. Pile them on a warmed serving plate and serve immediately, with ice cream if desired.

Meringue Fingers

These little coffee-time treats can be stored in an airtight container for several days—if they haven't all been eaten!

15 mins, plus 1 hr setting/cooling

65–70 mins

MAKES 30

INGREDIENTS

1 egg white

¼ cup superfine sugar

1½ tsp unsweetened cocoa

5 oz/140 g dark chocolate, broken into pieces

1 Line a cookie sheet with baking parchment. Whisk the egg white until it forms soft peaks. Whisk in half the sugar and continue whisking until stiff and glossy. Fold in the remaining sugar and the cocoa.

2 Preheat the oven to 250°F/120°C. Spoon the mixture into a pastry bag fitted with a ½ inch/1 cm/ round tip. Pipe fingers about 3 inches/7.5 cm long on the prepared cookie sheet, spacing them at least 1 inch/2.5 cm apart. Bake in the preheated oven for 1 hour, until completely dry. Remove from the oven and transfer to a wire rack to cool.

3 Put the chocolate in the top of a double boiler or in a heatproof bowl set over a pan of barely simmering water. Heat, stirring constantly, until the chocolate has melted and the mixture is smooth. Remove from the heat. Cool slightly, then dip the meringue fingers into the mixture, one at a time, to half-coat them. You can either coat one end completely, leaving the other plain, or dip the fingers at an angle so half the length is coated. Place the fingers on baking parchment to set.

Chestnut Cream Squares

These little cakes look wonderful, and are well worth the preparation time. The magical combination of flavors is out of this world.

45 mins, plus
11–11½ hrs
freezing/standing

55–60 mins

MAKES 30

INGREDIENTS

BOTTOM LAYER

3 oz/85 g dark chocolate, broken into pieces

6 tbsp sweet butter

4 tbsp confectioners' sugar

4 eggs, separated

½ cup superfine sugar

⅔ cup all-purpose flour

5 tbsp Morello cherry jelly

3 tbsp kirsch

DARK LAYER

3½ oz/100 g dark chocolate

generous ⅓ cup milk

4 tsp superfine sugar

¼ tsp vanilla extract

1 egg yolk

1 tbsp cornstarch

generous 2 tbsp confectioners' sugar

1¼ cups heavy cream

WHITE LAYER

2 cups heavy cream

1 tbsp confectioners' sugar

CHESTNUT LAYER

1½ cups chestnut paste

4 tsp dark rum

2 tsp superfine sugar

30 cherries, to decorate

1 Line a 12 x 10 x 2 inch/30 x 25 x 5 cm rectangular cake pan with baking parchment. Melt the chocolate in a heatproof bowl set over a pan of barely simmering water, then cool slightly. Mix the butter, confectioners' sugar, and chocolate together. Beat in the egg yolks, 1 at a time.

2 Preheat the oven to 350°F/180°C. Whisk the egg whites in a separate bowl until soft peaks form, whisk the superfine sugar in until stiff, then fold into the chocolate mixture. Strain the flour then fold into the mixture. Spoon into the pan and smooth the surface. Bake for 30 minutes.

3 Remove the pan from the oven, let cool, then cut around the edges with a knife. Invert onto a flat surface. Wash and dry the cake pan and line with baking parchment. Return the bottom layer to the tin. Bring the jelly to a boil in a small pan, strain, and cool. Sprinkle the Kirsch over the bottom layer, then spread with the jelly.

4 Melt the chocolate in a heatproof bowl set over a pan of barely simmering water. Remove from the heat. Pot the milk, superfine sugar, and vanilla into a pan and bring to a boil. Remove from the heat. Mix the egg yolk, cornstarch, and 2 tablespoons of the hot milk in a bowl, add to the pan of milk, and return to a medium heat. Cook, stirring, for 3–5 minutes, until thickened. Stir in the confectioners' sugar and melted chocolate. Remove from the heat. Beat the cream until thick, then stir it into the chocolate mixture. Spread over the layer in the pan, cover and freeze for 1½–2 hours.

5 When the dark layer is half-frozen, make the white layer. Whisk the cream with the sugar until thick, then spread over the dark layer. Cover and freeze for 8 hours.

6 Remove the cake from the pan, with the white layer uppermost. Beat together the chestnut paste, rum, and sugar. Press through a garlic press and spread over the white layer. Cut the cake into 30 squares and top each with a cherry. Refrigerate for 30 minutes before serving.

Mocha Rolls

Dark and white chocolate are combined with coffee and Kahlúa liqueur in these attractive sponge-cake rolls.

35 mins, plus 1½–2¼ hrs chilling/setting

50–55 mins

MAKES 16

INGREDIENTS

⅔ cup cold, strong, black coffee

1 tbsp gelatin

1 tsp Kahlúa or other coffee-flavored liqueur

1 cup ricotta cheese

10 oz/280 g white chocolate, broken into pieces

1 oz/25 g dark chocolate

SPONGE CAKE

3 eggs, plus 1 egg white

scant ½ cup superfine sugar

generous ¾ cup all-purpose flour

2 tbsp butter, melted

1 For the sponge cake, line the bottom of a 12 x 8 x 1½ inch/30 x 20 x 4 cm cake pan with baking parchment. Put the eggs, egg white, and sugar in a heatproof bowl over a pan of barely simmering water. Whisk until pale and thickened.

2 Preheat the oven to 350°F/180°C. Remove the mixture from the heat, then whisk until cool. Strain the flour over the mixture and fold in. Fold in the melted butter, a little at a time. Pour the mixture into the prepared pan and bake for 25–30 minutes, until the cake is firm to the touch and has shrunk slightly from the sides of the tin. Remove from the oven and transfer to a wire rack, still standing on the baking parchment, to cool.

3 Meanwhile, put 2 tablespoons of the coffee into a small heatproof bowl and sprinkle the gelatin on the surface. Let

it soften for 2 minutes, then set the bowl over a pan of barely simmering water and stir until the gelatin has dissolved. Remove from the heat. Put the remaining coffee, liqueur and ricotta in a food processor or blender and process until smooth. Add the gelatin mixture in a single stream and process briefly. Scrape the mixture into a bowl, cover with plastic wrap and chill in the refrigerator for 1–1½ hours, until set.

4 Carefully peel the baking parchment from the cooled cake. Using a knife, cut horizontally through the cake. Trim off any dried edges. Cut each piece of cake in half lengthwise. Place each piece between 2 sheets of baking parchment and roll lightly with a rolling pin to make it more flexible.

5 Spread the cut side of each cake piece with an even ¼ inch/5 mm thick layer of the coffee filling, leaving a ¼ inch/

5 mm margin all round. Cut each strip across into four pieces, giving a total of 16 pieces. Roll up each piece from the short end, like a jelly roll.

6 Put the white chocolate in a heatproof bowl over a pan of barely simmering water. Stir until melted. Remove from the heat. Place 1 roll, seam-side down, on a metal spatula and hold it over the bowl of melted chocolate. Spoon the chocolate over the roll to coat. Transfer the roll to a sheet of baking parchment and repeat with the remaining rolls.

7 Put the dark chocolate in a heatproof bowl over a pan of barely simmering water. Stir until melted. Remove from the heat. Spoon it into a waxed paper pastry bag fitted with a small, plain tip and pipe zig-zags along the rolls. Allow to set completely before serving.

Ladies' Kisses

These tiny cookies sandwiched together with melted chocolate are lovely at coffee-time or served as petits fours after dinner.

30 mins, plus 2–2½ hrs chilling/cooling

30–35 mins

SERVES 20

INGREDIENTS

scant ⅔ cup sweet butter

generous ½ cup superfine sugar

1 egg yolk

1 cup ground almonds

1¼ cups all-purpose flour

2 oz/55 g dark chocolate, broken into pieces

2 tbsp confectioners' sugar, to dust

2 tbsp unsweetened cocoa, to dust

1 Line 3 cookie sheets with baking parchment, or use 3 non-stick sheets. Cream the butter and sugar together until pale and fluffy. Beat in the egg yolk, then beat in the almonds and flour. Continue beating until thoroughly mixed. Shape the dough into a ball, wrap in plastic wrap and chill in the refrigerator for 1½–2 hours.

2 Preheat the oven to 325°F/160°C. Unwrap the dough, break off walnut-size pieces and roll them into balls between the palms of your hands. Place the dough balls on the prepared cookie sheets, allowing space for them to spread during cooking. You may need to cook the cookies in batches. Bake in the preheated oven for 20–25 minutes, until golden. Carefully transfer the cookies, still on the baking parchment if using, to wire racks to cool.

3 Put the chocolate in the top of a double boiler or in a heatproof bowl set over a pan of barely simmering water.

Melt over a low heat, stirring constantly. Remove from the heat. Remove the cookies from the baking parchment, if using. Spread the melted chocolate on the flat sides and sandwich them together in pairs. Return to the wire racks to cool. Dust with a mixture of confectioners' sugar and cocoa.

Chocolate Pistachio Cookies

These crisp Italian biscotti are made with fine cornmeal as well as flour, to give them an interesting texture.

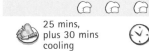

25 mins, plus 30 mins cooling 🕐 35 mins

SERVES 24

I N G R E D I E N T S

2 tbsp sweet butter, plus extra for greasing

6 oz/175 g dark chocolate, broken into pieces

2½ cups self-rising flour, plus extra for dusting

1½ tsp baking powder

scant ½ cup superfine sugar

½ cup cornmeal

finely grated zest of 1 lemon

2 tsp amaretto liqueur

1 egg, lightly beaten

¾ cup coarsely chopped pistachio nuts

2 tbsp confectioners' sugar, to dust

1 Lightly grease a cookie sheet with butter. Put the chocolate and 2 tablespoons of butter in the top of a double boiler or in a heatproof bowl set over a pan of barely simmering water. Stir over a low heat until melted and smooth. Remove from the heat and cool slightly.

2 Strain the flour and baking powder into a bowl and mix in the superfine sugar, cornmeal, lemon zest, liqueur, egg, and pistachios. Stir in the chocolate mixture and mix to a soft dough.

3 Preheat the oven to 325°F/160°C. Lightly dust your hands with flour, divide the dough in half and shape each piece into a 11 inch/28 cm long cylinder. Transfer the cylinders to the prepared cookie sheet and flatten, with the palm of your hand, to about 2 cm/¾ inch thick.

Bake in the preheated oven for about 20 minutes, until firm to the touch.

4 Remove the cookie sheet from the oven and allow the cooked pieces to cool. When cool, put the cooked pieces onto a cutting board and slice them diagonally into thin cookies. Return them to the cookie sheet and bake for a further 10 minutes, until crisp. Remove from the oven, and transfer to a wire rack to cool. Dust lightly with confectioners' sugar.

Candies & Drinks

There is nothing quite as nice as home-made chocolates and candies—they leave the average box of chocolates in the shade! You'll find recipes in this chapter to suit everybody's taste. Wonderful, rich, melt-in-the-mouth Italian Chocolate Truffles, Chocolate Marzipans, Nutty

Chocolate Clusters, and rich Chocolate Liqueurs—they're all here. There is even some Easy Chocolate Fudge, so there is no need to fiddle about with candy thermometers.

Looking for something to wash it all down? We have included delightfully cool summer chocolate drinks and for warmth and comfort on winter nights hot drinks that will simply put instant hot chocolate to shame. Enjoy!

Rocky Road Bites

Young children will love these chewy bites. You can vary the ingredients and use different nuts and dried fruit according to taste.

40 mins   5 mins

MAKES 18

INGREDIENTS

FILLING

4½ oz/125 g light chocolate

2½ oz/50 g mini multi-colored marshmallows

¼ cup chopped walnuts

1 oz/25 g no-soak dried apricots, chopped

1 Line a cookie sheet with baking parchment and set aside.

2 Break the milk chocolate into small pieces and place in a large mixing bowl. Set the bowl over a pan of simmering water and stir until the chocolate has melted.

3 Stir in the marshmallows, walnuts, and apricots, and toss in the melted chocolate until well covered.

VARIATION
Light, fluffy marshmallows are available in white or pastel colors. If you cannot find mini marshmallows, use large ones and snip them into smaller pieces with kitchen scissors before mixing them into the melted chocolate in Step 3.

4 Place heaping teaspoons of the mixture onto the prepared cookie sheet.

5 Let the candies chill in the refrigerator until set.

6 Once set, carefully remove the candies from the baking parchment.

7 The chewy bites can be placed in paper candy cases to serve, if desired.

Easy Chocolate Fudge

This is the easiest fudge to make—for a really rich flavor, use a good dark chocolate with a high cocoa content, ideally at least 70 percent.

1 hr 10 mins | 5 mins

MAKES 25 PIECES

INGREDIENTS

1 lb 2 oz/500 g dark chocolate

75 g/2¾ oz/⅓ cup sweet butter

1¾ cups condensed milk

½ tsp vanilla extract

1 Lightly grease an 8 inch/20 cm square cake pan.

2 Break the chocolate into pieces and place in a large pan with the butter and condensed milk.

3 Heat gently, stirring until the chocolate and butter melts and the mixture is smooth. Do not allow to boil.

4 Remove from the heat. Beat in the vanilla extract, then beat the mixture for a few minutes until thickened. Pour it into the prepared pan and level the top.

5 Chill the mixture in the refrigerator until firm.

6 Tip the fudge out on to a chopping board and cut into squares to serve.

COOK'S TIP
Store the fudge in an airtight container in a cool, dry place for up to 1 month. Do not freeze.

Fruit & Nut Fudge

Chocolate, nuts, and dried fruit—the perfect combination—are all found in this simple-to-make fudge.

⏱ 1 hr 10 mins   🕐 5 mins

MAKES 25 PIECES

INGREDIENTS

9 oz/250 g dark chocolate

2 tbsp butter

4 tbsp evaporated milk

3 cups confectioners' sugar, strained

½ cup coarsely chopped hazelnuts

⅓ cup golden raisins

1 Lightly grease an 8 inch/20 cm square cake pan.

2 Break the chocolate into pieces and place it in a bowl with the butter and evaporated milk. Set the bowl over a pan of gently simmering water and stir until the chocolate and butter have melted and the ingredients are well combined.

3 Remove the bowl from the heat and gradually beat in the confectioners' sugar. Stir the hazelnuts and golden raisins into the mixture. Press the fudge into the prepared pan and level the top. Chill until firm.

4 Tip the fudge out on to a chopping board and cut into squares. Chill in the refrigerator until required.

VARIATION

Vary the nuts used in this recipe; try making the fudge with almonds, brazil nuts, walnuts, or pecan nuts.

Nutty Chocolate Clusters

Nuts and crisp cookies encased in chocolate make these candies rich, chocolatey, and quite irresistible!

1½ hrs   5 mins

MAKES 30

INGREDIENTS

6 oz/175 g white chocolate

3½ oz/100 g graham crackers

⅔ cup chopped macadamia nuts or brazil nuts

1 oz/25 g preserved ginger, chopped (optional)

6 oz/175 g dark chocolate

1 Line a cookie sheet with a sheet of baking parchment. Break the white chocolate into small pieces and place in a large mixing bowl set over a pan of gently simmering water; stir until melted.

2 Break the graham crackers into small pieces. Stir the crackers into the melted chocolate with the chopped nuts and preserved ginger, if using.

3 Place heaped teaspoons of the mixture on to the prepared cookie sheet.

4 Chill the mixture until set, then carefully remove from the baking parchment.

COOK'S TIP

Macadamia and brazil nuts are both rich and high in fat, which makes them particularly popular for confectionery, but other nuts can be used, if preferred.

5 Melt the dark chocolate and let it cool slightly. Dip the clusters into the melted chocolate, allowing the excess to drip back into the bowl. Return the clusters to the cookie sheet and chill in the refrigerator until set.

Chocolate Cherries

These cherry and marzipan candies are easy to make. Serve as petits fours at the end of a meal or as an indulgent nibble at any time of day.

1½ hrs | 2 mins

MAKES 24

INGREDIENTS

12 candied cherries

2 tbsp rum or brandy

9 oz/250 g marzipan

5½ oz/125 g dark chocolate

extra light, dark, or white chocolate, to decorate (optional)

1 Line a cookie sheet with a sheet of baking parchment.

2 Cut the cherries in half and place in a small bowl. Add the rum or brandy and stir to coat. Let the cherries soak for at least 1 hour, stirring occasionally.

3 Divide the marzipan into 24 pieces and roll each piece into a ball. Press half a cherry into the top of each marzipan ball.

4 Break the chocolate into pieces, place in a bowl and set over a pan of hot water. Stir until all the chocolate has melted.

5 Dip each candy into the melted chocolate using a cocktail stick,

VARIATION

Flatten the marzipan and use it to mold around the cherries to cover them, then dip in the chocolate as above.

allowing the excess to drip back into the bowl. Place the coated cherries on the baking parchment and chill until set.

6 If liked, melt a little extra chocolate and drizzle it over the top of the coated cherries. Allow to set.

Chocolate Marzipans

These delightful little morsels make the perfect gift, if you can resist eating them all yourself!

50 mins

5 mins

MAKES 30

INGREDIENTS

1 lb/450 g marzipan

⅓ cup very finely chopped candied cherries

1 oz/25 g preserved ginger, very finely chopped

1¾ oz/50 g no-soak dried apricots, very finely chopped

12 oz/350 g dark chocolate

1 oz/25 g white chocolate

confectioners' sugar, to dust

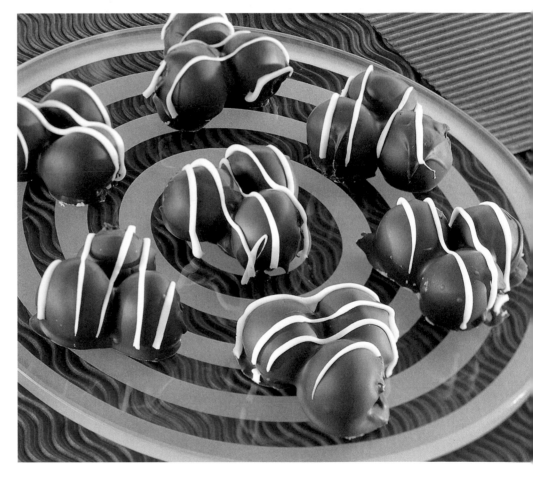

1 Line a cookie sheet with baking parchment. Divide the marzipan into 3 balls and knead each ball to soften it.

2 Work the candied cherries into one portion of the marzipan by kneading on a counter lightly dusted with confectioners' sugar.

3 Do the same with the preserved ginger and another portion of marzipan, and then the apricots and the third portion of marzipan.

4 Form each flavored portion of marzipan into small balls, keeping the different flavors separate.

5 Break the dark chocolate into pieces, place in a bowl and set over a pan of hot water. Stir until melted. Dip one of each flavored ball of marzipan into the chocolate by spiking each one with a toothpick, allowing the excess chocolate to drip back into the bowl.

6 Place the balls in clusters of the three flavors on the cookie sheet. Repeat with the remaining balls. Chill until set.

7 Melt the white chocolate and drizzle a little over the tops of each cluster of marzipan balls. Chill until hardened, then remove from the baking parchment and dust with sugar to serve.

VARIATION
Coat the marzipan balls in white or light chocolate and drizzle with dark chocolate, if you prefer.

Chocolate Liqueurs

These tasty chocolate cups are filled with a delicious liqueur-flavored filling. Use your favorite liqueur to flavor the cream.

🍰 1 hr 🕐 5 mins

MAKES 40

INGREDIENTS

3½ oz/100 g dark chocolate

about 5 candied cherries, halved

about 10 hazelnuts or macadamia nuts

⅔ cup heavy cream

2 tbsp confectioners' sugar

4 tbsp liqueur

TO FINISH

1¾ oz/50 g dark chocolate, melted

a little white chocolate, melted, or white chocolate curls (see page 15), or extra nuts and cherries

1 Line a cookie sheet with a sheet of baking parchment. Break the dark chocolate into pieces, place in a bowl and set over a pan of hot water. Stir until melted. Spoon the chocolate into 20 paper candy cases, spreading up the sides with a small spoon or brush. Place upside down on the cookie sheet and allow to set.

2 Carefully peel away the paper cases. Place a cherry or nut in each cup.

3 To make the filling, place the heavy cream in a mixing bowl and strain the confectioners' sugar on top. Whisk the

cream until it is just holding its shape, then whisk in the liqueur.

4 Place the cream in a pastry bag fitted with a ½ inch/1 cm plain tip and pipe a little into each chocolate case. Let chill for 20 minutes.

5 To finish, spoon the melted dark chocolate over the cream to cover it and pipe the melted white chocolate on top, swirling it into the dark chocolate with a toothpick. Let the candies harden. Alternatively, cover the cream with the melted dark chocolate and decorate with white chocolate curls before setting. Or place a small piece of nut or cherry on top of the cream, then cover with dark chocolate.

COOK'S TIP

Candy cases can vary in size. Use the smallest you can find for this recipe.

Chocolate Mascarpone Cups

Mascarpone—the velvety smooth Italian cheese—makes a rich, creamy filling for these tasty chocolates.

40 mins · 5 mins

MAKES 20

INGREDIENTS

3½ oz/100 g dark chocolate

FILLING

3½ oz/100 g light or dark chocolate

¼ tsp vanilla extract

7 oz/200 g mascarpone cheese

unsweetened cocoa, to dust

1 Line a cookie sheet with a sheet of baking parchment. Break the dark chocolate into pieces, place in a bowl and set over a pan of hot water. Stir until melted. Spoon the chocolate into 20 paper candy cases, spreading up the sides with a small spoon or brush. Place upside down on the cookie sheet and allow to set.

2 When set, carefully peel away the paper cases.

3 To make the filling, melt the dark or milk chocolate. Place the mascarpone cheese in a bowl and beat in the vanilla extract and melted chocolate until well combined. Let the mixture chill, beating occasionally until firm enough to pipe.

4 Place the mascarpone filling in a pastry bag fitted with a star tip and pipe the mixture into the cups. Decorate with a dusting of cocoa.

VARIATION

Mascarpone is a rich Italian soft cheese made from fresh cream, so it has a high fat content. Its delicate flavor blends well with chocolate.

Mini Chocolate Cones

These unusual cone-shaped mint-cream chocolates make a change from the more usual cup shape, and are perfect for an after-dinner chocolate.

🖐 40 mins 🕐 5 mins

MAKES 10

INGREDIENTS

2¾ oz/75 g dark chocolate

generous ⅓ cup heavy cream

1 tbsp confectioners' sugar

1 tbsp crème de menthe

chocolate coffee beans, to decorate (optional)

1 Cut 10 circles, 3 inches/7.5 cm across, out of baking parchment. Shape each circle into a cone shape and secure with sticky tape.

2 Break the chocolate into pieces, place in a bowl and set over a pan of hot water. Stir until melted. Using a small brush, coat the inside of each cone with the melted chocolate.

3 Brush a second layer of chocolate on the inside of the cones and chill until set. Carefully peel away the paper.

4 Place the heavy cream, confectioners' sugar and crème de menthe in a mixing bowl and whip until just holding

COOK'S TIP

The chocolate cones can be made in advance and kept in the refrigerator for up to 1 week. Do not fill them more than 2 hours before you are going to serve them.

its shape. Place in a pastry bag fitted with a star tip and pipe the mixture into the chocolate cones.

5 Decorate the cones with chocolate coffee beans (if using) and chill in the refrigerator until required.

Collettes

A creamy, orange-flavored chocolate filling in white chocolate cups makes a wonderful treat.

🕐 40 mins   ⏱ 5 mins

MAKES 20

INGREDIENTS

3½ oz/100 g white chocolate

FILLING

5½ oz/150 g orange-flavored dark chocolate

⅔ cup heavy cream

2 tbsp confectioners' sugar

1 Line a cookie sheet with baking parchment. Break the white chocolate into pieces, place in a bowl and set over a pan of hot water. Stir until melted. Spoon the melted chocolate into 20 paper candy cases, spreading up the sides with a small spoon or brush. Place upside down on the prepared cookie sheet and allow to set.

2 When set, carefully peel away the paper cases.

3 To make the filling, melt the orange-flavored chocolate and place in a mixing bowl with the heavy cream and the confectioners' sugar. Beat until smooth. Chill until the mixture becomes firm enough to pipe, stirring occasionally.

4 Place the filling in a pastry bag fitted with a star tip and pipe a little into each candy case. Chill until required.

COOK'S TIP
If they do not hold their shape well, use 2 cases to make a double thickness mold. Foil cases are firmer, so use these if you can find them.

Mini Chocolate Tartlets

Small tartlet shells are filled with a rich chocolate cream to serve as petits fours. Use individual tartlet pans to make the shells.

1½ hrs | 15 mins

SERVES 18

INGREDIENTS

1½ cups all-purpose flour

⅓ cup butter

1 tbsp superfine sugar

about 1 tbsp water

FILLING

3½ oz/100 g full-fat soft cheese

2 tbsp superfine sugar

1 small egg, lightly beaten

1¾ oz/50 g dark chocolate

TO DECORATE

generous ⅓ cup heavy cream

dark chocolate curls (see page 15)

unsweetened cocoa, to dust

1 Strain the flour into a mixing bowl. Cut the butter into small pieces and rub in with your fingertips until the mixture resembles fine breadcrumbs. Stir in the sugar. Add enough water to mix to a soft dough, then cover with plastic wrap and chill for 15 minutes.

2 Roll out the dough on a lightly floured counter and use to line 18 mini tartlet pans or mini muffin pans. Prick the tartlet shells with a toothpick.

3 Beat together the full-fat soft cheese and the sugar. Beat in the egg. Melt the chocolate and beat it into the mixture. Spoon into the tartlet shells and bake in a preheated oven, 375°F/190°C, for 15 minutes until the dough is crisp and the filling set. Place the pans on a wire rack to cool completely.

4 Chill the tartlets. Whip the cream until it is just holding its shape. Place in a pastry bag fitted with a star tip. Pipe rosettes of cream on top of the tartlets. Decorate with chocolate curls and dust with cocoa.

COOK'S TIP

The tartlets can be made up to 3 days ahead. Decorate on the day of serving, preferably no more than 4 hours in advance.

Mini Florentines

Serve these cookies at the end of a meal with coffee, or arrange in a shallow presentation box for an attractive gift.

30 mins   10–12 mins

MAKES 40

INGREDIENTS

⅓ cup butter

⅓ cup superfine sugar

2 tbsp golden raisins or raisins

2 tbsp chopped candied cherries

2 tbsp chopped candied ginger

1 oz/25 g sunflower seeds

¾ cup slivered almonds

2 tbsp heavy cream

6 oz/175 g dark or light chocolate

1 Grease and flour 2 cookie sheets or line with baking parchment.

2 Place the butter in a small pan and heat gently until melted. Add the sugar, stir until dissolved, then bring the mixture to a boil. Remove from the heat and stir in the golden raisins or raisins, cherries, ginger, sunflower seeds, and almonds. Mix well, then beat in the cream.

3 Place small teaspoons of the fruit and nut mixture on to the prepared cookie sheet, allowing plenty of space for the mixture to spread. Bake in a preheated oven, at 350°F/180°C, for 10–12 minutes or until light golden in color.

4 Remove from the oven and, whilst still hot, use a circular cookie cutter to pull in the edges to form perfect circles. Let cool and go crisp before removing from the cookie sheet.

5 Break the chocolate into pieces, place in a bowl over a pan of hot water and stir until melted. Spread most of the chocolate on to a sheet of baking parchment. When the chocolate is on the point of setting, place the cookies flat-side down on the chocolate and allow it to harden completely.

6 Cut around the florentines and remove from the baking parchment. Spread a little more chocolate on the coated side of the florentines and use a fork to mark waves in the chocolate. Allow to set. Arrange the florentines on a plate (or in a presentation box for a gift) with alternate sides facing upward. Keep cool.

Rum Truffles

Truffles are always popular. They make a fabulous gift or, served with coffee, they are a perfect end to a meal.

45 mins   5 mins

MAKES 20

INGREDIENTS

5½ oz/125 g dark chocolate

small knob of butter

2 tbsp rum

½ cup shredded coconut

3½ oz/100 g cake crumbs

6 tbsp confectioners' sugar

2 tbsp unsweetened cocoa

1 Break the chocolate into pieces and place in a bowl with the butter. Set the bowl over a pan of gently simmering water, stir until melted and combined.

2 Remove from the heat and beat in the rum. Stir in the shredded coconut, cake crumbs, and two-thirds of the confectioners' sugar. Beat until combined. Add a little extra rum if the mixture is stiff.

3 Roll the mixture into small balls and place them on a sheet of baking parchment. Chill until firm.

4 Strain the remaining confectioners' sugar on to a large plate. Strain the cocoa on to another plate. Roll half of the truffles in the confectioners' sugar until coated and roll the remaining truffles in the cocoa.

5 Place the truffles in paper candy cases and chill in the refrigerator until required.

VARIATION

Make the truffles with white chocolate and replace the rum with coconut liqueur or milk, if you prefer. Roll them in unsweetened cocoa or dip in melted light chocolate.

White Chocolate Truffles

These delicious creamy white truffles will testify to the fact that there is nothing quite as nice as home-made chocolates.

2¾ hrs   5 mins

MAKES 20

INGREDIENTS

2 tbsp unsalted butter

5 tbsp heavy cream

8 oz/225 g good quality Swiss white chocolate

1 tbsp orange-flavored liqueur, optional

TO FINISH

3½ oz/100 g white chocolate

1 Line a jelly roll pan with baking parchment.

2 Place the butter and cream in a small pan and bring slowly to a boil, stirring constantly. Boil for 1 minute, then remove from the heat.

3 Break the chocolate into pieces and add to the cream. Stir until melted, then beat in the liqueur, if using.

4 Pour into the prepared pan and chill for about 2 hours, until firm.

5 Break off pieces of the mixture and roll them into balls. Chill for a further 30 minutes before finishing the truffles.

6 To finish, melt the white chocolate. Dip the balls in the chocolate, allowing the excess to drip back into the bowl. Place on non-stick baking parchment, swirl the chocolate with the prongs of a fork, and let it harden.

7 Drizzle a little melted dark chocolate over the truffles if you wish and let them set.

COOK'S TIP

The truffle mixture needs to be firm but not too hard to roll. If the mixture is too hard, allow it to stand at room temperature for a few minutes to soften slightly. During rolling the mixture will become sticky but will reharden in the refrigerator before coating.

Italian Chocolate Truffles

These tasty morsels are flavored with almonds and chocolate, and are simplicity itself to make. Serve with coffee for the perfect end to a meal.

50 mins 5 mins

SERVES 24

INGREDIENTS

175 g/6 oz dark chocolate

2 tbsp amaretto liqueur or orange-flavored liqueur

3 tbsp unsalted butter

4 tbsp confectioners' sugar

½ cup ground almonds

1¾ oz/50 g grated chocolate

1 Melt the dark chocolate with the liqueur in a bowl set over a pan of hot water, stirring until well combined.

2 Add the butter and stir until it has melted. Stir in the confectioners' sugar and the ground almonds.

3 Let the mixture stand in a cool place until firm enough to roll into 24 balls.

4 Place the grated chocolate on a plate and roll the truffles in the chocolate to coat them.

5 Place the truffles in paper candy cases and chill.

VARIATION

The almond-flavored liqueur gives these truffles an authentic Italian flavor. The original almond liqueur, Amaretto di Saronno, comes from Saronno in Italy.

Candied Citrus Peel

The Mediterranean sun produces some of the most flavorful citrus fruit in the world, and this is a traditional way to preserve the peel.

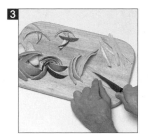

🍽 6½ hrs   🕐 35 mins

MAKES 60

INGREDIENTS

1 large unwaxed, thick-skinned orange

1 large unwaxed, thick-skinned lemon

1 large unwaxed, thick-skinned lime

3 cups superfine sugar

1¼ cups water

4½ oz/125 g best-quality dark chocolate, chopped (optional)

1 Cut the orange into quarters lengthwise and squeeze the juice into a cup to drink, or to use in another recipe. Cut each quarter in half lengthwise to make 8 pieces.

2 Cut the fruit and pith away from the zest. If any of the pith remains on the zest, lay the knife almost flat on the white-side of the zest and gently 'saw' backwards and forwards to slice it off because it will taste bitter.

3 Repeat with the lemon and lime, only cutting the lime into quarters. Cut each piece into 3 or 4 thin strips to make 60–80 strips in total. Place the strips in a pan of water and boil for 30 seconds. Drain thoroughly.

4 Dissolve the sugar in the water in a pan over a medium heat, stirring. Increase the heat and bring to a boil, without stirring. When the syrup becomes clear, turn the heat to its lowest setting.

5 Add the citrus strips, using a wooden spoon to push them in without stirring. Simmer in the syrup for 30 minutes, without stirring. Turn off the heat and set aside for at least 6 hours until completely cool.

6 Line a cookie sheet with foil. Skim off the thin crust on top of the syrup without stirring. Remove the zest strips, one by one, from the syrup, shaking off any excess. Place on the foil to cool.

7 If you want to dip the candied peel in chocolate, melt the chocolate. Working with one piece of candied peel at a time, dip the peel half-way into the chocolate. Return to the foil and allow to set. Store in an airtight container.

Cocochoc Pyramids

This is a traditional favorite. In this recipe, coconut ice is deliciously dipped in melted chocolate to make a two-tone treat.

🕭 35 mins, plus 1½–2½ hrs setting/standing

🕐 15–25 mins

MAKES 12

INGREDIENTS

⅔ cup water

2¼ cups granulated sugar

pinch of cream of tartar

generous 1 cup shredded coconut

1 tbsp heavy cream

a few drops of yellow liquid food coloring

3 oz/85 g dark chocolate, broken into pieces

1 Pour the water into a heavy-based pan, add the sugar, and stir over a low heat until the sugar has dissolved. Stir in a pinch of cream of tartar and bring to a boil. Boil steadily, without stirring, until the temperature reaches 238°F/119°C on a sugar thermometer. If you do not have a sugar thermometer, test the syrup frequently by dropping a small quantity into a bowl of cold water. If the mixture can then be rolled between your finger and thumb to make a soft ball, it is ready.

2 Remove the pan from the heat and beat in the coconut and cream. Continue to beat for 5–10 minutes until the mixture becomes cloudy. Beat in a few drops of yellow food coloring, then allow to cool. When cool enough to handle, take small pieces of the mixture and form them into pyramids. Place on a sheet of baking parchment and allow to harden.

3 Put the chocolate in the top of a double boiler or in a heatproof bowl set over a pan of barely simmering water. Stir over a low heat until melted, then remove from the heat. Dip the bottom of the pyramids into the melted chocolate and allow to set.

Dried Fruit Petits Fours

Irresistibly sweet and unbelievably tempting, these fruity little chocolates can be served with coffee at the end of a dinner party.

20–25 mins, plus 30 mins setting   5 mins

MAKES 30

INGREDIENTS

¾ cup ready-to-eat dried apricots

¾ cup ready-to-eat dried figs

¾ cup ready-to-eat dried dates

¾ cup coarsely chopped walnuts

3 tbsp finely chopped candied orange peel

3 tbsp apricot brandy, plus extra for moistening

confectioners' sugar, to dust

4 oz/115 g light chocolate, broken into pieces

4 tbsp chopped, toasted hazelnuts

1 Chop the dried fruits by hand or in a food processor. Place the chopped fruit in a bowl and add the walnuts, candied peel, and apricot brandy, and mix well.

2 Gather the mixture together and turn out on to a counter lightly dusted with confectioners' sugar. Divide the mixture into 3 pieces and form each piece into a roll about 8 inches/20 cm long, then cut each roll into slices about ¾ inch/2 cm thick. Moisten your hands with a little apricot brandy and roll each slice into a ball between your palms.

3 Place the chocolate in the top of a double boiler or in a heatproof bowl set over a pan of barely simmering water. Stir over a low heat until melted. Remove from the heat and cool slightly. Spear each fruit ball with a fork or skewer and dip it in the melted chocolate to coat it. Place on a sheet of baking parchment and sprinkle over the hazelnuts. Let stand for 30 minutes, or until set.

Double Chocolate Truffles

Marzipan, honey, and dark and light chocolate are combined into little morsels of sheer delight.

 25 mins, plus 1 hr cooling 10 mins

SERVES 60

INGREDIENTS

¾ cup sweet butter

⅔ cup grated marzipan

4 tbsp clear honey

½ tsp vanilla extract

7 oz/200 g dark chocolate, broken into pieces

12 oz/350 g light chocolate, broken into pieces

1 Line 2 cookie sheets with baking parchment. Beat together the butter and marzipan until thoroughly combined and fluffy. Stir in the honey, a little at a time, then stir in the vanilla.

2 Place the dark chocolate and 7 oz/ 200 g of the light chocolate in the top of a double boiler or in a heatproof bowl set over a pan of barely simmering water. Stir over a low heat until melted and smooth. Remove from the heat and let cool slightly.

3 Stir the melted chocolate into the marzipan mixture, then spoon the chocolate and marzipan mixture into a pastry bag fitted with a large, round tip and pipe small balls on to the prepared cookie sheets. Let cool and set.

4 Put the remaining milk chocolate into the top of a double boiler or into a heatproof bowl set over a pan of barely simmering water. Stir over a low heat until melted, then remove from the heat. Dip the truffles, 1 at a time, in the melted chocolate to coat them, then texture some of them by gently tapping them with a fork. Place on the cookie sheets to cool and set.

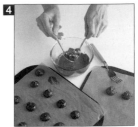

Rum & Chocolate Cups

Use firm foil candy cases, rather than paper ones, to make the chocolate cups, because they offer extra support.

25 mins, plus 1¾ hrs chilling/cooling

10–15 mins

SERVES 12

INGREDIENTS

2 oz/55 g dark chocolate, broken into pieces

12 toasted hazelnuts

FILLING

4 oz/115 g dark chocolate, broken into pieces

1 tbsp dark rum

4 tbsp mascarpone cheese

1 To make the chocolate cups, place the chocolate in the top of a double boiler or in a heatproof bowl set over a pan of barely simmering water. Stir over a low heat until the chocolate is just melted but not too runny, then remove from the heat. Spoon about ½ teaspoon of melted chocolate into a foil candy case and brush it over the bottom and up the sides. Coat 11 more foil cases in the same way and allow to set for 30 minutes. Chill in the refrigerator for 15 minutes. If necessary, reheat the chocolate in the double boiler or heatproof bowl to melt it again, then coat the foil cases with a second, slightly thinner coating. Chill in the refrigerator for 30 minutes more.

2 Meanwhile, make the filling. Place the chocolate in the top of a double boiler or in a heatproof bowl set over a pan of barely simmering water. Stir over a low

heat until melted, then remove from the heat. Let cool slightly, then stir in the rum and beat in the mascarpone until fully incorporated and smooth. Set aside to cool completely, stirring occasionally.

3 Spoon the filling into a pastry bag fitted with a ½ inch/1 cm star tip. Carefully peel away the confectionery cases from the chocolate cups. Pipe the filling into the cups and top each one with a toasted hazelnut.

Chocolate-Dipped Prunes

A much underrated dried fruit, prunes make delicious and very attractive after-dinner treats.

30 mins, plus 30 mins cooling

55–65 mins

SERVES 24

INGREDIENTS

scant 1 cup water

⅔ cup granulated sugar

2 cinnamon sticks, each 3 inches/ 7.5 cm long

1 vanilla bean

1 lb/450 g whole prunes

2¾ oz/75 g leftover sponge cake

¾ cup ground, toasted walnuts

5 tbsp slivovitch or brandy

½ tsp vanilla extract

3½ oz/100 g white chocolate, broken into pieces

1 Pour the water into a pan, add the sugar and stir over a low heat until the sugar has dissolved. Add the cinnamon sticks and vanilla bean, raise the heat and bring to a boil. Then lower the heat and simmer for 5 minutes.

2 Add the prunes, bring back to the boil and simmer for 5 minutes. Lift out 24 large, well-shaped prunes with a slotted spoon and set aside to cool. Simmer the remaining prunes for 30–40 minutes, until very tender. Meanwhile, slit the 24 reserved prunes and remove the pits, leaving a neat cavity for the filling.

3 Drain the soft-cooked prunes and discard the syrup. Remove the pits and place the prunes in a food processor with the sponge cake, ground walnuts, slivovitch (or brandy if using), and vanilla.

Process to a smooth paste. Divide the filling among the reserved prunes, carefully pressing it into the cavities and gently reshaping the prunes around it.

4 Put the chocolate in the top of a double boiler or in a heatproof bowl set over a pan of barely simmering water.

Stir over a low heat until melted, then remove from the heat. Dip each prune into the melted chocolate to half coat, then spoon the remaining chocolate into a pastry bag fitted with a fine tip. Pipe thin lines over the tops of the prunes, then place them on a sheet of baking parchment until set.

Mexican Chocolate Corn

If you can obtain Mexican chocolate, it is worth doing so, but otherwise use any good-quality, dark chocolate.

🍮 5 mins   🕐 10–15 mins

SERVES 6

INGREDIENTS

scant 3 cups water

½ cup tortilla flour

2 inch/5 cm piece of cinnamon stick

scant 3 cups milk

3 oz/85 g dark chocolate, grated

sugar, to taste

1 Pour the water into a large pan, stir in the tortilla flour and add the cinnamon. Stir over a low heat for 10–15 minutes until thickened and smooth. Gradually stir in the milk, then beat in the grated chocolate, a little at a time, until melted and fully incorporated. Remove and discard the cinnamon.

2 Remove the pan from the heat and ladle the mixture into heatproof glasses. Sweeten to taste with sugar.

Chocolate Eggnog

The perfect pick-me-up on a cold winter's night, this delicious drink will get the taste buds tingling.

10 mins   5 mins

SERVES 4

INGREDIENTS

8 egg yolks

1 cup sugar

4 cups milk

8 oz/225 g dark chocolate, grated

⅔ cup dark rum

1 Beat the egg yolks with the sugar until thickened.

2 Pour the milk into a large pan, add the grated chocolate and bring to a boil. Remove from the heat and gradually beat in the egg yolk mixture. Stir in the rum and pour into heatproof glasses.

Hot Brandy Chocolate

Brandy and chocolate have a natural affinity, as this richly flavored drink amply demonstrates.

10 mins   7–10 mins

SERVES 4

I N G R E D I E N T S

4 cups milk

4 oz/115 g dark chocolate, broken into pieces

2 tbsp sugar

5 tbsp brandy

6 tbsp whipped cream, to decorate

4 tsp unsweetened cocoa, to decorate

1 Pour the milk into a pan and bring to a boil, then remove from the heat. Place the chocolate in a small pan and add 2 tablespoons of the hot milk. Stir over a low heat until the chocolate has melted. Stir the chocolate mixture into the remaining milk and add the sugar.

2 Stir in the brandy and pour into 4 heatproof glasses. Top each with a swirl of whipped cream and sprinkle with a little strained cocoa.

Hot Chocolate Drinks

Rich and soothing, a hot chocolate drink in the evening can be just what you need to help ease away the stresses of the day.

SERVES 2

INGREDIENTS

SPICY HOT CHOCOLATE

2½ cups milk

1 tsp ground allspice

3½ oz/100 g dark chocolate

4 cinnamon sticks

generous ⅓ cup heavy cream,
  lightly whipped

HOT CHOCOLATE & ORANGE TODDY

2½ oz/75 g orange-flavored dark chocolate

2½ cups milk

3 tbsp rum

2 tbsp heavy cream

grated nutmeg

1 To make Spicy Hot Chocolate, pour the milk into a small pan. Sprinkle in the allspice.

2 Break the dark chocolate into squares and add to the milk. Heat the mixture over a low heat until the milk is just boiling, stirring all the time to prevent the milk burning on the bottom of the pan.

3 Place 2 cinnamon sticks in 2 cups and pour in the spicy hot chocolate. Top with the whipped double (heavy) cream and serve.

4 To make Hot Chocolate & Orange Toddy, break the orange-flavored dark chocolate into squares and place in a small saucepan with the milk. Heat the mixture over a low heat until just boiling, stirring constantly.

5 Remove the pan from the heat and stir in the rum. Pour into cups.

6 Pour the cream over the back of a spoon or swirl on to the top so that it sits on top of the hot chocolate. Sprinkle with grated nutmeg and serve at once.

COOK'S TIP

Using a cinnamon stick as a stirrer will give any hot chocolate drink a sweet, pungent flavor of cinnamon without overpowering the flavor of the chocolate.

Cold Chocolate Drinks

These delicious chocolate summer drinks are perfect for making a chocoholic's summer day!

5 mins each • 0 mins

SERVES 2

INGREDIENTS

CHOCOLATE MILK SHAKE

2 cups ice cold milk

3 tbsp drinking chocolate powder

3 scoops chocolate ice cream

unsweetened cocoa, to dust (optional)

CHOCOLATE ICE CREAM SODA

5 tbsp Glossy Chocolate Sauce (see
    page 103)

soda water

2 scoops of chocolate ice cream

heavy cream, whipped

dark or light chocolate, grated

1 To make the Chocolate Milk Shake, pour half of the milk in a blender.

2 Add the drinking chocolate powder to the blender and 1 scoop of the chocolate ice cream. Blend until frothy and well mixed. Stir in the remaining milk.

3 Place the remaining 2 scoops of chocolate ice cream in 2 serving glasses and carefully pour the chocolate milk over the ice cream.

4 Sprinkle a little cocoa (if using) over the top of each drink and serve.

5 To make the Chocolate Ice Cream Soda, divide the Glossy Chocolate Sauce between 2 glasses. (You can use a ready-made chocolate dessert sauce instead of the Glossy Chocolate Sauce).

6 Add a little soda water to each glass and stir to combine the sauce and soda water. Place a scoop of ice cream in each glass and top up with more of the soda water.

7 Place a dollop of whipped double cream on the top, if liked, and sprinkle with a little grated dark or light chocolate.

COOK'S TIP
Served in a tall glass, a milk shake or an ice cream soda makes a scrumptious snack in a drink. Serve with straws, if wished.

Index